D1253397

THE FAITHS MEN LIVE BY

Here are the religions, old and new, which Dr.
Potter examines and explains in this book:

Adventist

Animism

Assemblies of God

Baha'i

Baptist

Buddhism

Christianity

Christian Science

Christ Unity Science

Church of God in Christ

Church of the Nazarene

Churches of Christ

Churches of God

Confucianism

Congregational-Christian

Disciples of Christ

Divine Science

Eastern Orthodox

Episcopal

Ethical Culture

Evangelical-Reformed

Evangelical-United Brethren

Friends

Greek Catholic

Hinduism

Humanism

Islam (Mohammedanism)

Jainism

Jehovah's Witnesses

Judaism

Latter-Day Saints (Mormon)

Lutheran

Methodist

New Thought

Parseeism

Pentecostal Assemblies

Presbyterian

Religious Science

Roman Catholic

Rosicrucian

Salvation Army

Shinto

Sikhism

Spiritualist

Swedenborgian

Taoism

Theosophy

Unity

Universalist-Unitarian

Vedanta

Volunteers of America

Zoroastrianism

The Faiths Men Live By

by

CHARLES FRANCIS POTTER

ACE BOOKS, INC.
23 West 47th Street, New York 36, N. Y.

First Printing . . . April, 1954
Second Printing . . . June, 1954
Third Printing . . . January, 1955
Fourth Printing . . . June, 1955

An *ACE STAR* Book reprinted
by arrangement with Prentice-Hall, Inc.

Printed in the U.S.A.

CONTENTS

PREFACE

THIS BOOK is written to help people appreciate the good in religions other than their own. Incidentally, it might enable those of no particular faith to pick out one they like or formulate a private one. One can strengthen one's own religion by understanding other religions. Some faiths are peculiar to certain areas and temperaments, but there are universal values in any religion.

The present trend is toward unity. That very encouraging trend can be hindered or even blocked by ignorance of and prejudice against foreign religions; or world unity can be encouraged and fostered by sympathetic appreciation of other faiths.

It is true to some extent that "every man grovels in error," but too much stress has been put on that point by captious critics of religion. In this book the emphasis is rather on the more inspiring fact that "every man glimpses a truth."

Each chapter discovers in some religion values that can be appropriated by any reader, either to add to his own faith or to reaffirm neglected parts of it. Eternal truths emerge in new forms and fresh colors when seen in different settings.

He knows not his own faith who knows not his neighbor's.

In the six years I have been writing this book, I have noticed from time to time evidences of a growing recognition by the public of the need for a better understanding of religion and religions. What had been seen as a desirable ethical aim, namely, the democratic toleration of other faiths and an attempt to appreciate their good points, is becoming a pressing social and even political necessity.

The widespread controversy about religion, or the lack of it, in our public schools has engaged the attention of the press, the pulpit, and even the Supreme Court. "Released Time" from school in order for children to study the faith of their fathers was demanded and, in some localities, secured. In other communities sectarian religion was and is taught within the public school system in spite of the American constitutional insistence on the separation of church and state.

Confronted with the insistent demand for the teaching of religion in the public schools, educators in a department of the National Education Association have been pondering the dilemma for many months now, and very recently have come up with what may prove to be the wise solution. The

7

dilemma is—how can religion be taught without teaching some one particular religion and thereby discriminating against other religions?

The solution, heralded as "a new approach to the delicate problem of religion in education," is teaching *about* religion. In other words, it is proposed that Comparative Religion, once only an elective subject in universities and theological seminaries, and studied by only an infinitesimal portion of the population, be taught in our public schools to all.

If it were still the custom to dedicate books to people, I should dedicate this one to these educators who realize the great need for teaching our children and young people to appreciate the importance and function of religion and the various forms it has taken historically and is taking contemporaneously, forms so varied that anyone wishing to choose a religion or to enrich his own faith can find the spiritual help he needs, no matter what his temperament or type of personality.

Most certainly, since religion is so powerful an influence in the making of decisions, we shall never succeed in establishing the United Nations until we cast aside our prejudices and learn to appreciate the fact that the word "heathen" should be deleted from our vocabularies. All faiths have their deep wells of inspiration, and every religion of man deserves our reverent study.

The reader will find in this book an introductory chapter concerning primitive animistic and polytheistic religion. The ethnic or world faiths are given a chapter each, with the exception of the minor Jainism and Sikhism, which are appended to Hinduism, from which they stem.

The order of the chapters is roughly chronological, save that Christianity is put last of the world religions in order to introduce its divisions and denominations, of which the more important numerically are given separate chapters.

Mormonism and Christian Science thereafter are given ample space because of the general interest in them as the only two great religions recently founded and the only two originating in America.

In the Appendix are grouped a number of significant sects and important religious organizations.

CHARLES FRANCIS POTTER

INTRODUCTION

The Beginnings of Religion

THE PRIMITIVE FORM of religion called *animism*, the belief in nature powers and spirits, has left its mark on language, and probably also on the subconscious.

Anyone who has felt the apparently malevolent force of a great twisting cyclone, or has even seen its effects, can understand why, all through the West Indies and the northern coast of South America where these tempests frequently rage, the aboriginal Carib Indians feared and worshiped *Hurukan*, the evil spirit of the destructive whirling wind. The same sort of storm in another part of the world gets its name from the mythological spirit monster of hurricane and volcano called by the earliest Greeks, *Typhon*.

Fear of the mighty powers of nature is deeply rooted in every one, even the most sophisticated. The great American philosopher and psychologist, Dr. William James, in a letter written in 1906, shortly after a California earthquake, confessed:

> . . . the room was shaken like a rat by a terrier, with the most vicious expression you can possibly imagine, it was to my mind absolutely an *entity* . . . and it was impossible not to conceive it as animated by a will, so vicious was the temper displayed — everything *down*, in the room, that could go down, bureaus, etc., etc., and the shaking so rapid and vehement.

If the scholarly professor found it "impossible not to conceive" the earthquake "as animated by a will," it is hardly surprising to find that primitive men personified, or at least attributed partial or occasional intention to, the powers of nature, and tried to counteract or placate them as best they could; hence animism, the earliest form or stage of religion, apparently originated.

We smile patronizingly at the animistic Ainus of northern Japan for trying to make it rain by praying to the skulls of raccoons and then throwing water over each other. But we revert to the same sort of primitive religion when we say, "I haven't had a cold this winter," and then quickly knock on wood, thus unwittingly calling on the dryad or wood sprite of the tree, from which the wood came, to protect us from the evil spirit of virus influenza, lest we, as our grandparents put it, "catch a death o' cold." The Ainus are really, within their frame of reference, more rational than we, for they know that raccoons love water and are forever washing their food, whereas most of the many moderns who knock on wood can give no logical reason for doing so.

Our wood-knocking we think of as superstitious rather than religious, but superstitions are simply survivals of primitive religions, relics of former faiths and religious practices remaining emotionally fixed within those people who have supposedly abandoned such beliefs and customs and accepted a religion much higher in the scale. Just as the vermiform appendix, which causes us upright bipeds so much trouble, is said by scientists to be an atavistic remainder and reminder of our quadrupedal forebears or forelemurs, so the dozens of superstitions we modern men confess reveal that we are still loyal, at least emotionally, to the animistic faith of our fathers, and therefore should be much more understanding and sympathetic toward other religions which some of us, rather arrogantly, deem inferior to our own. When we consider the results of a survey which showed that only one-fourth of the Harvard University faculty were free from superstition, it would seem that the earliest forms of religion persist even among those cultured folk professing the most developed types, or claiming to have no religion at all.

Among the less intelligent or at least less literate adherents of the religions of today, the latent natural animism easily bursts through the thin veneer of the professed faith. Examples of twentieth-century animism are easily collected. In India, a bullock was sacrificed to a motorcycle, and a sheep to the machinery in a new industrial plant, a practice to be expected, perhaps, when the machine age is suddenly imposed on a people whose religion of Hinduism still contains more animism than any other ethnic faith, with the possible exception of Japanese Shinto.

A Russian peasant, upon seeing for the first time a small Ford tractor plowing, in one afternoon, a field requiring a week's hard labor by him and his horse, knelt before the miraculous machine, patted it reverently, and said the Russian equivalent of "Nice little Lord Jesus!" Not long ago a newly installed telephone switchboard in Spain was solemnly sanctified by sprinkling it with holy water, from time immemorial in many religions an approved technique for driving out the wizardry of evil spirits.

The use of water in religious ceremonies such as christening, blessing, aspersion, lustration, baptism, and especially exorcism, is a most interesting survival, somewhat sublimated, of the animistic element in primitive or pagan religion. To early man, water was alive; it was truly "living water." It moved; it made many sounds. As rain, it pattered; in the brook, it tinkled and murmured; the surf of the sea roared. Its power in storm and flood was evident. Usually, however, it was more helpful than harmful. It quenched his thirst and cooled and cleaned his body. So he used its beneficent powers to counteract evil forces. No evil spirit could cross running water or remain in it. The Hindu cleansed himself from sin by immersion in the Ganges, the Jew in the Jordan, and the Roman in the Tiber. Even now the priest of the Yoruba Negroes in Africa sprinkles the face of the newborn child with holy water taken from a vessel under a sacred tree.

Throughout the ancient world, in the childhood of mankind, practically all the races of primitive men baptized their children with or in sacred waters in order that the good or holy spirit of the water might drive away the evil spirits which were known to hover around at the dangerous times when such phenomena as birth, puberty, marriage, or death occurred.

Religion, therefore, in its earliest stage of animism, was man's brave attempt to use the few friendly factors in his environment to counteract the many hostile powers, and also, a little later, to persuade the helpful powers to accept his gifts of offerings and sacrifices and reward him by granting his desires and supplying his needs.

Animism, however, was the pre-deity period of religion. Man had not yet reached the concept of gods. But he had the idea that all things were alive, at least all things that moved, and acted to do things to him. He had no notion of there being any such thing as accidents: nothing ever just happened. Somebody or Something did it, and meant to do it. Everything he himself did, so he thought, he did "on purpose." He meant to do it and wanted to do it. So he naturally projected his own intentions and feelings upon the animal, object, or force of nature which had done something to him. If the earthquake shook him, as he shook his child, or as his dog shook a rat, then the earthquake also was alive, and did the shaking purposely. To put it in William James's language, it was "animated by a will."

The savage went back and kicked or shouted at the obstacle which had tripped him to punish it for its insolence: modern man still retains enough emotional animism to look back, at least, and glare at whatever he fell over. And mama spanks and scolds the "naughty door" that dares to bump the head of her precious child whom she thereby indoctrinates in the ancient pagan faith.

In its essence, then, animism is the primitive form of religion which assumes that material objects, animals, and all the phenomena of nature have each a living soul (Latin, *anima*). And because early man, once he reached the stage of animism, sought to placate the evil spirits and cultivate and please the good spirits residing in all things, animism has sometimes been called nature worship. But it must not be confused with pantheism, the much later and more developed philosophic belief that God is all, or that the whole impersonal universe is God.

11

It has been claimed by some students of the subject that there was a more primitive religion preceding animism, sometimes called animatism, centered around belief in *mana,* a sort of non-personalized spiritual force, called also by the Algonquin tribe of American Indians, *manito;* and by the Japanese, *kami. Mana* is a Polynesian word common in the Pacific Islands, and recent studies have tended to show that it and the related terms mentioned are not so much indicative of a particular stage of religious belief as they are omnibus words of very wide application to almost any phenomena of a magic or miraculous nature which excite wonder, awe, or admiration. Kami, for instance, may be spiritual power allegedly present, rather indiscriminately, in foxes, echoes, dragons, trees, mountains, and in people, either very noble or very wicked. Sometimes mana apparently means prestige; sometimes, energy. It seems to be the uncivilized man's equivalent of Bergson's *élan vital* or vital impulse, and much resembles in some of its more benevolent aspects the powers attributed to the Holy Spirit or Holy Ghost in the early Christian Church. Far from indicating a pre-animistic religion, it is a conception of that philosophically mature type which occasionally emerges among the semi-civilized intelligentsia.

The next step in the evolution of religion from animism is *polytheism,* although some scholars insert an interim of what they call "polydaemonism." They use the word "daemon" in the Greek sense of spirits who may be good, bad, or neutral; not in the Christian sense of evil devils. But since the daemons were impersonal spirits, polydaemonism was only one variety of animism, slightly more developed.

Polytheism was an easy step from animism, for, once spirits were granted the powers of will, wish, and intention, it took little more to think of them as manlike gods. The beneficent spirit who lived in and around the spring of living water soon became one of the gods of the tribe of men who used the spring. The rude cairn or hut they built over the spring became his shrine, and later his temple. And the same tribe would worship a god of the mountain, and later a god of their flocks and cattle; still later, a Baal of their gardens and crops. Perhaps, of old, they reverenced the mana-power in the square black stone which fell from heaven and buried itself with a great hissing and smoke in the wet sand near the spring. In due time men worshiped the god Allah, his consort the goddess Allat, and their two daughters Aluzza and Manat, also goddesses, in the temples which were erected near the sacred spring Zem Zem and the holy cube-shaped black stone, the Kaaba.

This worship of several gods and goddesses at Mecca was paralleled by many similar regions of polytheism such as the pantheon of Olympian gods at Athens. These gods and goddesses were, like the Vedic gods of India and the deities of Zoroaster's bright Persian heaven, personified virtues and forces of nature.

The next saltation, or forward step, in the evolution of religion, was from polytheism to *henotheism,* when one god was chosen as the greatest, though not the only god. Zeus headed the Olympian pantheon, and, as Jupiter (Zeus-pater), was acknowledged the greatest of the Roman deities. Allah became recognized as the leader supreme of all the gods and goddesses of Arabian Mecca, which was an easy transition, as most of them were his female kin. There was a period of henotheism among the early Israelites or Hebrews in Palestine, also, when the gods of the Canaanites and other tribes were reckoned as real gods, but Yahweh (Jehovah) was, by the Israelites, considered the El Elyon, or God Most High.

From henotheism to *monotheism,* belief in one God alone, was a natural emergence. As the greatest god of the henotheistic pantheon gradually absorbed the virtues and duties of the other gods and goddesses this change in status was possible. In other words, the worshipers gave to him the holy attributes of all the others and so his associates and rivals faded away. There came to Mecca a camel-driver named Kutam who asserted that there was but one God, the Great God Allah, the All-Merciful. When Kutam had made good his assertion by political and military as well as spiritual means, he was praised, and became known as Muhammad, the Praised One, and the great sentence of all Islam became, "There is no God but Allah, and Muhammad is his Prophet."

The three great monotheistic religions are Judaism, Christianity, and Islam, and the two latter inherited or derived their monotheism from Judaism, which claims to have been the first faith to adopt belief in one God only, or, to put it in theological language, the first people to whom the One God revealed Himself. Akhenaten (Amenhotep IV) of Egypt, 1388-1358 B. C., taught monotheism in his religion of Atenism, but that religion was soon swallowed up in the swamps of Egyptian polytheism. Some think that Moses may have studied Akhenaten's monotheistic faith in Egypt before Atenism faded out, and it is chronologically possible. But the Jews themselves claim that their monotheism dates back to Abraham, the founder of Judaism, whose time was long before that of Moses, and is given as early as 2300 B.C.

But whenever or wherever monotheism originated, it has not yet become universal, for polytheism and animism even now are the faiths of millions, and remnants of these old religions still exist in the consciousness and influence the conduct of many who profess to be pure monotheists.

13

1
HINDUISM

The World's Oldest Living Religion

ON THAT FATEFUL THIRTIETH day of January 1948, when Mahatma (Great-souled) Gandhi, struck by the assassin's bullets, fell backward mortally hurt, he murmured, *"Ai Ram, Ai Ram!"* (Oh Rama, O Rama!)

As Jesus on the cross nineteen centuries before had cried, *"Eloi, Eloi!"* (My God, My God!) so Gandhi, fatally wounded, called on his favorite Hindu God Rama, one of the many gods of the very ancient religion of India.

Gandhi might have called on the deity Vishnu, for Gandhi was a Vishnuite as well as a Ramaite. Indeed, Rama's relation to Vishnu is, for the Hindu, like that of Christ to God.

Gandhi might also have called on Allah, the God of Mohammed, or on Christ himself, for he believed in them both. Hinduism is not an exclusive religion, like the Western ones, but inclusive, adopting every good religious idea. That may be why it is the oldest religion.

True to the spirit of Hinduism, Gandhi accepted all great religions as his, and was therefore claimed by leaders of all religions as one of their own. The pacifists assert that Gandhi's "Holy Trinity" was Jesus, Tolstoi, and Thoreau.

Gandhi himself is already in the process of becoming a Hindu god. His legal name was Mohandas Karamchand Gandhi, but no one in India calls him that, and few know it. He was the Mahatma, the great-souled master and teacher, spoken of with reverent love as "Gandhiji" or "Mahatmaji," the "ji" meaning, as accurately as English can translate it, "beloved." Eighteen years ago there were already images of Gandhi in Hindu temples along with those of Rama and Krishna. His martyr death will doubtless speed his adoring disciples to make him, along with Rama and Krishna, another *avatar* or incarnation of the supreme deity Vishnu.

Within a few days after his death, devoted followers had made a large crater by scooping bits of soil from the spot where he fell. These spoonfuls of earth will be as carefully preserved and handed down to future generations as have been the splinters of wood now in existence believed to be pieces of the cross on which Jesus the Christ died.

A further step toward deifying Gandhi was taken when the ashes from his cremated body were scattered by his son on the waters where the Jumna and Ganges rivers join near Allahabad, a very ancient sacred place. The city was named Allahabad (abode of Allah) by the Moslem conquerors of that part of India, in 1572 A.D., but had already been called

Prayaga (the place of sacrifice) by the Hindus for many centuries before. When a Hindu's ashes are strewn at the sacred junction of waters, it is believed by some Hindus that he will escape the fate of being reborn as an animal and may attain immediate immortality.

Moslems, also, admired Gandhi, and will probably eventually include him in their list of saints, for he stood up for their rights against severe Hindu criticism, and, besides, he was a faithful reader of the Koran.

Christians have long called Gandhi "The Christ of India," for he not only read and reread, but followed literally (better than many Christians themselves) the non-violence principles of the Sermon on the Mount.

Since representatives of all great religions have said of Gandhi, "He was one of us in spirit," it may be that we should amend a familiar saying to read:

"In Christ, and Gandhi, there is no East or West."

If all other religious leaders could be as appreciative of their neighbors' faith as Gandhi was, instead of each insisting that his religion is the only true religion, this troubled world would be drawn closer together in friendship and understanding.

One reason why Hinduism is so tolerant of other religions is that it has no creed, no set of required beliefs. No one can be expelled from Hinduism for heresy. Nor can he be compelled to adopt any particular practices, rites, or sacraments, like going to church, or confession, or baptism. There are no strict rules about what one shall or shall not eat or drink or whom he may or may not marry. Particular sects and divisions within Hinduism may require of their members that they follow, in general, certain customs of the group, but there are so many subdivisions within Hinduism itself that a person can quite easily find a sect to suit himself. Or he can even start one of his own.

The late Dr. Kedernath Das Gupta, a widely-traveled Hindu who had the respect and admiration of men of all religions, once explained Hinduism this way:

> "Hinduism is a vast conglomerate religion consisting of many faiths. It might be termed a Fellowship of Faiths. A man is a Hindu who in good faith declares himself to be such. *The essence of Hinduism is 'Know thyself.'*"

When such freedom of choice within Hinduism is not only allowed but even encouraged, one would hardly expect to find any single belief, except perhaps belief in God, upon which the majority of Hindus agree. But there are many devout Hindus who are what Christians would call atheists. On the other hand, there are millions who believe not in

15

one God but many, and there are enough popular gods in India for a Hindu to worship a different one each day for a year.

Though Hinduism is divided over the question of one god or none or many, no Hindu would presume to criticize his neighbor for disagreeing with him on which god to worship, or how many. A man in India is measured by what he is and does, rather than by what he believes.

There are, however, seven beliefs which are commonly held by the majority of Hindus: Karma, Dharma, Reverence for asceticism, Reverence for the Vedas, Pantheism, Transmigration of souls, and Final liberation of the soul.

KARMA (pronounced *Kurma*) might well be phrased in the Christian language of Paul's Letter to the Galatians: "Whatsoever a man soweth, that shall he also reap," but the Hindus carry the principle further. They believe that every thought, word, or deed sets up a chain of cause and effect for whose consequences the individual will have to pay in this life or in some future life.

DHARMA is difficult for a Westerner to understand: one has to be born and brought up in India to have a feeling-consciousness of this word which represents the very heart of Hindu religion and social conditions. No one English word defines it and it carries much of the meaning in our several words — law, duty, religion, virtue, and even social custom. It means the way things are and ought to be. When a Westerner says that certain things "just aren't done," a Hindu would say that to do such things would "break Dharma."

It is because of belief in Dharma that the caste system has such a strong hold in India. There are many castes and sub-castes, but the four main ones are the Brahman (or Priestly), the Kshatriya (or Warrior-Ruler), the Vaisya (or Merchant-Farmer), and the Sudra (or Artisan-Laboring class).

As early as the Sacred Laws of Manu (250 B.C.), and probably before that, these castes were believed divinely ordained. In these Sacred Laws it is written that God made the Brahman from His head, the warriors and kings from His arms, the merchants and farmers from His thighs, and the craftsmen and laborers from His feet. Even the Hindu who does not believe in God believes in the caste system.

Intermarriage between castes is forbidden. Separate wells and different roads are used by those of widely separated castes.

The native Sanskrit word for caste is "varna" (pronounced *vurna*) which means "color," and gives us a clue to the origin of the caste system. It was probably established by the conquering light-colored Aryans when, thousands of years ago, they pushed down through the Khyber Pass from the Plateau

of Iran and overcame the dark Dravidians, the earlier inhabitants of India.

Gandhi tried to reform the caste system, and set a good
example by adopting into his own high-caste family a child
from the lowest outcastes and by working for the uplift of
the despised so-called "untouchables."

REVERENCE FOR ASCETICISM (SELF-DENIAL). Visitors from
America to India, such as our soldiers in the recent World
War, are at once surprised to find so many ascetics and beg-
gars, but fasting and begging are long-established features of
religion in India.

Gandhi's fasting has advertised the custom to the world.
We Americans are somewhat puzzled as to why it proved
such an effective weapon that it finally was an important
factor in bringing freedom to India. But the English know,
if we do not, that ascetism, martyrdom, and self-denial are
so highly esteemed in the religion of Hinduism that, had the
English permitted Gandhi to fast unto death, they would
have had a religious conflict on their hands throughout
India.

Begging on the street is a misdemeanor in American
cities. In India, it is a respected occupation because it is part
of Hinduism. The perfect religionist is supposed to pass
through four stages in his life. First, he is a young student,
then a married householder, then a forest-dweller or hermit,
and finally a religious beggar like the mendicant Christian
friars of the Middle Ages. He is considered very holy, for he
has given up all interest in family or fortune and asks but a
crust to keep him barely alive while he meditates on life and
death.

REVERENCE FOR THE VEDAS. The Vedas (Books of Knowledge) include all the many sacred scriptures of Hinduism.
Of the four original Vedas, coming down from long before
1000 B. C., the oldest is the Rig Veda, "the oldest document
among the world's living religions." It is a collection of over
a thousand verses, including the famous Gayatri, or prayer-
hymn to the sun, at least ten centuries older than Christianity
but still used daily by millions of Hindus:

> Let us meditate upon the adorable
> Glory of the Divine Life Giver!
> And may He direct our thoughts!

PANTHEISM. Underlying all sects of Hinduism is usually
discovered some form of pantheism, the doctrine that all is
God, or more definitely, that there is no God but the combined forces and laws of nature. Among the less educated,
this pantheism becomes a form of animism, the belief that
animals and even objects have souls. Stones and trees, springs
and mountains are considered sacred and are worshiped.

A logical extension of this belief is the idea that all life is so sacred that nothing must be killed. No matter how much an animal is suffering, it must not be put out of its misery. No gnat or mosquito will be killed by the most devout. Some sects will not eat after dark lest they accidentally swallow some minute form of life. And millions of Hindus will eat no meat, for to do so would be to share the guilt of the man who killed the animal.

The cow is particularly holy. An often-quoted verse from the sacred book, the Mahabharata, states:

All that kill, eat, and permit the slaughter of cows, rot in hell for as many years as there are hairs on the body of the cow so slain.

And Gandhi, who tried to reform Hinduism in some of its beliefs, such as the caste system, ardently defended cow worship, to the surprise of his American admirers, saying:

The worship of the cow is the Hindus' unique contribution to the evolution of humanitarianism. It is a practical application of the belief in the oneness, and therefore the sacredness, of all life.

Some aspects of Hindu cow worship offend Western ideas of sanitation and it would take more than Gandhi's idealistic defense to convince us that the practice was humanitarian in origin. As a matter of fact, no one knows the actual origin of cow worship for the Aryan invaders brought it with them to India, and it was then already ancient.

Our word "cow" comes directly from the corresponding Sanskrit "go" of the early Aryans, and that word "go" also meant in Sanskrit several other ideas, including earth, heaven, rays of light, and speech itself! So scholars have inferred that the cow very early became a sacred symbol of the fruitfulness, fertility and life of the earth.

TRANSMIGRATION OF SOULS. Most Hindus believe that after death they are reborn into some other person or animal. This is part of their *Karma*, and they go up or down in the life scale in proportion as they have been good or bad during the present life. This keeps on for long periods of time, perhaps for millions of years, until

THE FINAL LIBERATION OF THE SOUL in Nirvana, which is variously defined as "passionless peace" or as "absorption into the infinite" or as "final union with Brahm."

Naturally the question arises, How can the poor individual, bound to the wheel of *Karma*, ever hope to attain the great liberation?

Remember that Dr. Das Gupta said the essence of Hinduism is to "Know thyself." He said further:

The true knowledge of one's inner self leads to union

with the Supreme Being (or liberation) through what is technically called "Yoga."

Yoga is the direct answer to the question of how to attain liberation, how to know thyself; in fact the word means union—union with the universal spirit Brahm.

Yoga is correctly pronounced in one syllable, with the a silent, exactly as our word "yoke," its direct descendant, is pronounced in one syllable with silent e.

There are many varieties of yoga, each with its ardent disciples. The man who practices yoga is a yogi; the woman, a yogini. The five best known and most widely used paths to liberation are:

(1) Bhakti or Devotional Yoga, the Way of Love,
(2) Jnana or Intellectual Yoga, the Way of Knowledge,
(3) Karma or Action Yoga, the Way of Service,
(4) Raja or Meditation Yoga, the Way of Psychology,
(5) Hatha or Physical Yoga, the Way of Strength.

In all these various systems of yoga, and, in fact, throughout Hinduism, there is emphasis on the idea that the seeker for truth will find it nearer than he thinks, more likely within himself than outside.

Sri Ramakrishna, one of the greatest teachers of 19th century Hinduism, told many parables and religious stories, of which the following is a typical example:

A man woke up at midnight and wanted to have a smoke. Needing a light, he went to his neighbor's house and knocked on the door. When the neighbor asked what his midnight visitor wanted, he replied, "I wish to smoke. Can you give me a light?" to which the neighbor answered, "Bah! What's the matter with you? Here you have taken all this trouble to come over here, to say nothing of wakening me, to get a light, when in your own hand you hold a lighted lantern!"

"Likewise," continues Sri Ramakrishna with the moral "what a man wants is already within him; but he still wanders here and there in search of it."

JAINISM

The Jain (pronounced *Jine*) of 2500 years ago was a vegetarian pacifist nudist who refused to worship any god, and the million and a half Jains living today in India and Pakistan have compromised very little on their original faith except that now they practically worship the twenty-three prehistoric legendary Tirthankaras or saints, as well as the twenty-fourth, the historical Vardhamana (Mahavira), their probable founder, who distinctly and repeatedly forbade his followers to worship anyone.

Gautama Siddhartha, who became known as the Buddha (Enlightened One), was a younger contemporary of the Mahavira (Great Hero), lived in the same part of India, and was also a non-theistic humanist. Their early life-stories are similar—both were born to wealth and royal position and left wife, child and their luxurious palaces at the age of thirty for lives of poverty and self-denial as they sought to reform the barren ritualistic Hinduism of the sixth century B. C., and discover the meaning of human existence. Scholars have therefore suspected that the Mahavira story is but another version of the Buddha legend, and Jainism only a branch or outgrowth of Buddhism. But further study has revealed that Jainism is the older faith, and that Gautama, in his wanderings, may have followed, for a while, the ascetic teachings and practices of Vardhamana, only to abandon them and set up another kind of religion.

Jainism is really quite different theologically from both Hinduism and Buddhism, and much more modern and Western in point-of-view. It teaches self-reliance and asserts the individuality and indestructibility of the human soul, whereas Hinduism affirms that the soul of man is only part of the Universal Soul, and Buddhism that man is but a bundle of *khandas,* or elements, physical and mental, constantly changing, held together only by the desire for existence and finally dispersed when that desire is overcome.

The word Jain comes from *Jina,* a conqueror, not a military hero, but a victor over his own evil inclinations. The true Jina has overcome not only the four major passions of anger, greed, pride, and deceit, but also the lesser vices of disgust, worry, joy or sorrow, fear, sexual craving, and either like or dislike of material things. The Jain scriptures say:

"Difficult to conquer is oneself. But when that is conquered, everything is conquered."

The main doctrine of Jainism is *Ahimsa,* to refrain from taking life. Jains refuse to condone not only war and capital punishment, but also animal or bird sacrifice, vivisection, and the killing of animals, fish, or birds for sport or food. They admit that the nuts, fruits, and vegetables which they eat, also have life, but eating them is the least of sins, for plants are lowest in the life scale, having the fewest sense organs. Jains refuse to eat potatoes, however, believing they contain microscopical forms of life.

The strict Jain strains every cup of fluid he drinks, examines carefully every mouthful of food, watches every step he takes lest he crush an ant or beetle. The Jain monk even carries a little broom to sweep the path ahead of him. Nor does he light a fire, lest inadvertently he kill some insect in the air above it or in the ground beneath.

No follower of this faith will be a farmer, for in plowing he may kill or injure an earthworm. Of course he is never a butcher or fisherman, nor can he make or sell guns or fishing rods or tackle. He is usually, therefore, a monk, a teacher,

20

an artist, a trader, a business man or a banker. As a result, Jains are educated, literate, and prosperous, and influential in their communities far out of proportion to their comparatively small numbers. They are charitable, often in a way surprising to Westerners, for they erect and maintain hospitals and asylums for old, sick, and incurable animals, such as cows, which their religion forbids them to put out of misery. Yet humans have been permitted, under certain circumstances, and even encouraged at times, to commit suicide by starving to death after a series of fasts.

The nudism of the Jain is explicable partially because of Ahimsa, lest he crush an insect in the folds of his clothing. There are today two great divisions within Jainism, Swetambaras (White Clad) or lightly clothed, and Digambaras (Sky Clad) with no clothes at all, except where Moslem neighbors insist they wear loin cloths. The White Clad sect puts clothes on statues, but the Sky Clad people have nudist statues, and the colossal (60 feet high) one of Gomatesvara, the Tirthankara (ford-finder), in Mysore state, startles the tourists who come upon it.

The Digambaras are so orthodox and old-fashioned that they look down on all women, holding that no woman can attain to the Jain heaven (Nirvana) unless she is finally reincarnated as a man. Monks are warned not to let women catch them by their wiles, for then it soon is, "Fetch some nice fruit, the comb, the looking-glass. . . . Paint my feet; come and rub my back." The poor monks, trapped "like an antelope caught in a snare," cannot escape no matter how much they struggle. "Getting up at night, they lull the baby asleep like nurses, and though they are ashamed of themselves they wash the clothes like washer-women." This passage is from the second *Anga* (limb) or book of the Jain scriptures, of which there are thirty-three, forty-five, or eighty-four, according to various sects. But very few are known in English translations, and the Jains, except for a few scholars, never study their scriptures, but are happy to be able to recite the list of the names of their sacred books, like an American Sunday School child chanting "Genesis, Exodus, Leviticus, . . ." through to ". . . Third John, Jude, Revelation."

The Jain vow to abstain as much as possible from sex acts is another of the rules based on Ahimsa, the doctrine against the taking of life, for Jains are taught "that in every act of sexual intercourse 900,000 living beings, very minute, of the shape of the human being, and having the five senses, but no mind, are generated and killed." One would think that a little more scientific information might alter several of the Jainist religious doctrines, but probably, as in other orthodox religions, these loyal folk would develop a remarkable skill

21

in keeping their faith and their science in separate compartments.

If Mahavira could return to earth and see the modern Jains worshiping the statues of himself and the other Jainist saints in the great temples of Satrunjaya, one of the most beautiful of temple-cities in India or anywhere else, he would doubtless sigh, and then repeat his famous humanist text:

"Man! Thou art thine own friend! Why wishest thou for a friend beyond thyself?"

SIKHISM

Guru Nanak, the founder of Sikhism (pronounced seekism), was a dynamic combination of Martin Luther, Dwight L. Moody, and the Apostle Paul. He resembled Luther, his contemporary, for while the German was trying to reform Christianity, Nanak was doing his best to reform Hinduism. Like Moody, he was an evangelist, and just as Moody's preaching in the United States and England in the late 19th century was supported and supplemented by Ira D. Sankey's sweet singing, so Nanak's minstrel companion Mardana with his rebab, the Oriental ancestor of the violin, was a great assistance in spreading the new faith. And like the Apostle Paul, Nanak took four long missionary journeys, traveling, so his disciples assert, from his Punjab home in northwest India to Delhi, Benares, and the Himalaya Mountains on the first journey, then east to Madras and Ceylon, then far northwest to Kashmir and Peshawar, and finally to Baghdad and even the holy Moslem cities of Medina and Mecca in Arabia.

Of course, he had to be disguised as a Moslem to get into Mecca, but betrayed himself by sleeping with his feet toward the Kaaba, the sacred building which is the Holy of Holies of all Islam, and toward which the faithful bow in prayer daily. The infuriated Mullahs (Moslem priests) shouted at the infidel dog, "How dare you turn your feet toward God?" Nanak, who was never at a loss for an answer, confounded and silenced them by replying calmly, "Show me a place where God is not, and I will turn my feet towards that place."

Nanak was the first of the Ten Gurus (teachers) of Sikhism, but he was not quite the first in the Punjab region to suggest the idea that there could and should be a blending of the religion of Hinduism and that of their Moslem conquerors into one monotheistic faith. The weaver and poet Kabir, Nanak's older contemporary and perhaps his teacher, whose beautiful lines were in part incorporated later in the Sikh scriptures, and in our own day were translated into English in Rabindranath Tagore's *Songs of Kabir*, anticipated Nanak's main message of monotheism by his famous prayer,

22

"Oh God, whether Allah or Ram, I live by Thy Name."

The legend is told that at the death of Kabir there arose a dispute whether his body should be cremated according to Hindu ritual, or buried as is the Moslem custom. While they quarreled, he himself appeared unrecognized among them, and suggested that they lift the cloth covering the body, whereupon nothing was discovered but a heap of flowers. So the Hindus burned half the flowers and the Moslems interred the rest. The same story is told of Nanak, save that his followers, feeling ashamed, knelt together in one group around the fragrant mound of beauty.

The common legend testifies to the common purpose of the poet and the preacher—the proclaiming of monotheism —but it was Nanak's widespread missionary work, carrying the gospel of the One God idea and related democratic doctrines, which led to the establishment of the Sikh religion. The good Guru resolutely attacked and forbade to his followers (*Sikhs* means disciples) such ancient Hindu practices as the worship of idols, polytheism, the caste system, asceticism, long pilgrimages, child marriage, infanticide, and *suttee*, the custom whereby widows threw themselves upon their husbands' funeral pyres for cremation with the body to show their single-minded devotion to their lord and master. Nanak did much to elevate the position of woman, for he taught that in the sight of God all human beings, irrespective of sex, caste, or race, are equal. It has been said that his message, in a phrase, was simply the Unity of God and the Brotherhood of Man.

He would enter a town, and, after Mardana's rebab music had drawn a crowd, would proclaim cryptically, "There is no Hindu and no Musalman!" People wondered what he meant, and he told them. It was as simple as that. North, south, east, and west, he proclaimed that Allah of the Moslems and Brahma, Shiva, Vishnu, Kali, Krishna, and all the gods of the Hindus were really but one great God over all, and this God was a loving kindly Guru or Teacher. Sikhism at its best was a blending of Bhakti Hinduism (loving devotion to a personal God) with Moslem Sufism with its divine rapture of the God-possessed mystic.

But by the time of the last of the Ten Gurus of Sikhism, the quiet, peaceful, all-loving mysticism of the first Guru had been changed to a militant religion of trained warriors. The tenth Guru, Gobind Singh, who ruled from 1675 to 1708, felt obliged to train the Sikhs into an army lest the religion be wiped out. The ninth Guru, Tegh Bahadur, Gobind Singh's father, had been beheaded by the Mogul emperor Aurungzeb, who continued a terrible persecution of the Sikhs. But the persecution roused them to a great revival of their faith. They gathered spontaneously in great crowds to sing hymns, pray, and listen to the preaching. Moreover, they enrolled as soldiers, and submitted to rigorous training, women as well as men, and soon Guru Gobind Singh had a disciplined army to defend the faith.

The army was badly defeated in battle, but the Tenth Guru then established a sort of underground Gideon's Band of picked men who were chosen for their religious devotion as well as unusual strength and valor. They were given the Baptism of the Sword and added to their names the suffix "Singh" or Lion. They were also given the marks of the five K's. That is, they must wear *Kes,* long hair and uncut beard, *Kangha,* a comb for the same, *Kripan,* a short sword, *Kara,* a steel bracelet, and *Kach,* a pair of shorts or knee-length drawers. These all had symbolic meanings, such as saintliness, restraint, and dignity. The chosen Lions became the Brotherhood of the Pure, known as the Khalsa, and by their devotion and valor, the Sikhs finally established an independent state in the Punjab which lasted from 1764 until they surrendered to the British in 1849, and the last Sikh Maharajah, Dhulip Singh, presented to Queen Victoria the famous diamond Kohinur (Mountain of Light).

Under British rule they kept their religion, and recently, since that rule has ended, the Sikhs have, by a turn of fate, a state of their own again. When India was divided into the Republic of India and the Moslem state of Pakistan, the line was drawn through the Sikh section and many migrated into the East Punjab area. Seven Punjab states formed a Union, making a Sikh state on May 5, 1948. So the Sikhs have their state back, but when last seen, the Kohinur shone resplendent in the crown of Queen Elizabeth II at her recent coronation.

Sikhism is one of the smallest of the ethnic (world) religions, for its six million adherents seem few indeed compared with Hinduism's 250, Islam's 300, Confucianism's 400, and Christianity's and Buddhism's 500 million each, but it does outnumber Jainism's million and a half and Zoroastrianism's hundred thousand. And in only thirty years the Sikhs have doubled their 1924 membership of three million. They are found today mostly in the Punjab area where Kabir and Nanak gave them their initial impulse, but, since many of them are soldiers by profession, the wars of the twentieth century have had a scattering effect, and "congregations" of good size are to be found in Hong Kong, Singapore, London, Vancouver, and Stockton, California.

There has been a trend, of late, toward an increase of the Nanakpanthis, the so-called "easy-going" Sikhs who wish to return to the peaceful tenets of Baba (Father) Nanak. The influence of Mahatma Gandhi, after he took over the direction of the Indian National Movement in 1919 and preached non-violence, was somewhat responsible for a return to a sort of modified pacifism. And there has been for some years a trend back toward Hinduism on the part of some Sikhs. But the main body is growing faster than the population increase, and the Sikh religion is strong because of the fine characters and democratic principles of its people.

Anyone who visits the Punjab will do well to spend some time at the center of Sikh worship, the golden temple at Amritsar in its water-mirror setting. It is the greatest rival in breathtaking beauty of the Taj Mahal itself.

2

JUDAISM

The Mother of Religions

IN THE BANQUET HALL of the King of Syria stood a woman and her seven sons. King Antiochus Epiphanes was reclining on a couch, Roman fashion, beside a great dinner table heaped with rich viands. The centerpiece was a whole-roasted suckling pig, garnished with garlands of flowers.

"Come and eat with me," the monarch bade the woman and her sons, pointing to the vacant couches beside which they stood.

"Come," he urged with growing impatience, seeing them stand rigid and unmoving. "You would not refuse to eat with a king at his birthday feast! Now, would you?"

And when they remained silent still, the king flew into a rage, one of his too-well known fits of temper which had led those who called him Epiphanes (The Illustrious) to his face to call him Epimanes (The Maniac) behind his back. Now he snarled, with sinister tones:

"So-o-o, perhaps you do not appreciate the excellence of this banquet. Do you not know that it was especially in your honor that this pig was killed in sacrifice to Olympian Zeus upon the high altar of burnt-offering in your own Jewish temple here in Jerusalem? Ah! You shudder, madam! Have I moved your hard heart at last? Well, we shall soften up these stubborn sons of yours as well. Guards, bind them all and give them the lash."

The sadistic king watched his victims writhe silently under the whips for a dozen blows, and then demanded:

"*Now* will you eat of the sweet swine's flesh, or will you defy me further?"

Thereupon the eldest son spoke up to the king. He spoke quietly, but firmly, and even with a note of rebuke:

"We are fully prepared to die rather than transgress the laws of our fathers."

Welcoming the young man's defiance as furnishing an

25

excuse for venting his wrath, the infuriated king proceeded with a program of torture and mayhem which has no parallel in history. First, the man's tongue was cut out to pay for his defiance of the king. Then he was scalped, his hands and feet hacked off, and his still living body taken to the adjacent kitchen and cast into a huge heated pan, while his brothers and his mother were forced to look on until his life was extinct.

Yet, with the room still full of the horrible fumes, when the king asked if they would now eat the swine's meat which their religion forbade, they did not even answer him, but quoted to each other sustaining scripture from the writings of Moses.

Antiochus then vindictively ordered his slaves to tear the scalp from the second son, and then demanded of him:

"Will you eat, or do you prefer to have your body suffer thus, limb by limb?"

And when a courageous "No" was the answer, he was put through a long series of tortures, but with his last breath he cried to the king:

"Wretch, you are releasing us from this present life, but the King of all the world will raise us up to everlasting life because we have died for His Law."

The third son surprised even the king by coming forward and offering his hands to be amputated, saying with quiet self-possession:

"From Heaven I received these hands: for His Law I disregard them; from Him I hope to receive them back again."

When six sons in turn had thus died after the most shameful mishandling and anguish, the king decided to try different tactics with the remaining lad. He spoke kindly to him and promised him riches and a fine position as Friend of the King if he would only give up the religion of his people. But the boy acted as if he did not hear, so Antiochus called the mother to him and appealed to her to advise the child to save his young life by yielding.

She agreed to speak to the boy and did, but in the Hebrew tongue and in these words:

"My son, have pity on me who carried you nine months in the womb and nursed you three years and brought you up till now. Fear not this butcher. Be as brave as your brothers and accept death that by God's mercy I may receive you again with them."

Hardly had she finished when the youth shouted:

"What are you waiting for, O King? I will not obey your command, but I will obey the command of the Law which was given to our forefathers through Moses. But you, O unholy King and vilest of men, will receive as the judgment of God the rightful penalty for your arrogance!"

Then, according to the old Maccabean account:

". . . the king, falling into a rage and exasperated at being mocked, handled him worse than all the others. And last of all after her sons the mother died."

The record breaks off abruptly, as if the chronicler would mercifully spare us the details of the mother's death. We are left aghast at this tale of a monarch's inhuman cruelty but thrilled at the spiritual strength and fortitude of these heroic folk whose religion was dearer to them than life itself.

Unknown by name, but perhaps the most famous of all the many martyrs of the Jewish faith, this Hebrew widow and her seven stalwart sons who perished in the bloody pogroms of mad King Antiochus in 168 B. C. were typical of the thousands of Jews before and the millions since who suffered and perished in persecutions because of their most sacred faith.

Scattered abroad with no homeland of their own for nearly two thousand years, almost twice as long as the time they had that homeland in Palestine, the Jews are only now in the hard process of regaining a foothold there. Those who wonder at the desperate persistence of the boatloads of refugees daring death to win a home in Palestine might remember that for centuries every Jewish bridegroom under the wedding canopy has offered his bride a drink of wine, then has drained the glass, dashed it to the floor and crushed it with his heel, as a symbol that their happiness will not be complete until the Jews regain the Holy Land.

Through the long centuries in foreign lands round the globe, and notwithstanding their continual persecutions, the Jews have retained their characteristic religious and racial traits, and are still a center of the world's interest.

Moreover, unlike any other religion, Judaism has had within it enough spiritual strength, and to spare, to become the parent of two other great world religions, Christianity and Islam, commonly called Mohammedanism. Besides, two such diverse modern faiths as Mormonism and Ethical Culture both owe much to Judaism, and there are indications that it may yet bring forth new faiths for the new age, perhaps along the lines of Einstein's Cosmic Humanism. More than any other religion, then, Judaism is entitled to be called "The Mother of Religions."

What is there in Judaism, we must continually ask, what secret power is there in this ancient religion that it can keep begetting other religions and yet has so sustained its own adherents that their race not only survives persecution but even seems to thrive on it?

The name is not merely a pretty poetical tribute, either. Judaism was the religion of Jesus Christ himself, and his early disciples were, of course, Jews of his neighborhood. It is evident that he tried at first to establish a reform within Judaism rather than a new religion, saying:

"I came not to destroy the Law but to fulfill it."

The early Christian Church, since it was founded by Jews, naturally continued many Jewish beliefs and customs. Some were gradually dropped: others have been retained until this day. Animal sacrifice and circumcision of infants and converts were abandoned, after heated debates between Peter and Paul, but the Sabbath, changed from Saturday to Sunday, was retained, and the Passover meal which Jesus ate with his disciples just before his death became The Lord's Supper of the Christian Church.

Most important of all, Christianity took over the Hebrew Bible and made it the Old Testament of its own scriptures, thus adopting the One God of Righteousness, the Ten Commandments of Moses, and the social teachings of the great prophets of Israel. The Hebrew Psalms became Christian hymns.

Yes, Christianity ownes much to Judaism.

Similarly, though not to such an extent, Judaism influenced Mohammedanism, or, as its adherents prefer to have one call it, Islam. The Koran, the Bible of Islam, quotes from the Psalms of David and "The Scrolls of Moses and Abraham," and contains several stories which are plainly rather garbled versions of some in the Hebrew Bible. Kutam the Camel-driver heard these Bible stories on his travels before he became Mohammed (the praised one) and later told them to his followers as best he remembered them.

Like Moses, and probaby imitating him, Mohammed taught the Oneness of God and the foolishness of idolatry. He too taught that the Sabbath should be kept as a day of rest, but changed it to Friday. And finally, like the Jews, the Moslems trace their descent from Abraham, the Father of the Faithful, but through Ishmael rather than Isaac.

There may be a clue to the secret power of Judaism in the three-letter word which recurs again and again in all its literature. In every one of the responses of the martyr sons to the king the word "Law" occurs. The Law of God was to them the most important thing. Even a small part of it, a little dietary law prohibiting the eating of a certain kind of meat, is so important that a good Jew would die before breaking it.

But it is not merely Law as law—not Law for law's sake, that is so important to the Jew. The Law does not mean dry legalism to him. It is alive—personified in a spiritual sense. Recently when a group of New Yorkers in a hotel room

28

got onto the subject of religion, one said he was an agnostic; a Protestant said his God was the Loving Heavenly Father of Jesus; a Roman Catholic said his God was Jesus Christ Himself. Then a woman turned to a quiet young man, obviously Jewish, and asked him who his God was, expecting that, of course, he would say, Jehovah. But to the surprise of all he said:

"Our God is The Law." And he said it as if to introduce a very fine personal friend whom he much respected and admired.

The good Jew holds the Law more sacred than his own life, not because it is law but because to him it is the Law of God. Law is God's Word and God's Word is Law. Deity and righteousness are to him identical. God is righteous law personified; and the Torah, as the devout Jew calls the Law, is God objectified and made real to him.

That Hebrew word, *Torah*, which we rather inaccurately translate "Law," meant much more than that to the ancient Jews and still does to the Jews of today. Originally, it apparently signified "oral direction" or "instruction by word of mouth." It soon came to mean what God had told His people through the mouth of Moses and the prophets. It included not merely laws about property and morality, but sanitary regulations and dietary rules, medical treatment and even etiquette. And beyond and above all these, the Torah included religion, man's spiritual relation to God and man and nature.

The word Torah was later applied specifically to the Books of Moses, the so-called Pentateuch, the first five books in the Hebrew (and Christian) Bible—Genesis, Exodus, Leviticus, Numbers, and Deuteronomy. In their present form, these books date from much later than Moses, but through all their changes, his name has been associated with them.

Today, the Torah, in a restricted sense, means the rolled scrolls containing in Hebrew text the five Books of Moses, kept in a sort of sacred closet in the synagog. But in a wider sense it means the word and law of God and the teachings of the prophets, sages, and rabbis, explaining the will of God for His people.

The reason why the Torah seems like a living thing to a Jew is probably that it is so closely connected with his everyday life and habits. Even his diet is affected by his religion. Certain kinds of fish he may not eat. Pork is forbidden in the Torah. Probably Moses forbade eating it because in hot countries it spoils quickly. That is true also of the scaleless fish which are forbidden.

It has been said that Moses welded the Hebrew tribes into a nation, and led them from superstition to religion, by giving them a God. That is partly true, but it is nearer the truth to say that out of his own deep religious conviction Moses improved the Jews' idea of God by telling them of the Great God who had appeared to him in the Burning Bush.

To understand Judaism, one must understand Moses and know just what he did for the Jews, for he delivered them from more than Egyptian bondage. With only the aid of his brother Aaron, who was often more hindrance than help, he inspired an unorganized gang of slave workmen to desire freedom, talked their owner-employer into letting them go into the desert to worship, organized their escape and led them for forty years during which he turned this horde of fleeing refugees into a well-disciplined and armed nation with a legal code, sanitary laws, social system, economic system, and a religion which has lasted for three thousand years.

This great teacher, prophet, and organizer was the real founder of Judaism and probably the greatest of all Jews. Certainly he has influenced the human race more than any other one man—through his far-seeing laws clustering round the famous Ten Commandments.

Yet we do not know his name, nor where he was buried! "In a valley in the Land of Moab," on the edge of the land of promise, is all we know of his final resting place; and as for his name, the Jews gratefully called him "*Mosheh*," which means "Deliverer" and has become "Moses" in English. And this name, given in compliment, (as Gautama was called *Buddha,* The Enlightened, and Kutam, *Mohammed,* The Praised), has been used so much and so long that his original name has disappeared.

To understand *modern* Judaism, however, one must know about the work of another Moses, who, long after Bible times, in fact only eight centuries ago, revised and reinterpreted Judaism for his perplexed fellow Jews.

Moses Maimonides was born in Cordova, Spain, the Athens of the West, in 1135 A. D. When he was but thirteen, the city was captured by a Moslem general, and the boy wandered far to the east, studying many branches of learning until he became in time not only the acknowledged highest authority on the Talmud (the official Jewish commentary on the Law), but also the personal physician of Saladin, the greatest of the Sultans of Islam, who was himself a learned man.

This intellectual giant, Maimonides, did for Judaism what Saint Augustine and Saint Thomas Aquinas did for Christianity; namely, he systematized, revised, simplified, and explained its sacred literature and theology and reconciled both to the philosophy of the time.

Maimonides' *Guide for the Perplexed* greatly influenced Moslem and Christian as well as Jewish theology thereafter.

Moses Maimonides made Judaism forever his debtor by condensing its religious ideas to thirteen fundamental principles, as follows:

(1) Belief in the existence of God, the Creator;
(2) Belief in the unity of God;
(3) Belief in the non-bodily nature of God;
(4) Belief in the priority and eternity of God;
(5) Belief that God alone must be worshiped;
(6) Belief in prophecy;
(7) Belief that Moses was the greatest of all prophets;
(8) Belief that the Law was revealed from heaven;
(9) Belief that the Law will never be annulled and that God will give man no other Law;
(10) Belief that God knows the works of men;
(11) Belief in reward and punishment;
(12) Belief in the coming of the Messiah;
(13) Belief in the resurrection of the dead.

These Thirteen Articles were never adopted as a dogmatic test by an authoritative council of rabbis, and have often been adversely criticized, but they are widely accepted, are fairly representative of Jewish theological opinion, and are found in orthodox Jewish Prayer Books.

The Jewish observance of the seventh day of the week as the Sabbath, a day of rest and worship, is more strict than the observance of Sunday by Christians or Friday by Moslems. Because the Sabbath is a day of rest and the commandment says, ". . . in it thou shalt do no work . . . ," the more orthodox Jews interpret the prohibition so literally that on Saturday they will not carry a book, drive a nail, or light a fire. Strict observers of the Sabbath will neither turn on an electric lamp nor scratch a match to light a cigarette.

But the Sabbath is not primarily a day of prohibitions and kill-joy laws: it is really a pleasant day of light. Sabbath Eve is the time when the family is together for a joyful home meal. At sundown on Friday the mother of the household lights the candles, saying a prayer and a blessing as she does so:

"May our home be consecrated, O God, by thy Light."

When the men of the family return from the Friday evening service in the synagog, there is an exchange of "Gut Sabbas" (Good Sabbath) greetings and a common song of greetings to the Sabbath, for, to a Jew, the Sabbath, like the Torah, is almost a living being: it has a sort of personality of its own. Then there is Bible reading, wine drinking, hand washing, blessing of the children by the father, and, just before the family sits down to the evening meal, a blessing

31

of the food. Whatever else may be on the table, the *Hallah* is sure to be there, the special braided bread of the Sabbath.

It is a gay and happy meal, with the singing of songs and the asking of traditional questions, the answers to which everyone knows. The questions frequently concern national history and customs, so the children are taught almost without being aware of the process. The next morning the whole family attends synagog service and frequently the men of the family attend another meeting in the afternoon, a sort of study-class, where they discuss the writings of the rabbis, usually "Pirke Aboth," (Chapters of the Fathers), a collection of proverbs and wise comments on religion and life.

Thus with rest and worship, meditation and study of sacred writings, the Jewish Sabbath has continued through the centuries and has been adopted and adapted by other religions and even by those of no religion, at least to the extent of using it as a day of rest from labor, recognized now as one of the rights of man.

Besides the weekly Sabbath, there are a number of Jewish holidays which have come down from ancient times. Of these colorful fasts and feasts the four main ones are *Rosh Hashanah* or Jewish New Year, *Yom Kippur* or Day of Atonement, *Pesach* or Passover, and *Hanukkah* or Feast of Lights.

Jews celebrate their New Year in the fall, which may seem strange to some Gentiles, but the ancient Egyptians, Persians and Phoenicians all reckoned the year as beginning at the autumnal equinox, September 21st. With the Jews it comes in with the month *Tishri*, which may vary between September 6th and October 5th. For instance, September 28, 1954, is the first day of the Jewish year 5715, since the Jews count from the day of the creation of the world which they figured occurred in the fall of the year which Gentiles would call 3761 B. C.

The blowing of the *shofar* (ram's horn) in the synagog ushers in Rosh Hashanah, which means The Head of the Year. It is a Day of Judgment, not in the sense of the end of the world, but it is believed that on that day God enters in the Book of Life His Judgment on the deeds of each person during the year that has just passed. It is also a time when each person is expected to judge himself. In fact Rosh Hashanah begins ten days of self-examination, soul-searching and penitence which end on Yom Kippur. Rosh Hashanah itself is kept for two days, an interesting survival of the time when it took more than one day for the news to travel by signal fires and shofar blowing that the new moon which began the year had been officially seen.

The greatest of Jewish sacred days is Yom Kippur, the Day of Atonement, the tenth day of the New Year. In

Hebrew, *Yom* means day and *Kippur* means covering, hence Yom Kippur is the day of covering or atoning for sin. In former times a bullock and two goats were sacrificed as sin-offerings, but nowadays fasting and penitence have taken the place of the sacrifices. There is very rigid fasting from sunset to sunset for adults, but the younger children fast for only one meal. Some Jewish teachers have maintained that God "will regard the fat and blood lost by the fasting worshipers as though it were laid upon the altar."

On Yom Kippur nearly all Jews attend synagog services, even those who never go at any other time. Sometimes there are not enough synagogs to accommodate the crowds, so halls, ballrooms and even Christian churches are hired for the occasion.

Before a Jew can make his peace with God on the Day of Atonement, he must make peace with his brothers. He confesses all wrongdoing, and asks and secures forgiveness from all whom he may have wronged, before the final blast of the shofar which marks the sealing of the Book of Life, lest he be under the displeasure of God for the whole year until Rosh Hashanah comes round again and gives him another chance.

In contrast to the Day of Atonement is Pesach, or Passover, the springtime feast of rejoicing. Doubtless the Jews, in common with all races and nations, celebrated a vernal feast long before their captivity in Egypt, but it is now connected with their deliverance by Moses.

According to the ancient traditional history, Moses was unable to persuade Pharaoh to let the Hebrews go until God smote with death the first-born of all the Egyptians. Lest the angel of death should kill the first-born of the Jews also, it was arranged that each Jewish family should smear the doorpost of their house with the blood of a lamb. Seeing the blood, the angel of death would "pass over" the house without striking down the first-born there.

Shocked by the calamity, Pharaoh agreed to let the Jews go, but Moses urged them to make great haste lest Pharaoh change his mind. They did not tarry even to let the leaven raise the bread, but took with them the unleavened dough in the dough-troughs.

Hence it is that at the greatest meal of the year on Passover Eve there is on the table in place of the braided loaf of the Hallah a pile of the square thin crisp *Matzoth*, a sort of unleavened cracker or biscuit.

This great dinner is called *Seder*, or service, and every good Jew is supposed to "make" his Seder, that is, observe the complete long ritual prescribed by tradition for the whole evening. On the table are the old Seder symbols—for the "bitter herbs" of the Bible story there are horse-radish roots and parsley; for the sacrificial lamb, a roasted lamb bone; for the bricks which the Jews had to make in Egypt, a sort of red fruit-cake. There is also a roasted egg, which is rather interesting, since there is no mention of eggs in the Bible story of the flight from Egypt.

There is no mention of eggs in the Christian account of of the first Easter, either, but eggs have crept into the menu of the Christian breakfast on Easter morning. At any rate, the egg as a symbol of fertility, life, and hope, deserves a place at any springtime feast.

Hanukkah, the fourth of the greater Holy Days of the Jewish faith, comes at about the same time as the Christian Christmas. To the Jewish people, Hanukkah is the Feast of Dedication, instituted in 165 B. C. by Judas Maccabeus as he purified and rededicated the altar at Jerusalem after it had been polluted with a pagan sacrifice by mad King Antiochus of Syria.

This happy holiday is celebrated by Jewish children who light candles, one more each night for eight nights, the youngest child lighting the candle and saying the blessing for the first night. Hanukkah week is a time of story telling and game playing and gift giving. The children re-enact the stories of the Maccabean struggle for Jewish independence.

It is an interesting fact that the early Christian church observed Hanukkah, the feast of lights, for the first four centuries of the Christian era, until the celebration of Christmas on December 25th came in and gradually took its place.

There are so many similarities between the Jewish festivals of Hanukkah and Passover and the Christian celebrations of Christmas and Easter that in large cities where Jews and Christians live side by side, the children borrow customs from each other, with the result that a blending is taking place. In New York City, at the Easter-Passover season, Christians are learning to eat the unleavened matzoth supplied in the restaurants, and on Easter Sunday afternoon many Jews join the Christians in the Fifth Avenue fashion parade.

Perhaps this blending of festivals is a sign and foregleam of greater sympathy between religions.

There was a great Hebrew prophet named Jeremiah who has been called "the Moses after Moses and the Jesus before Jesus." The 53rd Chapter of Isaiah with its beautiful and moving description of the Suffering Servant of God, the Man of Sorrows acquainted with grief, despised and rejected of men, was very probably originally written about Jeremiah as a symbol of the true spiritual quality of Judaism, but Christianity has adopted it as a prophetic portrayal of Jesus of Nazareth.

It is very significant that when Jesus questioned his dis-

34

ciples as to who men thought he was, the reply was that some took him for Jeremiah come again to life! That is not to be wondered at, for Jesus quoted Jeremiah frequently and evidently admired him greatly.

If Christian and Jewish religious schools were to study the Book of Jeremiah simultaneously for a year, with special reference to his being the logical link between Moses and Jesus, these two great religions would discover that they have more in common than the followers of either religion realize.

In fact, the more the adherents of any religion learn about any other religion, the more they will discover the similarities and common ground in all religions, and feel a closer kinship to those of other faiths. On such sympathetic understanding rests our hope for the future peace of the world.

3

ZOROASTRIANISM

The Religion of Purity and Light

ALMOST EVERYONE is familiar with the children's game, London Bridge, popular the world over in many versions. Some students of folklore claim that the game is a survival and dramatization of the Zoroastrian concept of what happens to the soul after death.

The followers of Zoroaster, the ancient Persian prophet, believe that three days after death the soul comes to the Chinvat Bridge, the Bridge of the Decider. There, a great conflict takes place between good and evil forces to see which will have possession of the soul. After a great tug-of-war, one side or the other wins, and the man either goes off to prison for his misdeeds, or, if he has led a good life, he meets his conscience, in the form of a beautiful lady who leads him safely across the Chinvat Bridge to Paradise.

As the game London Bridge is usually played, two children clasp hands high to form the arch of the bridge, through which the other players march, singing verse after verse of "London Bridge Is Falling Down." At the line, "Here's a prisoner I have got," the two guards seize the child then passing through, and all sing, "Off to prison you must go," with the constant refrain, "My fair lady." The two leaders then take the prisoner aside and ask him to choose which side he wishes to belong to. When all the players are caught, they line up behind their leaders for a tug-of-war.

Certainly, the bridge itself, the lines "Here's a prisoner," "Off to prison you must go," and "My fair lady," combined with the decision the child must make, and the tug-of-war are all reminiscent of the Zoroastrian teaching. This is just one of the many ways by which this strange religion, evidently doomed to die out as a separate faith, has woven itself into other religions and even into our folklore.

Of all the great religions of the world, Zoroastrianism has the fewest members today. The hundred and twenty thousand living followers of Zoroaster, the Persian Prophet of the seventh century B. C., seem but a mere handful compared with the hundreds of millions of Christians, Buddhists, Hindus, and Moslems. Yet Zoroastrianism is considered still great by all experts on religion today, for two excellent reasons.

First, the small colony of Zoroastrians in Bombay (called by the Hindus "Parsees" when they arrived in India a thousand years ago as refugees fleeing from the Moslem invasion of Persia) is composed of the most intelligent, ethical, cultured, prosperous, and generous people on earth, highly admired and respected by all who know them. Their philanthropic gifts from each person average highest of all religions.

If a religion is known by its fruits, and if we measure the greatness of a faith by the quality of its people rather than by their number, then Zoroastrianism is truly great. Its followers really live up to their belief that the four virtues of man are *liberality, justice, friendliness,* and *sincerity,* and that the three great duties of man are:

1. To make him who is an enemy, a friend.
2. To make him who is wicked, righteous.
3. To make him who is ignorant, learned.

Second, scholars also reckon Zoroastrianism still great because many of its original teachings were adopted and are taught today by other religions—Judaism, Islam, and Christianity.

If a Christian were asked on a quiz program what great world religious leader

    (1) was prophesied centuries before birth as "The Saviour,"
    (2) was born of a virgin,
    (3) was saved in infancy from a jealous ruler,
    (4) astonished learned men by his youthful wisdom,
    (5) began to preach when thirty years old,
    (6) was tempted by the devil in the wilderness,
    (7) cast out demons,
    (8) cured a blind man,
    (9) performed many other miracles and
   (10) preached a Supreme God of truth and goodness,
he would probably answer:

"Jesus the Christ; for so the Bible teaches."

Yet if that same ten-fold question were asked, word for word, of a Parsee, he would answer, just as promptly:

"Zoroaster; for so the Zend-Avesta teaches."

And besides these remarkable parallels between the lives of two great founders of religion who lived nearly seven hundred years apart, Christians should know that the religion of Zoroaster, although not mentioned in the Bible by name, was closely connected with the life and death and teachings of Jesus himself! And in rather beautiful ways.

St. Matthew tells us in his gospel that:

> when Jesus was born . . . there came wise men from the east to Jerusalem saying, Where is he that is born King of the Jews? for we have seen his star in the east, and are come to worship him.

Who were these strange visitors to the cradle of the Infant Jesus? Some translators of Matthew's Greek call them "magi," "magicians," or "astrologers," rather than "wise men." But the best scholarship identifies them as Zoroastrian priests. Indeed, their reference to "his star" proves the point.

For Zoroastrians have a beautiful and interesting theory that every good man has a double in heaven, who grows as he grows on earth and becomes united with him when he dies. This double is called his *fravashi*, is supposed to be a sort of guardian angel or guiding star, and appears in the sky as a star when he is born. The greater the man, the brighter the star.

According to the apocryphal Book of James, the *Protevangelium*, which did not quite get into our Bible but parts of which are as old as some books that did, the Wise Men said:

> We saw a very great star* shining among those stars and dimming them so that the stars appeared not: and thereby we knew that a king was born unto Israel, and we came to worship him.

Jesus himself evidently believed and taught the Persian idea of the heavenly doubles, for he called a little child unto him and then said to his disciples:

> Take heed that ye despise not one of these little ones; for I say unto you, That in heaven their angels do always behold the face of my Father which is in heaven.

One of the Zoroastrian ideas adopted by Jesus is revealed by his words as he was dying on the cross, when he promised the penitent thief, "Today thou shalt be with me in Paradise." Now the Hebrew word for the place where both good and bad people went after death was *Sheol*. Paradise, as a sep-

---

* Astronomers have recorded over thirty novae or temporary bright stars. On February 23, 1901, a nova was the brightest star in the sky, but by July it had almost disappeared.

arate very beautiful place for the good, was not known to the Jews until their exile in Babylon and the conquest of that city by the Zoroastrian king Cyrus. The very word is from the Persian *pairidaeza*.

From Zoroastrianism the Jews also adopted many other ideas which Christianity took over later, such as the last judgment when the good shall be separated from the bad, the coming of the Messiah or Anointed One, the resurrection of the dead, the belief in evil spirits, and the final triumph over Satan the Adversary, or the Devil.

Perhaps this concept of the devil was one of Zoroaster's greatest contributions to Jewish and Christian theology. Before the Jews were taken into captivity in Babylon in 586 B. C., they had no personal devil in their religion. In 538 B. C. Cyrus, the Zoroastrian Mede, conquered Babylon and let the Jews go home to Palestine, where they remained under Zoroastrian rule for two hundred years until Greek Alexander the Great came into power.

Since Zoroaster was the first, of all teachers, to teach the doctrine of a chief demon, Angra Mainyu, the Adversary, and since the Jews after their return from captivity began to mention in their writings a personal devil whom they called Satan, which in Hebrew means the Adversary, and since, still further, Christianity took over Satan from the Jews, along with much other Persian theology, it is plain that Zoroastrianism today is not altogether confined to the remaining Parsees in India.

The followers of Zoroaster have, through the centuries, laid more and more emphasis on the idea of purity and consequently have paid increasing reverence to fire. This has led to their being called "fire-worshipers," which they vehemently deny, claiming, that they are no more fire-worshipers than Christians are cross-worshipers. Just as the cross is the symbol of the sacrifice of Christ for the sins of men, so fire is to the Parsee a symbol of the purity and righteousness of his god Ahura Mazda, and he permits no other symbol or representation. One of their writers has explained the matter in a most inspiring sentence:

> Think not that our fathers were worshipers of the fire itself: they fixed their eyes on the splendor of the exalted flame while they humbled their spirits before God.

The sandalwood fires kept ever burning in Parsee temples are sister symbols of the eternal light in Jewish synagogs and the ever-shining candles in many Christian churches.

Light and fire played a major part in the life of Zoroaster, according to the legendary accounts of him. He was conceived when the Glory of God "came down from the endless light and mingled with the mother of Zoroaster" who was then fifteen. For the three days before his birth, his radiance within his mother was so great as to illuminate the whole village. When he was born, his face was shining with light, and instead of crying and wailing as most infants do at birth, he laughed outright.

When he was a young man, he experimented with fire and lights in a cave where he made a miniature solar system, the first planetarium. He studied the stars and was the Father of Astrology. His call to preach came one bright morning when he stood at sunrise by the River Daiti and saw coming toward him a tall shining angel who took him up to a heaven so bright that he and the angel cast no shadows. There he met the great God Ahura Mazda, the Lord of Light and Purity, who taught him the principles of the true religion and commissioned him to preach it.

For many years Zoroaster traveled throughout the Iranian plateau, later known as Persia, preaching the Gospel of Light and calling on men to fight darkness with light, evil with good, to worship Ahura Mazda and help him defeat Angra Mainyu, the Lord of Darkness and Evil. To symbolize the new religion, we are told, Zoroaster carried with him "a cube of fire." The character of "a cube of fire" is unknown. The best guess is that it was a block of some porous substance which he dipped into an inflammable liquid, perhaps some form of the precious petroleum for which the nations of the world are even now contending in that very area. And when Zoroaster died at the age of seventy-seven, leaving behind a chain of centers of Mazda worship, each with its pot of eternal fire, his death came, so the Greeks who greatly admired him tell us, either by a stroke of lightning or by a flame from heaven.

The modern Parsee devotion to their religion of purity and light is beautifully shown in the *Naojote* ceremony, a most impressive occasion in the life of a Parsee, for it is his or her initiation into the sacred religion of Zoroastrianism and at the same time the recognition of his or her independence. Thereafter the boy or girl can without assistance pray and observe certain religious customs and ceremonies. In fact, the very word "naojot" means "new priest."

Moreover, it is the beginning of the serious education of the child, and the Parsees look upon education as a kind of light—an illumination of the mind—for they say:

"Education is the light-giving eye of man."

This beautiful initiation ceremony may take place as early as the age of seven, or it may be postponed to any age below fifteen, especially if the child is not yet deemed intelligent enough to understand the ceremony and assume his responsibilities. But the Naojote must take place by the age of fifteen lest the child be claimed by the Evil Spirit because he or she is guilty of the sin of "running about uncovered." The reference is to the being covered by the *sudrah*, or sacred shirt, the putting on of which is the main feature of the ceremony.

The child to be initiated is not seated before the officiating white-robed priest until he has been properly prepared for the ceremony by memorizing prayers and by a very careful bathing. Beneath his shawl, the candidate is naked to the waist. Beside them the eternal sacred sandalwood fire is burning.

The ceremony begins by the priest putting a new sudrah in the child's hands. All present pray. The child prays again, usually the Lord's Prayer of Zoroastrianism, called the *Honover*, (short for *Ahuna vairo*, the first two words in Persian), which runs in English:

"The will of the Lord is the law of righteousness."

The priest and the child now rise and the former very slowly and in carefully prescribed manner puts on him the sacred shirt and ties round him the sacred cord, both priest and child repeating prayers and reciting scripture all the while.

The sudrah must be made of the choicest white cambric, symbolic of innocence, light, and purity, and must be of two pieces of cloth stitched with seams down the side under the arms, so that the wearer represents the living present between the back past and the front future.

The most important part of this sacred shirt, however, is the pocket, which is in a strange place for a pocket—high in front, just below the throat. It is the bag or purse of righteousness, and is a symbol of both thrift and goodness, reminding the young initiate to keep his pocket full of money and the symbolic purse full of good deeds.

Christianity tells its converts not to lay up treasures on earth where moth and rust corrupt, but to lay up treasure in heaven where thieves do not break through and steal. But Zoroastrianism teaches its young initiates to do both. In fact, it is the only great world religion which openly reckons money-making and money-saving to be a virtue. To be sure, it also teaches and practices money-giving and charity more than any other religion.

The sacred cord, which the priest winds round the child's waist three times, symbolizes the three principles of Zoroastrianism, good thought, good speech, and good work. He ties it with four knots, two in front and two in back, typifying the four elements—fire, air, water and earth. There are three tassels on each end of the cord, representing the six sacred festivals which the child must hereafter observe each year. It is made of seventy-two threads, one for each chapter in the Yasna, one of the sacred books.

The sacred shirt and cord must always be worn, except when bathing, but the cord must be untied and retied right after rising in the morning, after every "call of nature," before prayer, after bathing, and before every meal. It must always be tied correctly, accompanied by the recitation of scripture verses and prayers as each knot is tied. A Zoroastrian youth can never forget his religion. Even when he puts his shirt on, he must look into the pocket to see if there are any good deeds there which he has put in recently.

In the Christian wedding ceremony, no knots are actually tied, although we often say "the parson tied the knot," but in the Parsee ceremony there are plenty of knots. A cloth is wound round the couple and tied with a double knot. A twisted cord is then wound around them seven times and knotted seven times over their clasped hands.

If an American is inclined to smile at such exaggerated knot-tying, let him remember that the United States divorce rate is now about one divorce to every three marriages whereas, among the Parsees, divorce is practically unknown.

It is regrettable that a religion with so much of good in it should have so few followers today. Within a century after Zoroaster had died, his faith had overrun Babylonia, Medea, Persia, and all the Near East; and Xerxes, a Zoroastrian king, had led a mighty army to the very gates of Athens. Yet apart from about ten thousand in remote parts of Iran, and perhaps as many more scattered throughout the world, the hundred thousand in India, mostly in or near Bombay, are all that are left.

One reason for this lack of growth is the refusal of Parsees to do any missionary work. In fact, one cannot become a Parsee by profession of faith, but only by inheritance, and, like the educated and well-to-do of all lands and faiths, the Parsees have few children.

Parsees differ from people of other religions in the matter of fasting. Instead of considering it a virtue, they call it a sin! In their sacred scriptures it is written:

Abstain from the keeping of fasts. . . . He who fasts commits a sin, and must, by way of expiation, give food to a number of poor people. . . . No one who does not eat has strength to do works of holiness. . . .

The greatest emphasis in the Zoroastrian religion, however, is on the virtue of purity. They believe:

Purity is for man, next to life, the greatest good. . . . The Religion of Mazda cleanses the faithful from every evil thought, word, and deed, as a swift-rushing mighty wind cleanses the plain.

This almost fanatic devotion to ceremonial purity accounts for their unique method of disposing of the bodies of the dead. Since they reverence the earth as well as the fire, they neither bury nor cremate corpses, but expose them on *dakhmas*, "Towers of Silence," in secluded places where birds come and devour the flesh, and the bones are left to dry. Twice a year the bones are collected and cast into the central well of the dakhma where they are eventually reduced to dust by the action of sun, rain, and air.

To some of us, that seems anything but a proper method of treating a dead human body, but the Parsees consider our burial customs very wicked, since one of their sacred books proclaims that burying the dead is "a sin for which there is no atonement." Some Parsees, however, have been advocating modernizing their disposal practices to bring them into line with present-day hygiene, and have suggested that bodies could be consumed by electricity; but that raises the question whether electricity may not be a form of fire, and therefore subject to the ancient taboo.

Zoroastrians have a great body of sacred writings, commonly called the *Zend-Avesta*. The most recent are in the modern Persian language, and prescribe the proper performance of rituals in the light of theology. The next older group of scriptures are in Pahlavi, a form of Persian current between the third and ninth centuries A. D., and include theological dogmas and commentaries on still more ancient Avestan texts.

These latter, the classical scriptures, written in one of the oldest of Aryan languages, cognate and contemporary with Sanskrit, form the *Avesta*, the Bible proper of the Zoroastrian faith. It is largely liturgical in nature, containing litanies, prayers, purification ceremonies, and hymns. Of the oldest group of seventy-two hymns, seventeen *Gathas*, or psalms, are attributed to Zoroaster himself, and are the oldest and most revered scriptures of all. In these most ancient sacred writings, singularly enough, modern folk of any religion can discover precious gems of faith that sparkle as brightly today as when they were first created by the Sage of Old Iran, such as this beautiful humanistic psalm:

> And through this Teaching I grow true and wise,
> When difficulties come, my faith in man
> Leads me to be and do what Thou hast taught—
> To be my own true self and do my best.

There are glimpses of universal truth and beauty for anyone who will study Zoroastrian beliefs, such as their concept of the rainbow. In the Jewish and Christian religions, children are taught that the rainbow was God's promise to Noah and his descendants that there never would be another world flood. When admiring the ....ctrum colors of the arc in the sky, one might recall also .ne Zoroastrian idea that the rainbow is "a signal of friendly greeting from spiritual beings in the heavens unto human beings on the earth."

And since someone with poetic imagination and a knowledge of comparative religion named the electric lamp after the Persian God of Light, Mazda, it can be said that in one way, at least, the faith of Zoroaster still illumines the world.

4

BUDDHISM

The Religion of the Middle Way

THERE CAME TO THE BUDDHA one day a weeping woman who carried a child on her hip and said:

"Lord Buddha, give me medicine to cure my child." And he, looking at the child and her, saw that the child was already dead and that she knew it, but he said:

"Very well, I will cure the sick one. Go into yonder village and bring me mustard-seed, but you must borrow it from a house where death has never entered." At sunset she returned and said:

"Lord Buddha, I understand. I was selfish in my grief, but you have cured my sick mind. Give me but leave to bury my little one and then I will come and follow thee."

From that day, 2500 years ago, until today, countless millions have also followed the Buddha and found peace of mind. Who was he, and what was his message?

He was a prince of India, Gautama Siddhartha, who, at the age of thirty, left his palaces, his wife and his little son, and went out into the world as a poor beggar to find the answer to human suffering.

He found his answer, not in temple sacrifices, nor in the fasting and privations of hermit monks, but in what we today call psychology. It dawned on him one morning that if suffering is due to unfulfilled desire, the way to peace is to stop desiring.

This is the core of his message—right thinking will bring peace of mind. This is what his half-billion followers believe now as they repeat their consoling creed:

> I take refuge in the Buddha:
> I take refuge in the Doctrine:
> I take refuge in the Brotherhood.

The life story of the Buddha is as strange as it is beautiful. There is a legend regarding his miraculous birth.

It was a wonderful dream that came to the young queen bride of India that late summer afternoon as she rested on

43

the couch in the great state bedchamber—such a strange
dream that when she told it to her husband, King Suddhodana, he summoned his wise men, the Brahmans, and
gave them gifts that they might interpret the meaning of
Queen Maya's dream.

Now the realm of King Suddhodana was the fair land of
the Sakya people, where the southern slopes of the Himalayas
meet the fertile plains of northern India; and as the queen
lay on the great bed, she could look through the window and
see in the distance the snowy peaks of the greatest of all
mountains.

In her dream, four courtly kings came and carried her,
bed and all, to a tableland of those Himalayas and set the
bed down beneath a great tree. Four queens then came and
bathed her, clothed her in wondrous raiment, touched her
with dainty scents, and decorated her with garlands of ex-
quisite flowers. They led her to a silver mountain, whereon
was a golden mansion, wherein was a sacred bed.

And as she lay upon that bed, she heard a trumpeting and
she beheld a glorious white elephant enter in the chamber.
His trunk shone like silver and with its fingerlike tip he held
a beautiful white lotus. Circling the bed slowly rightwise
three times, he then touched her right side with the lotus
and she seemed thereby in some strange fashion to conceive.
The psychic shock wakened her.

The Brahman wise men were no psychoanalysts, for this
was the sixth century B. C., but they were canny in their own
way and after due deliberation told the king:

"Fear not. The queen has conceived a son. If this son
dwells in a house, he will become king of all the world. If he
leaves his house and goes forth, he will become a Buddha, a
remover of the veil of ignorance from the world."

Today, all over the world, wherever even a dozen Buddhists may live, the birthday of the Buddha, Queen Maya's
son, is celebrated early in the month of May, a festival of
great rejoicing amid many beautiful blossoms. For he was
born among the flowers in a pleasure grove.

The queen was traveling in a golden palanquin to her own
family home for the birth. Beside the road there was, so
the ancient Buddhist scriptures tell us:

> a pleasure grove of sal-trees named the Lumbini
> grove. At that time from the roots to the tips of the
> branches it was one mass of flowers, and from within
> the branches and flowers hosts of bees of the five colors
> and various flocks of birds sported, singing sweetly.
> When the queen saw it, a desire to sport in the grove
> arose. . . . She went to the foot of a great sal-tree, and
> desired to seize a branch. The branch like the tip of a

supple reed bent down and came within reach of her hand. Stretching out her hand she seized the branch. Thereupon she was shaken with the throes of birth. . . . So the attendants set up a curtain for her and retired. Holding the branch and even while standing she was delivered.

And on that same May day of 563 B. C. were also born, we are told, the famous horse Kanthaka which the Buddha was to ride, his favorite elephant, his charioteer, his future wife, and even the bo-tree under which he was later to receive enlightenment.

As of every great religious leader, marvelous stories of his infancy are told. For instance, at his birth two streams of water fell from the sky—one hot and one cold—for his washing. Saints and kings acted as midwives, transferring him from a golden net, via an antelope skin, to a silken cushion, from which he rose immediately and took seven steps!

A wise man named Asita living in the Himalayas had seen a sign in the sky and came to behold the infant, rejoicing when he noted that the newly born Prince Gautama Siddhartha had all thirty-two of the traditional bodily marks of a great man, including projecting heels, prominent ankles, black hair curling toward the right, forty teeth, eyelashes like an ox, white hair between the eyebrows, and a head the shape of a cap.

The boy was reared in almost fantastic luxury and with the greatest of care. Of his youth he said later:

I was extremely delicate, O monks. Pools were made, all for my sake; in one were blue lotuses, in another red, in another white. Night and day a white parasol was held over me so that I should not be touched by cold or heat, by dust or weeds or dew. I had three palaces, one for the cold months, one for the hot, and one for the four rainy months when, entertained by female minstrels, I did not leave the palace at all.

Naturally, the over-pampered young man became restive under such restraint. As far as was possible his father kept from him all knowledge of the pain, suffering, disease and death in the world, but it takes more than walls to keep information from reaching an inquiring mind.

One spring day a flock of wild swans, headed north for nesting, passed over the garden prison of the prince. A hunter outside the wall shot the leading swan and it fell at the boy's feet, its wing transfixed by an arrow. The wondering lad soothed the bird's fright, removed the arrow, and salved the wound. He refused to give up the swan to the hunter who claimed it as his rightful prey, and a suddenly convened court upheld the boy on the ground that he who saves a life has more right to it than he who seeks to take it.

But the arrow had hurt the boy more than the bird, for it brought pain to his heart with the fear that there was sorrow that he knew not of, and strange conflicts in the world that lay beyond the walls of the palace gardens. He determined to find out, and pressed his father so hard that King Suddhodana finally gave him permission when he was sixteen years old to take a ride within the confines of the royal farm.

The king had removed anything which might give evidence of sorrow or pain to the innocent prince Siddhartha. All the ploughmen and milkmaids were singing, as in a well-staged musical comedy which indeed it was; but when the young prince returned to his summer palace after the day at the farm, he sat booding sorrowfully, and his father asked him why.

He had not known, the boy said, how hard men and women had to work for their daily bread. He had felt pain himself when the ploughmen goaded the straining oxen galled by their heavy yokes. He had seen a young frog seize and swallow a beautiful butterfly, only to be swallowed itself by a snake which in turn was carried aloft in the talons of a hawk which fell dead from the arrow of a boy who had to fight a larger lad for the prize.

So the boy prince Siddhartha pondered on the misery of existence and on the pain and death which lurked for every living thing, and wondered what might be done about it as he himself grew pale and thin with sympathetic sorrow. His father then consulted wise men who smilingly suggested that sometimes metal chains could not hold a young man whom a fair maid's tresses would bind fast. Perhaps the cure for a sorrowful despairing love of all living things was the sweet love of the dearest of all beings who live.

It was the first beauty show of which we have record, this "court of pleasure" which the king arranged. The most beautiful girls of all north India were commanded to perfume and bedeck themselves and parade before the sole judge, the young prince. There were to be lavish prizes for all; but the girls knew, if Prince Siddhartha did not, that he was the grand prize, to be had by the maid who would win his attention and love.

Clad in gorgeous silken saris with fresh flowers in their dark hair, hundreds of graceful girls sauntered seductively before him, and took from the prince the gifts he gently and smilingly but very impartially and almost indifferently offered them. When the last gift was gone, he sighed with relief, then started with embarrassment when he noticed that there still was one girl left. But what a girl!

The other girls had passed him with eyes downcast in

retended modesty. This radiant maiden, fairest of all in form and features, met his gaze fullface and smiled frankly and understandingly at the predicament in which they found themselves because of some miscount. The prince, no longer indifferent, apologized for the lack of a remaining gift, but offered a substitute of his own. As Sir Edwin Arnold tells it:

—therewith he loosed
The emerald necklet from his throat, and clasped
Its green beads round her dark and silk-soft waist;
And their eyes mixed, and from the look sprang love.

The scheme had worked, and King Suddhodana in great glee soon sent messengers to beautiful Yasodhara's father asking her hand for Prince Siddhartha.

But there were other young men already interested, it appeared, and the girl's father rather favored them as more manly young fellows than the pampered Siddhartha, so he sent back word to King Suddhodana that only if the youth could excel all others in archery, swordplay and horsemanship could he have the hand of the fair Yasodhara.

Whereat the king was sad, for he knew that among the other suitors were Devadatta the best archer, Ardjuna the most expert with horses, and Nanda the best swordsman in all the lands of the Sakyas. How could his cloistered son compete with these?

But Prince Siddhartha assured his worried father that he had no fear of the rival suitors, for love would make his eye keen and his arm strong. It was not on love alone that the young man was depending however; unknown to the king he had been secretly practicing and learning the required skills.

When the great day of the tournament came, Siddhartha surprised everyone but himself by winning easily all contests, so that men marvelled then and thereafter that a youth nurtured amid rose-bowers could vanquish men hardened by hunting and war.

The wedding was magnificent with all the symbolical ritual of the Sakya people, and King Suddhodana felt that married life would lessen the prince's melancholy meditations on the sorrows of existence. The king, however, did not trust to love alone, but built for the young couple a most magnificent palace for a wedding present, so designed that it was really a prison in disguise, with thick walls and surrounding forests to shut out the world of men.

All the attendants were sworn to cheerfulness and forbidden to mention pain or sickness or death or even old age. Not a wilting flower or dead leaf was permitted to suggest the temporal nature of all living things. The king had ever in mind the queen's dream and its interpretation by the wise men—that the boy, if a house-dweller, would become an even greater king than his father, but, if a wanderer, would be a holy prophet. Suddhodana was trying to insure the succession to his throne.

For ten years the king's marriage-trap and palace-trap kept the prince captive, but the king longed for a third trap —a child to hold the prisoner secure. And when Siddhartha's little son came, the grandfather was very happy. He was not even suspicious when the young father named the child *Rahula*, which means fetter or shackle.

It seems that Siddhartha, now twenty-nine years of age, had secretly made several short exploratory trips outside the palace grounds on his favorite horse Kanthaka, and had seen a very sick man, a very old man, and a corpse on the way to the cremation fire. These sights, new to him, had confirmed his boyhood suspicions of the existence of much misery and sorrow in the world. He determined to go forth and find out the truth for himself. If all men were likely to suffer and sure to grow old and die, what was the purpose of it all?

So, leaving behind his vast wealth and all the great expectations upon his succession to the throne, and stealing one last fond look at his wife and the week-old son sleeping together in the moonlight, he rode quietly away by night on Kanthaka, with the groom Chandaka running along beside holding by the stirrup. This flight from the palace is called in Buddhism "The Great Renunciation."

At dawn he dismounted, cut off his beautiful long hair with his sword, bade a touching farewell to his horse, and sent the weeping groom back riding the horse and bearing the sword and princely garments to King Suddhodana as a sign that his only son had "gone out" to save the world.

Then, clad in a coarse yellow robe, he set forth on foot, carrying only his begging-bowl, a razor, a needle, a rope girdle, and a water-strainer, as countless thousands of Buddhist monks have "gone out" in the twenty-five centuries since.

Of this very limited equipment, Gautama Siddhartha considered the water-strainer the most important item, not because he feared contracting disease from bug-infested drinking water, but because he feared he might unwittingly kill the poor bugs by swallowing them! He had already determined that there was enough death in this unhappy world and he was not going to be the cause of destruction of any living creature if he could in any way help it. He later made the very first of his ten commandments, "Thou shalt not take life."

. From prince to pauper, or from playboy to philosopher, history knows no more sudden or complete transition.

For six years and through three kingdoms, Siddhartha sought the solution of the riddle of existence. He sat at the feet of the sagest of men, Brahmans and yogis alike, and found no answer. He went to the priests in the temples and studied the system of salvation by sacrifice for sin, and departed sadly saying:

"How can a new evil atone for an old one? Can the killing of an innocent animal erase the sin of a man? That would be religion at the expense of moral conduct."

In the jungle of Uruvela, Siddhartha found five *bhikkhus*, ascetic hermit monks who practiced strict self-discipline by fasting and the subduing of the senses, and they assured him that this was the path to peace. Enthusiastically the young man adopted their way of life and soon became their leader, for he surpassed them in austerity. When they limited themselves to a handful of chick-peas a day, he took but half as much. Then he cut down that much by one pea less a day until he became a mere skeleton, and people came from far to see the holy man who had conquered his senses, and lived on three peas a day. He tells us:

"When I touched my belly, I could feel my backbone. My ribs stuck out like the rafters of an old shed. When I sat in the sand I made a mark like a camel's footprint."

When he got down to one hemp seed a day and his skin had turned from light brown to a dirty black like a mangura-fish, and he could not take three steps without falling, and yet he had not attained to superior knowledge and insight, he decided at last that there must be some better way of doing it.

There came to him then, as he lay swooning and dreaming of the rose-apple tree in his father's palace garden, a girl of whom we know nothing save this her act of womanly mercy and that her name was Nanda, the herdsman's daughter. Here was a poor starving man. It might be a holy thing to fast, but there was a limit to such things. So she held his head up and slowly fed him warm rice gruel; then later, good cooked rice with sour milk. He began to feel better as life returned to his weak limbs and clarity to his mind.

But his five disciples were doubly shocked at finding him eating a full meal and in the company of a woman. So they left him alone as a backslider.

He was glad to be left alone as he wished to think. Six years before, he had abandoned his home and family to seek the meaning of human existence. First he had tried philosophy, studying under the wisest men of the day, but to no avail. Then he had examined the priests with their temple practice of seeking salvation from sin by sacrifice and had found that equally fruitless. For several years since, he had been practicing self-torture by fasting and other forms of asceticism, but he saw now that that had been "time spent in trying to tie the air in knots." What then was the answer?

Like a flash it came to him one night as he sat in meditation under a *bo*-tree. His solution seems very simple to us in this day of psychology, and it is hard for us to conceive how new and wonderful it seemed to him 2500 years ago.

The "Great Illumination," as it was later called, was simply the discovery that *since pain is caused by desire, the way to peace is to stop desiring.*

Of course, there was more to it than that. Prince Guatama Siddhartha, who was thereafter called The Buddha, that is, the Enlightened One, formulated his Great Illumination for teaching purposes into The Four Noble Truths and the Eightfold Path, which interlock because the Fourth Noble Truth is the Eightfold Path:

(1) The First Noble Truth is that all who live suffer.
(2) The Second Noble Truth is that all suffering is due to desire, which can never be satisfied.
(3) The Third Noble Truth is that therefore suffering will end when all desires are suppressed.
(4) The Fourth Noble Truth is that the Middle Path of Moderation which leads to the end of suffering is the Noble Eightfold Path of
    (a) Right Views,
    (b) Right Resolves,
    (c) Right Speech,
    (d) Right Conduct,
    (e) Right Occupation,
    (f) Right Effort,
    (g) Right Awareness,
    (h) Right Meditation.

It is doubtful if many Americans would accept Siddhartha's Buddhistic recipe for happiness by suppressing desire, but we can adapt and adopt his general principle in the light of modern psychology and say that peace of mind can be attained by the control of emotional desires within reasonable limits.

Again, it is to be noted that what the Buddha preached was really salvation by psychology. He was the first prophet, so far as we know, to proclaim that inner peace comes to man by the control of his own mind rather than from outside gods.

When morning came, the prophet rose from his seat under the bo-tree (a large variety of fig-tree) determined to go forth and preach his newly discovered gospel of the Middle Way of salvation through mind-control. His first converts were two traveling traders who that morning gave him rice and honey-cakes for his breakfast. He then went to the place to which his five former followers had retired, and quickly converted them.

Buddhist tradition maintains that the five monks were saved by listening to the Buddha's famous first sermon, the "Sutta of Turning the Wheel of the Doctrine," in which he announced and explained the Four Noble Truths and the Eightfold Noble Path. This sermon has often been compared to Jesus' Sermon on the Mount.

The prophet soon had sixty disciples whom he sent out to preach far and wide. The success of the new doctrine was immediate, for India was in great need of a reformation in religion. The old Hinduism had become a corrupt system of priest-ridden superstition preying upon the ignorance of the people.

Seven years after he had left home, Siddhartha returned at the request of his aging father who had begged to see him once more before he died. King Suddhodana was shocked to see the yellow-robed monk who would have nothing to with the royal feast of welcome and insisted on begging his food from door to door. But the Buddha converted his father, his wife, and even his seven-year-old son. Indeed, the faithful Yasodhara had kept informed of all her absent husband's adventures and had followed his example of fasting and wearing a coarse yellow robe in the midst of the palace splendors.

For forty-five years more, until his death at eighty, Gautama Siddhartha the Buddha preached all over north India, sometimes accompanied by crowds of disciples, but often "he wandered lonely as a rhinoceros."

Like the great teacher he was, the Buddha put his message into simple forms, easy to remember. Besides the Four Noble Truths and the Eightfold Noble Path, he taught that there are Four Intoxications and Five Hindrances which prevent virtue.

The Four Intoxications are caused by (1) Sensuality, (2) Pride of Life, (3) Ignorance and (4) Speculation or Idle Wondering. Any one of these would produce in time a sort of mental haze like that of a drunken man. The Five Hindrances are (1) Fleshliness, (2) Crankiness (3) Laziness, (4) Worry, and (5) Hesitation. These latter are not often listed as sins in the western world, but there is no doubt that the Buddha was right in calling them hindrances to the good life.

The Ten Commandments of Buddhism differ greatly from the Ten Commandments of Judaism and Christianity.

They have no reference whatever to God or to the Sabbath; and the duties of man to man are much stricter. They are usually recited in this order:

(1) Thou shalt not take life. Compared with the Mosaic commandment, "Thou shalt not commit murder," ° this is much more inclusive. It prohibits all animal sacrifices, the killing of animals for food, the hunting of animals, and all war. All Buddhists are conscientious objectors by their first commandment, which is one reason why Buddhism was driven out of India by the warlike followers of Mohammed.

(2) Thou shalt not take what is not given. This is like the "Thou shall not steal" of Moses, but is interpreted as meaning also that one should not cause others to steal by carelessly putting temptation in their way. It means, too, that one should be generous, even to the extent of giving one's life for others.

(3) Thou shalt not be unchaste. Not merely adultery, but impurity, is prohibited and, in the case of Buddhist monks, marriage is forbidden.

(4) Thou shalt not lie. It is interesting to note that while the Mosaic code forbids bearing false witness against one's neighbor, the Buddhist commandment includes any kind of falsehood, misrepresentation, deceit, slander or gossip. Furthermore, on the positive side, this commandment is said to mean that one should speak only good of another and what is likely to cause harmony rather than trouble.

(5) Thou shalt not drink intoxicating liquors. This is interpreted to imply also that it is wrong to approve of others' drinking and wrong to act so as to drive others to drink.

These first five commandments are for all Buddhists, lay-members or monks, but there are five rather interesting ones for the monks alone:

(6) Thou shalt not be intemperate in eating and not eat after noon.

(7) Thou shalt not engage in nor witness dancing, singing, or plays.

(8) Thou shalt not use garlands, perfumes, or ornaments.

(9) Thou shalt not use high or luxurious beds.

(10) Thou shalt not accept gifts of gold or silver.

There is no record of the Buddha's ever praying or ever teaching his disciples to pray. The nearest to a prayer there is in Buddhism is the statement which must be made by a convert, which is called The Refuge, or the Buddhist Trinity:

°Mistranslated "Thou shalt not kill" in the King James Version.

> I take refuge in the Buddha.
> I take refuge in the Dharma.
> I take refuge in the Sangha.

The Dharma is the Teaching or Doctrine of Buddhism, and the Sangha is the brotherhood of the Believers.

As for the future life, Buddhists believe in *samsara*, which means the stream of existence in the ocean of births and deaths, but it is often translated transmigration of souls, or reincarnation. They hold that at death the soul is reborn in another body, and so on and on until one attains *Nirvana*. One life is not enough for the conquering of desire: it may take thousands, and some of the lives may be subhuman.

Nirvana does not mean, as has been commonly supposed in the West, that the soul is annihilated or wiped out completely. Nothing so irritates a scholar from India. A learned pundit friend of mine once said to me:

> Nothing in Buddhism has been so completely misunderstood as the teaching about Nirvana. . . . The human spirit itself is neither extinguished, nor is it absorbed into the universal spirit as a drop of water is merged into the ocean, vanishing as an individual entity. It is merely freed from the limitations of earthly attachments and personality, and it then enjoys transcendental bliss.

Buddhism took on a new lease of life under Asoka the Great, Emperor of India, who was converted about 270 B. C. and forthwith and with great energy and intelligence strengthened and promoted the teachings of the Buddha. He built temples all over India wherein were deposited tiny fragments of Gautama Siddhartha's bones. He set up an educational system and sent Buddhist missionaries to all parts of the great Greek Empire which Alexander the Great had recently established, and to eastern Asia as well. Buddhism spread to Ceylon, Tibet, Burma, Siam, Java and all Malaysia, China, and Japan, and still exists in those countries.

The faith of the Buddha has had a tremendous influence in China ever since it was first planted there in the first century B. C. Even today rejected wives, disappointed fathers, lovesick youths, discouraged business men, and aging mothers "take refuge in the Buddha" and find peace of mind.

It does not appeal to all psychological types, but the fact remains that it must be reckoned in point of numbers the greatest religion the earth has ever known. If all types and sects of Buddhism are included, estimates of the present numbers run as high as five hundred and twenty million as compared with five hundred million for all branches and sects of Christianity, its nearest rival. Both these estimates are probably overgenerous, but it should be remembered that Buddhism had over five and a half centuries' head start over Christianity, which it therefore far outnumbers if the total individual followers down through history are counted. Christianity, however, is far more widespread than Buddhism, which has always been mostly confined to the continent of Asia.

The Buddha, like Jesus and Confucius, was a teacher who knew the importance of proverbs, wise sayings, parables, and stories. Some of his popular sayings are:

"He who fills his lamp with water or his life with lust will dwell in darkness."

"To keep the body in good health is a duty: otherwise the mind is not strong and clear."

"Our deeds, good or evil, follow us like shadows."

"The fowl in the coop has plenty to eat, but will soon be but food himself. No one feeds the wild crane, but the heavens and the earth are his."

"Three things cannot be long hidden, the sun, the moon, and the truth."

"Mind is the source of happiness or unhappiness."

"No man can purify another man."

"Overcome anger by love, evil by good, the greedy by generosity, and the liar by truth."

"Long is the night to him who is awake; long is a mile to him who is tired; long is life to the foolish who know not the true religion."

"Let us live happily then, not hating those who hate us."

Of the thousands of stories said in the East to have been told by the Buddha or about him, the following three are a fair sampling.

Two young wild geese liked a turtle very much but they found him too talkative. When they flew south for the winter they invited him to go along with them. He said he would like to go to a warm country but he had no wings. They told him, however, that they could manage to take him if he would promise to keep his mouth shut and say nothing to anybody. He agreed, so the geese brought a stick and told the turtle to take tight hold of the middle of it with his jaws and keep his mouth shut till they told him he could open it. Then each goose took hold of an end of the stick in his bill and flew slowly away with the turtle hanging on in the middle. As they took off they flew low over a village and the children saw them and were amused, saying:

"Oh, look at the geese carrying a turtle by a stick. Did you ever see anything so funny in your life!" Whereat the turtle retorted:

"Well, what of it? Mind your own business!" And of course, when he let go the stick to talk he fell from the sky and died as he struck the ground at the feet of the children, who said:

"That just shows what happens to you when you can't keep your mouth shut."

Very popular among Buddhists is the Tale of the Impudent Ape. Now the Impudent Ape was old and wise and clever, but very mischievous. He knew seventy-two magic tricks, could travel anywhere by riding the clouds of the sky, and could change into any shape he wished. He made so much trouble that people sent for the Lord Buddha to tame him.

And when the Lord Buddha came out of the West, the Impudent Ape shouted:

"Who are you that you dare approach me unbidden?"

"I'm the Lord Buddha," he said very kindly, "and I have come to cure your impudence and make you tame." But the ape said, with bragging and breast-beating:

"I'm the Impudent Ape and I have secret knowledge and seventy-two magic tricks and I shall live forever and I am afraid of nobody!" And the Lord Buddha said with a smile:

"I have heard you can travel far and fast on the white clouds of heaven." And the Impudent Ape said "Watch me!" and he turned great somersaults on the white clouds of heaven fast and far like a whirlwind until he saw on the horizon five tall and beautiful pink pillars rising to the skies like mighty towers. And he thought he had reached the end of the world, so he made a mark on the middle pillar and then hurried back to the Lord Buddha and bragged:

"Ha! Ha! I went to the end of the world and back and if you don't believe me, go and see for yourself the mark I left at the base of the middle tower." The Lord Buddha smiled again and held out his hand and the Impudent Ape saw the mark he had made where the middle finger joined the palm of the Lord Buddha's hand. And thereafter the Impudent Ape troubled men no more.

Still another of the favorite *jatakas*, or legendary stories, chanted by the Buddhist monks of Ceylon on full-moon nights according to the ancient custom, is the Tale of the Very Strong Ox.

The owner of a Very Strong Ox once boasted to the men of a nearby village:

"I will forfeit to you a thousand pieces of silver if my Very Strong Ox cannot pull a line of a hundred wagons!"

They laughed at him, but agreed when he insisted; and he put up his silver and harnessed the ox to the first of a long line of one hundred ox-carts. Then he beat and goaded the ox and shouted:

"Get up there, you lazy ox! Pull, you wretched beast!"

But the Very Strong Ox did not even attempt to pull the wagons, no matter how much his owner beat and cursed him, and the man lost his silver.

That night as his master was silently and sadly feeding him, the Very Strong Ox turned his head and said, reproachfully:

"Master, why did you beat and curse me today? You never treated me like that before." And the surprised owner said:

"I am exceedingly sorry, O Very Strong Ox, and I assure you I will never act like that to you again."

"Then, Master," said the ox, "since you have always been kind to me until today, and since you promise not to forget ever again, I will pull those hundred wagons tomorrow."

And on the morrow the master said:

"Good ox, my noble animal, show our friends how very strong you are." Then the Very Strong Ox bowed his mighty shoulders to the yoke and pulled steadily until the last of the hundred carts came to where the first had been. And the men of the village gave the man back his silver and shouted:

"Your ox is the Very Strongest Ox in the world." And the Very Strong Ox never had to speak to his master again.

5

CONFUCIANISM

The Religion of Self-help

THE THREE beautiful daughters of the House of Yen stood before their honorable father and heard him say:

"Here by my side stands Commandant Shuliang Ho of the House of Kung. He is old, having passed his seventieth year, but he is tall and brave and strong, and of ancient noble lineage. Which of you, my daughters, will be his wife?"

After an embarrassing silence, having given her older sisters a chance to speak, the youngest girl, Chentsai, said:

"Honorable father, you know it is for you, not for us, to decide that." And the understanding father said to her gently:

"Very well. You will do."

So Seventy married Seventeen; and the bride, knowing that her elderly spouse had had nine daughters and never a son by his first wife, forthwith made pilgrimage to the sacred Mount Ni (Ni-chiu) to pray for a son.

The birth-stories tell, among other charming incidents, that when Chentsai climbed the mountain, all the leaves on the trees stood stiffly upright, and when she came down, they all bowed low. And that night a good spirit made to her this annunciation:

"Your son shall be the wisest of men. But you must bring him forth in a hollow mulberry tree."

So for months she searched for a hollow mulberry tree, saying nothing to anyone of the prophecy lest she be thought vain, but as her time drew near, she asked her husband if he knew of such a tree anywhere about. He told her that there was, to his knowledge, no such tree, but that an old dry cave in a nearby hill had long been known as the "Hollow Mulberry Tree."

Now this cave was in the town of Tsou, in the land of Lu, in that section of China which is now called Shantung, and, in that "Hollow Mulberry Tree," Chentsai brought forth her first-born son as October was browning into November, in the twenty-second year of Duke Hsiang of Lu, or by our reckoning 551 B.C.

First she named her baby "Chiu," for the mountain she climbed before his birth, (Ni-chiu), and later called him "Chung-Ni," for the first part of the mountain name. But neither of these names stayed by him, for he early showed the wisdom which the good spirit had prophesied, and even while he was still a youth, people began calling him Kung the Teacher or Kung the Master, which in the Chinese tongue is Kung Fu Tse.

And his wisdom so greatly grew until the end of his days that his countrymen truly have called him "the wisest of men."

In 1949 A.D. hundreds of millions of the Chinese people celebrated the twenty-five hundredth birthday of Chentsai's baby, who became the most famous man of China, the great sage, philosopher, and religionist whom they call Master Kung, and whom the West calls by the Latin form of his name, Confucius.

The celebration was a family party as well as a national festival, for the still illustrious Kung family today boasts direct descendants of Confucius to the seventy-sixth, seventy-seventh, and seventy-eighth generations, many of them now living in the same section of Shantung province where their revered ancestor was born.

If a man's own family so diligently practices the virtues he preached that his descendants furnish a large proportion of the leaders of the land for twenty-five centuries, then surely the teachings of such a man are precious and ought to be pondered well by the people of all countries and all religions.

Perhaps the reason why the people of China have remembered so well down through the centuries the lessons taught by Confucius is that he sugar-coated the moral medicine with sweet stories and tasty proverbs. He was able to do so because, from early youth, he had enriched his mind with the lore of his ancestors, both the wisdom written in books and the family stories preserved by word of mouth.

The first tale he heard was of the giant Kung who was as brave and selfless as he was strong. Doubtless the boy heard this story when he was but three years old, at the time of his father's funeral, and tales were told of family heroes.

It seems that this giant warrior of the clan of Kung was sixty years old but still of great strength and valor when he and his fighting men besieged the city named Pei-Yang. The crafty defenders left the city gate open to lead the attackers into an ambush. Kung's foremost men rushed in, but he was somewhat suspicious and followed more slowly. His fears were well grounded, for the defenders dropped the portcullis, a heavy gate sliding in vertical grooves, thus trapping the advance guard.

But Kung sprang forward with a warning shout to his men, caught the descending portcullis and held it by almost superhuman strength until they had all crawled under it on hands and knees back to safety.

This story of the valiant soldier was well remembered by the boy who was later known as Master Kung, for the great hero was his own father, Kung Shuliang Ho.

Of the boyhood of Confucius little is known save that he was exceedingly studious. He quickly learned all that his teachers knew and at the age of fourteen he was teaching the other boys. In one of his later books, *The Analects*, he states: "At fifteen I had my mind bent on learning."

This indicates that he had very early decided on becoming a scholar as his life ambition. But he had to help his widowed mother meanwhile. In later years, referring to this period, he said:

"When I was young, my circumstances were so poor that I became skilled in many practical matters."

In fact, he was so efficient and faithful at whatever he attempted that at the early age of seventeen he was given a responsible government position in charge of grain storage and supervision of the town grazing lands. When asked how he liked his position, he replied that it was easy, as all he had to do was to be sure his figures were correct and that the oxen and sheep were kept fat and strong.

It was not as simple as all that, for he soon found that much of his time was wasted in trying to pacify the shepherds and cowherds who were continually quarreling. It interrupted and delayed his study of the classics to which he devoted every spare minute.

The wisdom of the ancients kept him calm and dignified: why not try it on the quarrelsome men? But he knew they could not possibly understand the high philosophical language and ethical fine points which were his own delight. So this boy, still in his teens, condensed into one golden sentence the essence of ethics and the philosophy of religion, saying:

"Do not do to others what you would not want them to do to you."

It sounds exceedingly simple, and it is, but it takes the highest type of genius to discover the simple basic rules and formulas. Confucius himself probably did not realize at the time how important his little formula was: he only knew that it worked with the herdsmen, but later he made it the essence of his teachings. Today it is, as it has been now for many centuries, a central doctrine in all the religions of the world, and is usually called "The Golden Rule."

By the age of nineteen, Confucius was successful enough to afford marriage. A year later, at the birthday of his son, the Duke of Lu sent the young father two sacred carp with which to celebrate. Confucius, with one of the finer touches of Oriental ceremonial courtesy, thanked the Duke by naming his son, not for the Duke, but for the carp! The boy was known as "Li" (The Carp) for the rest of his life.

In later years, one of Confucius' disciples, wondering if the son of the famous teacher enjoyed any special advantages, asked Li if his father had ever given him any inside secret information beyond what he taught to his regular classes.

Li answered rather dryly that his father had honored him with extra-curricular instruction. Once, his sire had stopped him as he was hurrying by and asked if he had read the *Odes* (a book of ancient classical poems), and when he had said, "Not yet," his father had dismissed him with:

"Until you read the *Odes*, you will not be worth talking to."

When Confucius was twenty-four his mother died and he went into retirement to mourn her for over two years. During that time he evidently pondered his life purpose and decided to give up his government position and become a full-time teacher. He had already been doing some teaching successfully on the side, and when he applied himself diligently to his vocation, he attracted a large following which gradually grew until there were three thousand.

His was a traveling university, for he rode in an ox-cart, his pupils walking alongside. As Socrates walked with his students about Athens and as Jesus spoke from the stern of a fishing boat to his disciples in the boat and on the shore, so did the earlier Confucius dispense wisdom from an ox-cart. He took his texts and lesson subjects from little incidents which happened along the road.

Master Kung stopped the cart one day to question a woman who was weeping at a roadside grave. She explained:

"At this spot some years ago my husband's father was killed

by a tiger. Likewise my husband later. Now I have just buried the mangled body of my son." And Confucius said:

"Why then do you stay in such a dangerous vicinity?"

"Because, sir," she replied, "although there are tigers here, at least the government is not too harsh." Whereupon, the sage turned to his followers and said impressively:

"Listen, my children, and note this well. Fiercer than a tiger is a government which oppresses."

Again, as they traveled, they heard choking sounds from a clump of trees—as of one strangling. Confucius leaped from the cart and was the first to reach the man and unknot the cord by which he had tried to kill himself. When he could speak, the frustrated suicide said:

"I'm a complete failure. As a son, I did not reverence and care for my parents. As a citizen, I failed the state by traveling abroad and neglecting my civic duties. My friends and even my son have turned from me, wretch that I am. So I tried to end my worthless life."

"And you were wrong," said Confucius, "very wrong, for you brought all your misery on your own head when you neglected the care of your parents, which is the first duty. But all is not lost. Act from now on as if you had just discovered today the true value of life and how to conduct yourself properly: you may yet reach the goal of wisdom."

Wisdom is the virtue Confucius liked to emphasize. The other four of his famous Five Cardinal Virtues are Humanity, Uprightness, Decorum, and Truth. He was the first to make Humanism a religion.

Confucius continued this traveling school for more than a quarter-century, until, at the age of fifty-one, he had a chance to return to official life by becoming a magistrate in his homeland of Lu. Again, as in his youth, he was very successful, and was promoted to Minister of Works and then Minister of Justice. His rule was so wise that, according to Chien, the great Chinese historian who wrote three hundred years later:

"After three months, the butchers did not adulterate their meat; things lost in the streets were not stolen; and even foreigners did not have to go to the police and felt perfectly at home."

Things were going too well: a neighboring prince feared that Lu would outstrip and swallow up the state of Chi, so he sent to the Duke of Lu a magnificent present to distract him from the path of Confucian virtue.

Eighty exceptionally beautiful girls, trained in the arts of music, dancing, and love, together with a hundred and twenty high-bred horses, were brought to the delighted Duke of Lu from his devoted friend and neighbor, the Duke of Chi.

Thereafter for many days the Duke of Lu and all his court forgot all their civic duties. Wine, women, song, and horse races were the ruin of the Duke, and Confucius left him in disgust.

For thirteen years he wandered, as his fifty-five years of age lengthened to sixty-eight, seeking far and near some prince who wanted a state manager, but to no avail. He was often in want, but never discouraged. Then he went back home to Lu to complete his literary labors. From sixty-eight to seventy-two he worked hard and finished his compilation of the Chinese classics and one original book which he rather pathetically called, *Spring and Autumn, the Annals of the State of Lu.*

Discouraged and disappointed at the very end of life, more at the condition of the country than his own sorrows, he said:

> Ah! the Taishan (mountain) is crumbling!
> The strong beam is yielding!
> The philosopher is withering like a plant!

Seven days later, in the spring of 479 B. C., Confucius went to join his ancestors. Two of his few remaining disciples prepared his body for burial in the old way, putting three pinches of rice into the mouth and dressing the body in the robes of a Minister of State. Burial was to the north of the city. Three mounds were raised and a tree planted.

Now that he was dead, the people realized their loss. Many princes sent messages and tokens. The common people moved to the vicinity of the grave, built houses around it until a village and then a city arose, known as Kungli—Kung's Town. For generations, seasoned sacrifices and games were held there and a temple erected where his musical instruments, his gowns, caps, books, and even his old ox-cart were preserved.

His fame and recognition grew with the years. In 195 B. C. the Emperor of China offered up a sacrifice at Confucius' tomb. In the year 1 A. D. he was given the title of "Duke Ni, All-complete and Illustrious," and in 267 A. D. elaborate sacrifices in his honor were ordered four times yearly. In 1906, by imperial rescript, he was actually deified as the third God of China, along with Heaven and Earth!

In the great temple of Confucius at Peking the emperors of China twice a year for many centuries conducted a solemn ritual of praise and sacrifice to Confucius. In 1914 the first president of the Republic of China, Yuan Shih Kai, took the emperor's place.

The simple humanistic ethical religion of Master Kung has thus changed with the passage of years. He who claimed no divine revelation from on high and taught self-culture by honesty, self-control and the practice of the Golden Rule would doubtless be shocked and hurt if he came back to earth and found men worshiping him as a god. And he would be amused as well, for he had a delightful sense of humor, the rare kind which enabled him to laugh at himself.

Once a disciple confessed to Confucius that when asked to describe his great teacher, he found such a task too much for him. The sage smiled and said:

"Why didn't you just tell him that I am only a chap who forgets to eat when chasing knowledge, who forgets his grief when he captures it, and who just doesn't notice that old age is coming on?"

Confucius got separated from his disciples on another occasion and when they searched for him they were told:

"There is a tall man standing by the east gate of the city. He has a high forehead like Yao or some other of the ancient sages, tall and majestic, but for all that, he looks as forlorn as a lost dog."

"I don't know about my resembling the majestic sages of old," said the Master after they had found him and told of the stranger's description of him, "but to say I looked like a forlorn lost dog, he was quite right. That's capital!"

It is by his wise and witty proverbs and epigrams, however, that Confucius is best known and Confucianism was best propagated, understood, and adopted throughout China. In that ancient land it is said that a man may be a Buddhist, a Taoist, a Moslem, or even a Christian, but at heart he is always a follower of Good Master Kung, by whose precepts remembered deep in his subconscious the man of China makes his important decisions. Here are a few of those proverbs, each of which should be introduced by the well-known formula, "Confucius said . . ."

It is fault to cling to a fault.

What the superior man seeks is in himself; what the the small man seeks is in others.

A poor man who does not flatter, and a rich man who is not proud, are passable characters; but they are not equal to the poor who yet are cheerful, and the rich who yet love the rules of propriety.

Learning undigested by thought is labor lost: thought unassisted by learning is perilous.

If you recompense injury with kindness, with what then will you recompense kindness? Recompense injury with justice and kindness with kindness.

If the ruler were not covetous, the people would not steal.

Why should I feel hurt that men do not know me? Rather should I feel hurt that I do not know men.

If either wealth or poverty are come by honestly, there is no shame.

Be loyal to yourself, charitable to neighbors, nothing more.

A bow never loosened is useless.

The goody-goodies are the thieves of virtue.

By knowing the kind of faults a man has, you can tell his character.

There is no use trying to carve a piece of rotten wood.

To think twice is quite enough.

I do not expect to find a saint today: if I find a gentleman I shall be quite satisfied.

A man who has a beautiful soul always has some beautiful things to say, but a man who says beautiful things does not necessarily have a beautiful soul.

He who brags without shame will have great difficulty in matching his living to his bragging.

Easy talker, trouble maker.

When bad people dislike you, you may be a good person.

Words are easy to let out of your mouth, hard to recall.

Do not worry about people not knowing your ability: worry about not having it.

Don't admire a thoroughbred's strength: admire his temper.

Some rice plants that blossom bear no grains.

Plan ahead or find trouble on the doorstep.

It is man that makes truth great: not truth that makes man great.

When I really want true manhood, there it is right by me!

Humility is near to moral discipline; simplicity of character is near to true manhood; loyalty is near to sincerity of heart.

The superior man understands what is right: the inferior man understands what will sell.

The superior man develops upwards; the inferior downwards.

Listen much, . . . look much, . . . watch attentively, . . . and you will rarely have cause to repent.

In my relations with men, I listen to their words, but I look to their actions.

If a man makes no efforts to develop his own mind, I shall not develop it for him.

If three of us travel together, I shall find two teachers.

Since the end of World War II a tremendous ideological battle has been waged in China between the philosophy or religion of Communism and the old Confucianism, which is also both philosophy and religion. The Communist line is directly opposed to the intense family loyalty which has been a feature of Confucianism for twenty-five centuries. Communism is also destructive of the family-based system of moral order, and attempts to set up a contrary system. If Confucianism is forced to yield, it will probably continue to function, though greatly altered and under strict government control. It will be a long time before Confucianism disappears, if ever, for it has continued to exist for centuries alongside invading Buddhism and Christianity.

6

TAOISM

The Religion of the Way of Nature

WE KNOW tantalizingly little about the personal life of Lao Tse,° the great founder of Taoism,° which, with Confucianism and Buddhism, makes the third religion of China today. But what little we do know reveals one of the most remarkable of all the thinkers who have ever trod this planet!

There is a beautiful legend that his mother was a virgin who conceived when her eyes were struck by the light of a shooting star. The legend is doubtless a poetical way of saying that Lao Tse's life and teachings were so pure that he could not have been born in the ordinary way.

And a thousand years after his death, when the emperors of China were cherishing his teachings more than did the rulers of his day, another legend became current, namely, that he was born a little old man with white hair, and that he had been carried in his mother's womb for eighty-one years! That, of course, was a graceful Oriental tribute to his great wisdom.

What was there in the air in the sixth century B. C.? Did cosmic rays from some distant bursting sun strike this old earth and stir up the genes and chromosomes of the sons and daughters of men so that they begat and brought forth geniuses—prophets and philosophers and founders of religions?

For Lao Tse, living from 604 B. C. to approximately 517 B. C., had as his contemporaries probably the most illustrious group of men who ever lived at the same time. To name but seven of these immortals of the sixth century B. C., and the list could easily be doubled, there were in India, Gautama Siddhartha, the founder of Buddhism, and Mahavira, who founded Jainism. It was then that Zoroaster in what is now Iran and Confucius in China founded the religions which bear their name. Pythagoras in Greece was establishing his strange brotherhood of philosophers and mathematicians. And, of the great prophets of Israel who flourished in that

°*ao* is pronounced like *ow* in *cow*, and *t* like *d*, hence *Lowdzuh* and *Dowism*.

magic century, we should name at least Jeremiah and Ezekiel, whose writings enrich the Hebrew and Christian Bibles.

These seven men have left us precious fruits of their genius, writings now enshrined in the world's sacred literature, but the eighth one, Lao Tse, belongs well up on the list. The eighty-one short chapters of his one little book, the *Tao-Teh King*, compare favorably, for condensed wisdom, with any writing of his contemporaries. One has to turn to Emerson's *Essays* to find anything like Lao Tse's *Little Talks About Tao* as the book should be named. Take for example:

> There is nothing more yielding than water,
> Yet nothing equals it for wearing down the hard.
> Thus the weak can overcome the strong,
> And the gentle can conquer the hardhearted.
> This all know, but no one practices.
> Therefore the Sage says:
> "Who will take on himself the reproaches of men
> Shall save the state;
> And he who will bear the burden of the world's woes
> Shall be the King of the World."
> This paradox is true.

Students of history find it difficult to explain the source of Lao Tse's greatness and wisdom. Lao Tse was not his real name. Just as Yeshuah of Nazareth was called Christ (the Anointed), and as Gautama Siddhartha was named Buddha (the Enlightened), so little Li Err grew up to be called Lao Tse (the Venerable Philosopher). As a boy and young man, there was nothing to distinguish him from the typical Chinese boy of that time.

In Chinese, the name Li Err doesn't sound as untruthful as it does in English. The family name (always placed first in China) was Li, which means "plum." His given name Err means "ear." The plum tree is a symbol of immortality and little Plum Ear was said to have been born under a plum tree, "in the hamlet of Good Man's Bend, in Grinding County, in the Thistle District, in the State of Everywhere."

Little is known about Lao Tse because he kept himself away from people, living practically as a hermit. To be sure, he became custodian of the secret archives of his state, a sort of state librarian, but since he lived in a time when wars abounded and few people could read, he might just as well have lived alone in a cave.

When he was ninety years old, he took his life savings, bought a little cart and one black ox, and started west. When he reached the gate at the northwest boundary of the state, the gate-keeper, Yin Hsi, begged of him:

"Sir, since it pleases you to retire forever from among us, I beg of you as a personal favor to write me a book."

So he who had never written a book, he who had lived among books all his life until he had grown to hate them, tarried at the northwest gate of the State of Chou until he had written a little book of only five thousand Chinese characters or letters, making eighty-one short chapters, each a little poem.

And when Yin Hsi read the little book, he laid it reverently on the best table within the gate-house and came to where Lao Tse sat in his cart, waiting to resume his journey, and silently climbed in beside him.

The black ox pulled the little cart through the high gateway, and soon the great philosopher and his single convert were but a dot on the horizon and never heard of again.

But the book remained. It was in two parts, one about the *Tao* and one about *Teh*. Now Tao is hard to translate into English and has been interpreted to mean Way, Word, Reason, Creative Principle, and even God. Christian missionaries to China translated the first verse of St. John's Gospel, "In the beginning was the Tao, and the Tao was with God, and the Tao was God." But the Tao is not a personal God; it is rather the cosmic energy, the vital impulse, or the natural producing force in the universe.

The word Teh is easier to translate, for it means virtue, but it is virtue in the sense of vitality, virility, or power. And since the word *King* means book, the *Tao-Teh King* is simply a book telling about the power you get by letting nature teach you how to live. Mr. Ralph Waldo Trine's book-title "In Tune with the Infinite" would be a good interpretation of the central theme of the *Tao-Teh King*.

Four hundred years after Lao Tse left his little book behind him and vanished into the West, the Emperor Ching-Ti officially recognized it as a "classic." Four hundred years after that, the Emperor Ming-ti lectured on it regularly to his court and punished "any official who either stretched, yawned, or spit during the address."

The book did not reach Europe until 1823 A. D. in a French translation, and it is only lately that we are getting good English translations, with such scholarly appreciation as:

"—so clear and simple and so surprisingly in accord with the latest philosophy and science. . . . In purity, spotless. . . . So lofty, so vital, so restful, at the roots of strength. . . . Pithy sayings of mystical and universal wisdom."

Some of the most striking sentences from this great book, selected as acceptable and helpful to American readers, are these:

Without going out of the door, one can know the whole world. Without peeping out of the window, one can perceive Tao. The more one runs about, the less he learns.

There is no greater crime than seeking what men desire.

There is no greater misery than discontent.

There is no greater calamity than greediness.

Fame or wealth or your personality, which is nearer and dearer to you? Gain or loss, which is worse? Indulgence means waste and hoarding invites loss. He who knows when to stop will be able to go on.

Repay injury with kindness. To those who are good to me, I am good. And to those who are not good to me, I am also good. And to the insincere I am also sincere. Thus all get to be sincere.

My words are very easy to know, and very easy to practice. Yet all men do not know and practice them, because they know too much. The sage wears sack-cloth but carries jewels in his bosom. He knows himself but does not show himself.

The best soldier is not warlike. The best fighter is never angry. The best conqueror takes part in no war. The best employer does not look down but up to his employees. This is the virtue of non-contesting. This is the secret of bringing out other men's ability.

It has been noticed that Lao Tse spoke much as Jesus did. In fact, a German scholar has found 268 parallels between verses in the *Tao-Teh King* and verses in the Bible.

But Lao Tse would be the last one to praise any book, even his own. His emphasis was always on thinking and meditating deeply and getting a sort of mystical feeling-consciousness of truth, rather than merely reading and studying. He despised "learning for learning's sake."

He shocked Confucius greatly on the one occasion on which it is known they met, when Confucius was thirty-four and Lao Tse eighty-five. The contrast in their ages was no greater than that in their philosophy.

Confucius was a man of action, a great student of the classics, and also a busy young social reformer and politician, bent on getting the wisdom of the ancients into the constitution of the state. He had an entire code of ceremonies and rituals collected from the past which he was trying to get the Chou rulers to put into effect. Having heard that Lao Tse, the keeper of the state archives, was a wise man, he sought his help, but he made the mistake of going to the library in an elaborate gown and with considerable pomp. Lao Tse listened a while and then said:

"Those men you speak of are long dead and their bones mouldered to dust. Ancient ceremonies and old-time forms cannot revive China. Obedience to the letter must give way to the life of the spirit.

"Put away your polite airs and vain display of raiment.

The wise man seeks a quiet retired life. If you have a treasure, do not show it to everybody, but only to a chosen few.

"But have you, my young friend, yourself learned the Divine Way? Do you know the Tao?"

And Confucius confessed sadly:

"Alas, no, for though I have been a seeker many years, I have not yet found it."

"No one can give it to you," replied Lao Tse. "If it could be presented to men, who would not gladly give it to his prince, or his parents, or his brethren? Who would not delight to give it to his children?

"I will tell you why you have not obtained it. You cannot seize it by pursuing it. It will come itself into your heart if you give it a sanctuary there."

Like the Rich Young Man in the Bible story, who had too many possessions to give up, Confucius turned away sorrowful from the pure mysticism of Lao Tse. For days afterward he remained sadly thoughtful, and when his disciples asked him why, he said:

"When I meet a man whose thoughts fly about lightly as a bird, I can wing him with an arrow. When I meet one whose mind ranges like the running deer, I am the hound to bring him down. Even if he dives deep like a fish, I am the angler to land him. But when I meet this one whose thoughts mount on the wind and rush through the heavens like the Dragon into infinity itself, what can I do? I can only listen and wonder with troubled and perplexed mind."

The greatest of the disciples of Lao Tse, Chuang Tse, lived two centuries after his master and probably saved the Tao teachings from oblivion by the clever parable-stories he told to illustrate them. Like his teacher, he emphasized the truth that good and evil are relative terms. What seems bad may be good. His great story of the cripple deserves wider circulation:

"The poor cripple's back was so bent that his chin was sunk in his navel. His shoulders were higher on either side than the top of head. His spine seemed to point at the sky. His thighbones were like extra ribs.

"But he made a good living, not in spite of but because of his condition. His peculiar shape made it easier for him than for other men to sharpen needles, wash clothes, and clean rice. And when government agents came round to conscript citizens for labor-gangs, he was not chosen. When there was a levy of soldiers, he did not need to hide. When alms were given to the poor, he received more than anyone else. His apparent misfortune was really his greatest blessing."

I like the parable of the walrus, the centipede, the snake, and the wind:

"The walrus, envying the centipede, said to him, 'I have

only one leg, but I manage to get around on it, rather clumsily. How can you manage all those legs at once?' 'I don't manage them,' replied the centipede, 'it's my subconscious.' But the centipede envied the snake, saying, 'You have no legs and I have a hundred, yet you move much faster than I. How come?' And the snake said, 'It's a gift—my natural mechanism. What use have I for legs?' But the snake really envied the wind, for he said, sadly, 'Now I wriggle along pretty well, but I should, for, after all, I have a form. Now you, O wind, come sweeping down swiftly from the north and pass on to the south sea faster than anyone can travel, and yet you have no form. How come?' And the wind replied to the snake, 'It's true that I can travel swiftly, and I uproot great trees and destroy huge buildings. But I'll tell you my secret sorrow—any small child who points at me or kicks at me excels me, for I have neither eye nor mind.' "

When the wife of Chuang Tse died, his friend Hui Tse went to comfort him, but was surprised to find the great teacher of Tao seated on the ground, legs widespread with a huge metal basin between them, on which he was beating time as he sang loudly.

"What do you mean by acting thus unseemly?" demanded Hui Tse. "You have lived with your wife so long as to see your eldest son grown to manhood. It is bad enough that you shed no tear, but to drum on a basin and sing is surely going too far."

"Not at all," answered Chuang Tse, calmly. "At the hour of her death, I did feel badly, but I soon recollected that she had already existed without form or substance before her birth. Then substance was added to her spirit, and the substance took its natural form, and the next stage was birth. Now, by another change, her spirit has left her substance— a change as natural as the sequence of spring, summer, autumn, and winter. She is now lying peacefully and naturally asleep in eternity, I should only proclaim myself foolishly ignorant of these natural laws."

One of the most characteristic stories told of Chuang Tse is a fish-story. He was angling on the bank of the Pu River when there visited him two high officials sent by the ruling prince. They brought noble gifts and the royal invitation for him to become prime minister. But, without even turning his head, he went on fishing and said:

"I have heard that the prince has in a chest on the altar of his ancestral temple a sacred tortoise which has been dead now for three thousand years. Do you tell me now, please, would that tortoise rather be dead and have its dried body venerated, or be alive and wriggling its tail in the mud?"

"Why, of course," said the officials in unison, "it would prefer to wriggle its tail in the mud."

"Then please go back to the prince," said Chuang Tse, "and tell him that I, too, prefer to wriggle my tail in the mud."

When his followers came to Chuang Tse and asked him to expound to them what a good Taoist should think about death, he told them two connected parables, one about the Lady Li Chi and one about his own dream of the butterfly. Said he:

"You ask about the dread of death. How do we know but that our love of life may be a delusion? Perhaps the man who fears death is like a little child who has lost the way home! The Lady Li Chi was the daughter of a border warden, and only an ignorant peasant lass, so she dreaded to go to the palace of the Prince of Chin when he asked the rustic beauty to be his bride. She wept until the bosom of her dress was soaked with her maiden tears. But when she came into his palace, so unlike anything she had ever seen before, and shared his wonderful bed, and ate such delicious food, she understood how foolish she had been to weep. And so perhaps the dead repent of having craved for longer earth life. It may be that death is the great awakening when we shall learn that this life was but a dream.

"Once upon a time, I, Chuang, dreamed that I was a butterfly. I fluttered to and fro exactly like any butterfly. I was utterly unconscious of my human personality, and was aware only of my butterfly notions and motions. Suddenly I waked up, and lay there, fully conscious of being a man, myself, Chuang, once again. But ever since, I have not been sure whether in my sleep I was a man dreaming I was a butterfly, or whether now I am a butterfly dreaming he is a man! Yet between me and the butterfly there is certainly a difference, so this is a good example of the transformation of things in the change we ignorantly fear and call death."

There are fifty million Taoists today, mostly in China, divided into two groups, both of which have departed considerably from the simple teachings of Lao Tse and Chuang Tse. The Northern school goes in for metaphysical speculation, meditation, and breathing exercises similar to Hindu yoga. The Southern school is mostly concerned with magic, occultism, divination, and exorcism, and its priests get quite an income from selling charms, incantations, magic medicines, and amulets.

They even rearrange the location and position of buildings to counteract the bad influence of the devils who are blamed for family troubles and business failures. They have a leader who is called by them the Tien-shih, and by Europeans and Americans "the Taoist Pope." This head of the clan, living on the vast grant of land in the Kiangsi Hills, formerly given by the emperor to the Taoists, is not, like the Roman Catholic pope, the chief priest of a unified hierarchy, but the best magician of them all. Lower priests come to him to be solemnly endowed with his occult magical powers.

But this type of Taoism is rapidly disappearing with the spread of scientific knowledge among the Chinese. Philosophical Taoism, however, of the kind originally taught by Lao Tse and Chuang Tse, will long hold its honored place in the Orient in spite of Communism and will gain increasing recognition in the rest of the world. A religion or philosophy, call it what you will, which emphasizes naturalness and simplicity, which offers the consolations of mysticism to the unfortunate and bereaved, and which exalts the importance of physical and spiritual health and sanity, has much to teach the confused and distressed peoples of the earth today.

From the distance of over twenty-five centuries ago we can hear the Venerable Philosopher saying to us:

He who knows other men is observant: he who knows himself is intelligent. He who overcomes others may be strong, but he who overcomes himself is mighty.

Govern a nation as you would cook a small fish, that is, very little.

Where troops have been quartered, brambles and thorns spring up.

The greater the number of laws, the more thieves.

Excessive piety is no piety at all.

Faithful words are often not pleasant; pleasant words are often not faithful.

He who stands on tiptoe wabbles: he who straddles cannot walk well: he who boasts has no real merit.

The more you give, the more you have.

Be gentle, and you can be bold: be frugal, and you can be liberal: be humble and you can be a leader of men.

7
SHINTO

Japan's Way of the Gods

SHINTO IS AS OLD as Christianity, if not older, but in its early days it was that primitive form of religion, animism or nature worship. There is still enough of animism in Japan for people to think certain things may have souls and should be treated with respect, especially peculiar and outstanding objects like volcanoes and queer-shaped trees, just as Americans have named a well-known geyser, "Old Faithful."

But contact with Confucianism and its ancestor worship, and with the Buddhist priests who came down through Korea in A. D. 552, and more recently with Christianity, has changed the religion of the Japanese people so much and in so many ways that it is hard to separate the different faiths. Modern Shinto is really a mixture and is even now rapidly changing, because of World War II and the impact of Communism on the whole East.

What is left of original Shinto is hardly a religion at all, but rather a collection of ancient festivals, pilgrimages to old shrines, and the faithful but rather mechanical observance of time-worn customs and rituals. But there is the charm of the antique about it, and the patina of aging beauty is still attractive. The old legends of the gods and goddesses of the polytheism which followed the animistic period are still repeated, and crowds throng the shrine at Ise to worship Amaterasu the goddess of the sun, from whom, in unbroken line, the emperors of Japan are believed to have descended through the first one Jimmu Tenno, to whom in 660 B.C. she presented the mirror which is alleged to exist even now in her Ise shrine.

When an occidental refers to the Japanese religion as Shintoism, as many do, it is as if an Oriental spoke of "Christianism," for the "to" in Shinto means religion or way, and Shin-to is two Chinese words meaning The Way of the Gods, which in the Japanese language becomes *Kami no Michi*. The word *kami*, however, means much more than gods, and has been applied to anything strange and powerful, from the ancient deities to odd animals, queer birds, tigers, echoes, thunder, national prestige, the royal family, and even sexual power.

In fact, the early Japanese religion was phallic, and parts of the oldest Shinto scriptures, the *Ko-ji-ki* and the *Nihon-gi*, are not usually translated into English, but into Latin for scholars; for many sections are offensively frank about the details of natural functions. But modern Shinto has so evolved that today there is among all classes of the Japanese people such an appreciative reverence for the beauties of nature that it shows in all their art and poetry, and it can truly be said that they worship the holiness of beauty and the beauty of holiness.

The western world as a whole has not yet really accepted aesthetics, the study of beauty, as a requisite part of religion. So, many a tourist goes about the island kingdom looking for its religion, and finding little of the occidental type, concludes Japan has no faith. But the original nature-worship, with all its crudities, has been sublimated into the appreciation of beauty, and aesthetics is the real religion of the Japanese millions whatever other faiths may have been superimposed.

Children are taught the art of flower arrangement, and a whole Japanese town will turn out to admire and discuss the new plum and cherry blossoms, to contemplate the many varieties of blooming azaleas and chrysanthemums, or to compete for prizes for the best poems about the peonies.

The reverence for beauty is particularly noticeable in their idea of art. To them art is not merely a painting on the wall of a museum, or a statue in a park. Art must be everywhere and in everything. The commonest articles of daily use should be well-designed things of beauty—artistic in shape and color. The comb, the razor, the spoon, the tongs are, of course, functional; but they must be pleasing to the eye also and graceful in the hand. To the sensitive son of Japan, ugliness is a sin.

The age-old animism—the belief that objects around them are alive—leads the Japanese people to think that the creative artist really puts some of his own life into his paintings. One enthusiastic critic wrote of a great artist at work:

"If in mid-stroke of his brush a swift sword had severed it, it would have bled."

One of the most revealing of Japanese legends tells of the trouble certain peasants were having because a wild animal was getting into their gardens at night and ruining them. Early one morning one of the peasants, lying in wait, saw a huge black horse eating some vegetables and trampling the rest. Calling his fellow gardeners, he led the chase of the animal. It easily outdistanced them, but they saw to their surprise that it apparently entered a temple in the distance. When they reached the temple, they found it empty, and they were about to leave when one of them noticed on the wall a painting by their great local artist Kanaoka—a painting of a black horse partly obscured by a cloud of vapor. Upon examining it more closely, they found that the horse was steaming from recent exertion! Excitedly they called Kanaoka, who immediately took his brush and painted on the picture a rope tying the horse to a post, and their gardens have not been molested since.

When another great artist was but a small child, so the legend goes, he was punished for childish mischief by being bound and thrown into an empty temple. With his grimy tears for ink and his right great toe-nail for a brush, he drew on the white temple floor a sketch of a pair of rats so lifelike that they gnawed through the rope and set the talented child free.

In a religion of beauty, the priest must be a poet. In Japan there have been thousands of poets, and anyone, from a ditch-digger to the emperor, can write a poem—and usually does. The poems are not rhymed, but must contain a single beautiful thought, expressed in a rigid, brief form. One popular kind is the *tanka*, which is strictly limited to five lines or phrases which total exactly thirty-one syllables.

Even shorter is the *hokku* which contains just seventeen syllables, like this one:

> If a fal-len blos-som re-turns to the branch,
> It is a but-ter-fly.

Just as the American Indians believe that after death the spirit of the warrior goes to a Happy Hunting Ground, so the Japanese hold that the souls of their departed children play with bright flowers and gay butterflies in a heavenly garden. A famous hokku, touched with the pathos of bereavement, was written by the woman poet Chiyo shortly after the death of her little son:

> How far, I wonder, did he wander,
> Chasing the dragon-flies to-day?

The animistic belief leads to colorful religious celebrations full of symbolism and drama, such as the *tsuina*, or demon-expelling ritual, which is the ancient Shinto New Year's Eve ceremony and is mentioned historically as early as A.D. 689. The demons that are driven out are the evil influences of winter and the diseases they bring with them.

Formerly, in the court of the emperor (Mikado) an old man was dressed up as the Demon of Pestilence in a horrible costume and driven round the palace and, finally, away from it by bands of masked youths armed with staves and bow-and-arrows, which must be made of peach-wood, to which, according to Shinto, all evil spirits are allergic. After the driving out of the demon of disease, thousands of small placards were thrown to the crowd watching the drama. The lucky persons securing these cards in the ensuing scramble pasted them over their house-doors to keep away disease during the coming year.

The modern celebration of tsuina is more of a household affair, with the head of the family officiating, but the idea is the same, plus additions like evergreen trees outside the door and a sacred rope over it trimmed with ferns, holly, bean-pods and fish-heads. We might think they had borrowed the pine trees and holly from our American Christian year-end customs, as we borrowed them from the Druids and Teutons. But no, in Shinto they have their own explanations. The holly is used because the prickles on it keep away the demons.

On New Year's Eve, for a proper tsuina, the head of the household scatters parched beans, shouting "Out with the devils" and then whispering "In with the luck." Sometimes the women of the house pick up the beans, one for each year of their age, and fling them backward out of doors to drive away bad luck and hit the devils in the eye and blind them. There is another interpretation that the beans drive away the winter diseases and welcome the beneficent spring influences. (The Japanese New Year is later than ours and comes at the beginning of spring.) Perhaps Tennyson had the tsuina in mind when he wrote:

> Ring out the old, ring in the new,
> Ring out old shapes of foul disease,
> Ring out the want, the care, the sin,
> Ring out the false, ring in the true.

Shinto shrines are usually open day and night and are very well attended, especially at the many festivals. They are fenced-in squares of which, in the center of the enclosure, is the *haiden*, or worship-sanctuary. The worshiper must approach the shrine through one or more *torii*, the sacred gateways seen in all Japanese landscape pictures, consisting of a slightly curved horizontal bar of wood, mounted on two upright posts, with a cross-brace just beneath the bar. Torii means bird-roost, which describes but does not explain the gateway, which is evidently to guard and protect the shrine from evil spirits.

Going through the torii, the worshiper draws near the haiden, but does not enter it. Standing before it, he first washes his hands and rinses his mouth at a little font. Then he claps his hands and reaches up and pulls a rope which rings a bell to let the gods know he is present. Finally he bows his head in a brief prayer, tosses a coin or a little package of rice into the large offering-box, and leaves the shrine.

The apparent emptiness of the Shinto shrine impresses all strangers. There are no visible idols, pictures, or images of deities. It has been said, in some disappointment, that a visitor will find nothing in the shrine and even that cannot be seen. But in every place of worship there is somewhere concealed a holy object too sacred to be polluted by the curious eyes of sight-seers.

If the visitor did, by some mischance, get a look at the sacred thing, he would not be likely to recognize it as the *shintai*, or "god-body," the mere presence of which makes the whole shrine holy. For it would be something apparently worthless, like a lock of hair, a paper wand, a string of old beads, or perhaps an ancient mirror. But this insignificant object is very important to the Japanese Shintoist, for to him it is a holy talisman, filled with powerful kami, from which emanates magic strength. He fears, respects, and worships the kami-power. For Shinto cannot be understood until it is classified as a religion so old that it antedates the time when men personified the kami- or mana-filled object into a man-shaped god. The shintai is really a sort of fetish, and the devout Shintoist still lives in the era of such fetishes and magic charms.

So, on the way back from the shrine, the Japanese worshiper usually purchases a little sacred charm to take home and put on his god-shelf. It may be a lover's talisman containing two bits of silk thread tied together, labeled "The Charm of the God of Union," or an "Easy Birth Charm," or even an amulet insuring against fire, earthquake, burglary, and intestinal worms!

As a contrast to this primitive variety of animistic Shinto, there are many modern sects, more or less Shintoistic. It is true that Shinto was discontinued as the official state religion of Japan at the close of World War II, but that decree was simply the establishing of the historic principle of the separation of church and state. Actually, however, not one Shinto shrine was closed: the religion was only disestablished nationally and reorganized. It cannot be taught in the schools, and the shrines are no longer tax-supported, but it was not abolished as a national faith. It has to compete with Buddhism, Confucianism and Christianity, but it is allowed as much freedom of worship as any other religion.

All these old religions have plenty of competition in present-day Japan, for since World War II the government has registered two hundred and thirty new religions, including all sorts of faith-cures and health cults.

Even before the war, there were, besides official State Shinto, thirteen recognized fellowships or denominations of Sect Shinto, self-supported religious or denominational Shinto. These fellowships differed greatly according to the beliefs of their founders, and were really separate little religions with preachers, teachers, churches, schools, welfare agencies, and publishing houses.

The fastest-growing of these, and most interesting to Americans probably, is *Tenri Kyo*, a faith-healing and success cult with five million members, ten thousand churches, and sixty-two thousand religious workers of various kinds.

Tenri Kyo much resembles the American religion, Christian Science. It was founded by a very remarkable woman, now known affectionately by her followers as Grandmother Miki, who lived at about the same time and just about as long as Mother Eddy.

The two words Tenri Kyo are translated as "The Teaching of Divine Reason" (or Science). The final reality is this Divine Reason. Sickness is due to negative evil. Everyone should have a full, free, happy, healthy life here and now. "The root of sickness is in the mind," is an oft-repeated saying.

Grandmother Miki's third and last book was dictated when she was eighty-six, two years before her death in 1887. It is a book of allegories, somewhat resembling Bunyan's *Pilgrim's Progress,* but more mythological and as imaginative as science fiction. She named it *The Ancient Chronicle of the Mud-sea,* and to a first-time reader it is about as clear as its subject, but commentators and interpreters have done much for it. Few indeed are the sacred books of any religion which are in all parts crystal clear in meaning to new readers of today. It is apparently advantageous sometimes when writings are sufficiently vague and ambiguous to permit variety of interpretation as successive generations of disciples arise.

The founder of Tenri Kyo was a good housewife (with six children) and she summed up her religion as "Sweeping Away the Eight Dusts." Anyone of any religious faith wishing to find something helpful for his own spiritual life in the best of Modern Shinto would do well to brush away from his own soul Grandmother Miki's Eight Dusts: Covetousness, Stinginess, Love-selfishness, Suspicion, Getting Even, Bad Temper, Haughtiness, and Self-Desire.

It may be that the rapid growth of the Tenri Kyo cult is due to the fact that the Eight Dusts supply the need of a moral code which has been notably missing in historic Shinto, for there has been nothing like Judaism's and Christianity's Ten Commandments or Buddhism's Eightfold Path and Five Prohibitions. One Shinto theologian claimed that the Japanese people were so moral anyway that they needed no code. Others have pointed to *bushido,* the code of the warrior or sumurai, which inculcated the feudal virtues of courage, loyalty, endurance, and self-sacrifice to the point of *hari-kiri,* suicide for honor's sake. But this code was confined to the nobility, and its establishment owed as much to the ethical teachings of Confucius and Buddha as to the Shinto faith.

Besides Tenri Kyo, however, there are other new sects of Shinto which also show remarkable growth, numbering millions of followers. They, too, are developing new ethical teachings. They emphasize sincerity, without which social stability and world peace is impossible. They also stress the great importance of purification. Dr. Daniel Holtom, a Baptist teaching missionary who became the greatest expert on Shinto, finds this new ethical emphasis in the modern Shinto cults most encouraging, and says:

"Their doctrine of purification, beginning in a primitive, external cleansing from ceremonial defilement, and ending in the expulsion of all negative and unsocial attitudes and the attainment of inner peace and unselfish mutuality, ultimately reaches the true heights of genuine personal and social religion."

The Religion of Beauty and Temperance

THE MOST BEAUTIFUL BUILDING in the world, by common consent of all artists, is the Taj Mahal, erected three centuries ago in India near the city of Agra on the holy river Jumna—the same sacred river, by the way, into which the ashes of the great Gandhi were recently cast.

Shah Jahan called his beloved wife "Mumtaz Mahal," which means "The Crown of the Palace," and when she died in 1631 the grief-stricken husband began building the beautiful tomb, completed seventeen years later, which is now known by her abbreviated name. All the world, which loves a lover anyway, has admired ever since this supremely graceful tribute to his beloved paid by the royal lover who later shared it with her.

Its exquisitely proportioned walls are of white marble inlaid with gold and precious gems which spell out in Arabic various appropriate verses from the Koran. For the Taj Mahal and the Pear Mosque nearby, probably the next most beautiful structure in the world, are the expression in architecture of the genius and spirit of the religion of harmony, peace and beauty preached by Mohammed and called by him, "Islam."

Islam, Mohammed's Moslem religion, the latest of the great world faiths to be founded (622 A.D.), is based on belief in the merciful Allah, the One God. It is practiced by worshiping Allah, by reading, reciting, and following the commands of the Koran, the holy book Mohammed dictated, by alsmgiving, daily prayer, and by a pilgrimage at least once in a lifetime to the Holy City, Mecca.

Islam means "submission" to the will of Allah, and is the preferred name for the religion of Moslems (submitters). In the interest of interreligious friendship and understanding, non-Moslems should be careful not to refer to Islam, the religion of the Moslems, as "Mohammedanism" nor to its followers as "Mohammedans." The founder himself insisted on this point, lest his disciples worship him, the Prophet, as well as or instead of the one God, Allah. And he was more successful than most other prophets in avoiding posthumous deification. But the fulsome eulogies of ardent Moslems often come close to calling their Prophet a god, and sometimes the Koran is so highly praised and adored that Moslems have been called "Koranists."

As the jewelled verses from the Koran stud the walls of the Taj Mahal, so the literature of Islam is thickly set with gems of thought like the following, which would be hard to excel in any other religion:

"If thou hast two loaves of bread, sell one and buy white hyacinths for thy soul."

or the prayer of Rabiah, the Moslem woman saint:

"Oh God, if I worship Thee from fear of Hell, burn me in Hell, and if I worship Thee from hope of Paradise, shut me out of Paradise, but if I worship Thee for Thine own sake, then withhold not from me Thine everlasting beauty."

What sort of person was this Mohammed who established this religion of Islam and whose utterances became the Koran, the Bible of that faith?

According to the pious legends surrounding the birth, childhood and young manhood of The Prophet, many marvelous miracles occurred, but these stories so much resemble the infancy narratives and accounts of miracles told in the Christian writings, especially in the apocryphal books, that the reader suspects that the followers of The Prophet borrowed from the scriptures of the rival religion, Christianity.

Like Enoch, the patriarch, father of Methuselah, Mohammed is believed to have ascended into heaven and interviewed the prophets and even God Himself. Like Jesus the Christ, he is said to have healed the sick and to have fed his followers by a miracle.

But the true life story of this remarkable founder of the great religion of Islam, the story which emerges as we brush away the cobweb of myths, is more interesting than the legends.

Mohammed's father died before he was born and his mother soon after. He was adopted by his grandfather at the age of six and the grandfather died two years later, leaving the lad to Abu Talib, the boy's uncle. But Abu Talib, though he loved the boy, was too poor to support little "Kutam," as he was apparently then called, and the boy picked up a living by what would be called "hitch-hiking" today. He attached himself to camel caravans and, like a sort of land-sailor, saw the world, earning his way by odd jobs.

His home town, Mecca, was an ideal place for that sort of thing, for it was an Arabian holy city and the goal of pious pilgrims, hence a busy center of trade with many travelers constantly coming and going.

Soon the lad was an expert camel driver and by the time he was twenty-five his skill and success in conducting great caravans from Mecca in Arabia to Palestine, Syria, Egypt and even Mesopotamia, attracted the attention of the wealthy Meccan widow Khadijah, who first hired him and then married him. She was fifteen years older than he, but they are said to have had seven children after she was forty.

When Kutam himself was about forty, he would never

have been taken for a man about to found a religion. He was a successful business man—caravan agent for Khadijah and a produce merchant on his own.

Then came the flood which damaged the Kaaba, the Arabs' sacred building which contained in its wall the holy Kaaba stone, the black meteorite worshiped by all Arabia. The flood dislodged the Black Stone and when the water subsided there was much debate as to who should have the honor of replacing the holy stone. The rival clans finally agreed that the honor should fall on the first man who might enter the sacred court. And that was Kutam.

He must have been surprised, but quickly showed the shrewdness which served him and his religion so well later. Taking off his cloak, he spread it on the ground and carefully placed the stone upon the center of it. Then he called the rival clan chiefs and told them to take hold of the edges of the garment and thus lift the stone to the level of its proper location in the wall. As they did so, he skilfully slid the stone into place amid loud praises.

Thus Kutam became "The Praised One," which in Arabic is "Muhammad," which has become in English many words —Mahomet, Ahmad, Mahound, Mahmud, but usually Mohammed.

His contact with the Kaaba Stone did something to this successful business man. Just what, psychologists may consider. At any rate, the market soon missed Mohammed, and Khadijah had to care for both children and caravans.

Like many a prophet before him, Mohammed had retired into the wilderness to meditate. In a cave on the slopes of Mount Hira he pondered on religion—in fact on three religions.

On his caravan routes he had encountered many Jewish traders and they had told him stories of their religious heroes: Abraham, Moses, and David. In Syria he had encountered Christians who preached their faith to him. And all around him was the ancient religion of Arabia, a combination of animism, which worships stones and springs, and polytheism, which worships many gods and goddesses.

Mohammed, as he pondered in his cave, evidently decided that the primitive religion of his own people needed to be improved and made more like Christianity and Judaism. But he didn't think those two religions were perfect either, not in the form he had contacted them. The more he thought about it, the more puzzled he became. Then strange things began to happen.

Most prophets and mystics tell of a great light shining upon them at the height of their religious crisis. So we are told by Moses, Zoroaster, Buddha, Jesus, Paul, and others. Mohammed reported no lights, but resounding bells and vague voices murmuring. Then came trance-like fits and seizures. Someone or more seemed to be trying to use his own voice to tell him and others something important. He decided to tell Khadijah about it.

The rest is history. Khadijah listened, was convinced of a divine revelation, and stood by her husband. A little group soon was formed and listened secretly to the divine spiritualistic communications. Some of these messages they memorized; others they wrote down hastily on flat stones, ribs of palm-leaves, bits of leather, and even dry shoulder-blades of sheep.

Thus came into existence the sacred book the Moslems call Alcoran and we call the Koran. It is more read than any other book in the world. The Christian Bible may be a "bestseller" in America, but nearly a quarter-billion followers of The Prophet Mohammed read or recite long sections of Alcoran *five times a day*, every day of their lives from the time they can talk!

Into the ear of the new-born babe is whispered the Fatiha, the beautiful first sura (chapter) of the Koran; which opens:

Praise be to God, the Lord of the Worlds,
The Compassionate, the Merciful,
The King of the Day of Judgment,
Thee do we worship, and to Thee do we cry for help.
Guide us to the straight path, . . .

and this Fatiha is repeated before beginning any important undertaking, at all solemn occasions, by the bed of the sick, and it is the utterance on the lips of the dying Moslem.

To a non-Moslem the Koran is a rather puzzling book. The Jew is surprised to find Miriam, the sister of Moses and Aaron, identified as the same person as Mary, the mother of Jesus! The Christian wonders as he finds the Holy Trinity listed as Jehovah, Mary, and Jesus, instead of God the Father, God the Son, and God the Holy Ghost. It seems strange too to find the claim in the Koran that the Comforter or Advocate who was promised by Jesus to come after him, and who is taken by Christians to be the Holy Ghost, is really the Prophet Mohammed! By a coincidence, the Greek word "Paraklete" which is translated into English as Comforter becomes in Arabic "Ahmed," which is one of the names of Mohammed.

There is one command of Moses which Mohammed and his followers have obeyed more carefully than Jews or Christians. Leviticus 19:27 states, ". . . neither shalt thou mar the corners of thy beard." Moslems take that so literally that the orthodox ones will never let their beards be cut or trimmed, and the most devout save every hair shed by their beards and put the hairs in tiny caskets which are interred with their bodies.

So if a Moslem swears "by the beard of the Prophet," or by his own beard, it is a most sacred oath "as in the presence of Allah," like a Christian swearing on the Bible.

When you call the attention of a Moslem to any discrepancies between the Bible and the Koran, you will meet with a ready answer. Various books of revelation have been sent by God through Gabriel—to Adam, Seth, Enoch, and Abraham. The Taurat (Torah) was sent to Moses, the Zabur (Psalms) to David, the Injil (Evangel) to Jesus, and last of all and superseding all, Alcoran to The Prophet. Where the other books differ from Alcoran, they have been tampered with, say the Moslems.

The burden of Mohammed's message to Mecca, when he began to preach his new religion, was, "There is no God but Allah, and Mohammed is His Prophet." But the Meccans clung to their old gods and especially their goddesses. Allat, Aluzza, and Manat; and poor Mohammed found himself a prophet without honor in his own country. Open persecution developed when he called the Kaaba worship idolatry and endangered the profitable tourist trade with the pilgrims who came to Holy Mecca. Mohammed became Public Enemy Number One.

He fought the opposition valiantly for several years and then fled to Yathrib, two hundred miles north, where a warm welcome awaited him, and a fresh start. From the Year of the Flight, Anno Hegirae, the followers of Mohammed date their era. The year 622-623 A.D. is for them the year one A.H. August 30th, 1954 A.D., for instance, begins the year 1374 A.H. (You would expect it to be only 1332 A.H. by subtracting 622 from 1954, but the Moslem year is the old lunar year of only 354 days.)

They liked Mohammed so much in Yathrib that they renamed the city for him, *Medinat al nabi,* the City of the Prophet, soon shortened to Medina. For eight years Mohammed trained the whole city to be the missionaries and warriors of the new religion. To win the many Jews in Medina he ordered his followers to face Jerusalem when they prayed. But the Jews remained Jews, so Mohammed changed the "*kiblah*" or direction in prayer to Mecca, which was a notification to the Meccans that he intended ultimately to take over that holy place.

The Meccans replied by sending nine hundred warriors to capture Mohammed. He met them with three hundred picked men and roundly defeated the nine hundred. It seems that he had had a revelation that all his followers who died in battle for the faith would be immediately translated to a Paradise of unspeakable bliss. It worked very well, then and thereafter. In 630 A.D., or 8 A.H. the Prophet rode into Mecca at the head of an army of 10,000 well-trained fighting missionaries. He gave Mecca the same treatment as Medina, and in two years Islam was supreme throughout Arabia. Then the Prophet suddenly sickened and died.

But his disciplined army of followers went marching on with almost incredible speed of conquest. The Prophet's friend and disciple Omar led the growing Moslem army on to take Damascus in 635, Jerusalem in 636, the Euphrates region in 637, all Egypt in 640, and when Omar was assassinated in 644, his armies were at the gates of India. Then, with new leaders, they spread west, taking all North Africa and even Spain. Charles Martel stopped them at the Battle of Tours in France in 732, but for centuries they held what they had gained. About the year 1000 they entered India and built a great Mohammedan empire with the capital at Delhi.

Today at least three hundred million people, one-eighth of mankind, follow the teachings of Mohammed. There are ninety millions in Pakistan and the Republic of India, and many other millions in China, the Malay Peninsula and all the East Indies. Java is Moslem in faith and has been so for centuries. So, of course, has practically all the Near East. The great continent of Africa is gradually, and of late rapidly, becoming Islamic. And there are Moslem communities in Japan, Australia, England, and the United States.

Why has this religion spread so rapidly? Perhaps it grew at the outset because Mohammed preached a simple creed, not too hard to accept and follow. The five duties, or Five Pillars of Islam, as they are called, are:

    (1) Repetition of the Kalimah, or Creed: There is no God but Allah, and Mohammed is His Prophet.
    (2) Pray five, or at least three, times a day.
    (3) Almsgiving.
    (4) Fasting during the month of Ramadan.
    (5) Pilgrimage to Mecca at least once.

These duties are rather liberally interpreted. Take almsgiving, for instance, of which the Prophet is reported to have said.

"A camel lent out for milk is alms, good words are alms, and your smiling in your brother's face is alms."

Fasting for a whole month seems a hardship when, as by some Moslem sects, even swallowing saliva is considered breaking the fast. But the interpretation is that one may eat in the darkness of night and until the dawn light permits one to tell a black thread from a white one.

Since the Moslem year is lunar, the month of Ramadan revolves through the seasons, and when it comes in the summer, the long days make daylight fasting quite difficult. In 1918, when a British ship sailing into the Arctic region had as sailors Moslem lascars, the poor fellows waited in vain for the daylight to pass, since it was the month of Ramadan. Several of them starved to death rather than break their sacred fast, and the ship had to be hurried south to save the lives of the rest of them.

In that connection, it is interesting to note that the school authorities in Pittsburgh, Pennsylvania, were recently sued by Moslem parents seeking to restrain them from requiring the Moslem children to attend school on Friday, the Moslem Sabbath.

As for the required pilgrimage to Mecca, the last of the five duties, it is quite an elaborate ceremonial lasting ten days in Mecca itself, to say nothing of the journey there and back, but in cases of proved inability, a substitute pilgrim may be hired.

The fourth sura or chapter of the Koran states:

"God is minded to make His religion light unto you: for man was created weak."

Mohammed was always willing to compromise. There is a charming legend that once, taking Jesus's statement literally, he tried by faith to move a mountain, but vainly. So he said, "If the mountain will not come to Mohammed, then Mohammed will go to the mountain."

There was an intuitive knowledge apparent in Mohammed's mind which enabled him to sense what people wanted in a religion, and he gave it to them. He would make concessions to spread the faith. He knew that men like women and that women like property. So he allowed the men plenty of women on earth (no more than four wives at once) and all the beautiful damsels they wanted in Paradise. And to the women he gave property rights eleven centuries before Christendom began thinking of it. Perhaps Khadijah had something to do with that.

That an ancient orthodox religion should be still spreading today with missionaries winning converts all over the world is due doubtless to the fact that Islam has kept reinterpreting the Koran and the commentaries theron in the light of new truth. The followers of The Prophet have ever been hospitable to science: indeed, during the so-called Dark Ages of the Christian world, the light of learning was kept aflame in the Moslem world. The mathematical sciences, such as algebra and astronomy, were established and developed by Moslems. The whole civilized world now use Arabic figures, 1, 2, 3, etc., instead of the Roman numerals, I, II, III, and IV.

The western conception of a Moslem missionary as a fanatic with a sword in one hand and the Koran in the other is untrue. Modernistic and Humanistic movements among the followers of The Prophet have made considerable headway in changing their religion from a series of orthodox formalities to an ethical faith in harmony with modern science. The Moslem missionary today preaches world peace, world brotherhood, temperance, the uplift of woman, and the breaking down of racial barriers. And there is considerable truth in his claim that while Christiantiy *preaches* temperance and the brotherhood of man, Islam really abstains from all forms of alcohol and *practices* racial equality. This last-named feature may be the reason why the Prophet is rapidly gaining followers among American Negroes.

There has always been a dramatic challenge in the life-story of Mohammed and the romantic history of the Moslem missions. Perhaps the spirit of Islam with all its idealism, sometimes ruthless but always beautiful, was best caught by the Moslem free-thinker astronomer and poet, Omar Khayyam, when he wrote:

> Ah, Love, could you and I with Fate conspire
> To grasp this sorry Scheme of Things entire,
> Would we not shatter it to bits—and then
> Remould it nearer to the Heart's Desire!

9
CHRISTIANITY

The Faith of the Martyrs

THE CHIEF OF POLICE had driven out to the city line to meet the prisoner—had even taken him into his own carriage that he might reason with him, while the guards trotted behind.

Now, however, the official was getting exasperated. Why was he so stubborn, this patriarch?

"Look here," the chief said, "I'm trying to save your life. The mob in the arena is yelling for your blood. And all you have to do to get your freedom is to curse this Christ of yours and say, 'Caesar is Lord.' Three little words will save your life. What do you say, fellow?"

The old man refused again, quietly but firmly, to deny his Christ, and the officer, completely out of patience, pushed him roughly from the carriage. Bruised by the fall, the old man rose to his feet without a word and limped on, the guards marching along beside him again.

In the arena the Proconsul himself gave him another chance, while the crowd kept shouting, "Loose a lion on him!"

"Swear by the genius of Caesar and I will set you free." The old man stood silent. Meanwhile, the Asiarch, the ruler

85

of the games, touched by the prisoner's dignity, refused to loose a lion, insisting that the games were officially over. Disappointed and angry, the mob yelled:

"Burn him alive then!"

The Proconsul weakened, but tried again:

"Abjure your faith, or I cannot save you. It's your last chance. Curse your Christ!"

Down through the ages has resounded the noble reply of old Polycarp, Bishop of Smyrna, that winter day of 155 A.D.:

"Eighty and six years have I served Him and He has done me no wrong. How can I blaspheme my King and Saviour?"

Reluctantly the Proconsul gave the sign for death by fire, marvelling that instead of quailing at such a fate, the old bishop actually looked exalted. Polycarp was so calm that he thoughtfully laid aside his robe that it might clothe another when he was gone, and even tried, fumblingly, to unlace his sandals, a task usually performed by his devoted disciples.

And as the crackling flames ended his earthly life, the martyr stood looking steadfastly into the sky, uttering prayers and praises to Christ his King.

This story of the martyrdom of Polycarp is told in a letter written shortly afterward by eyewitness members of the Church at Smyrna to the Church at Philomelium, and they add:

"And so afterward we took up his bones, which are more valuable than precious stones and finer than refined gold, and laid them in a suitable place, where the Lord will permit us to gather ourselves together, as we are able, in gladness and joy and to celebrate the birthday of his martyrdom. . . ."

Polycarp was a Christian, a real Christian, and if you react with a thrill to his story, you begin to comprehend the faith called Christianity, whether or not that be your own faith. His name in Greek means "much fruit," and his faith was truly fruitful, leading his followers to celebrate in joy the date of his martyrdom and to seek to follow his example. Similarly, three centuries later, the followers of Patrick, the Patron Saint of Ireland, began celebrating his heavenly birthday, the 17th of March, as they still do, because they "reckoned that the time of his entry into the world of bliss was more to be celebrated than his advent into this vale of tears."

Understand Polycarp and you understand Christianity, because Polycarp was a living link in the chain of Christian men and women by and through whom the faith has been transmitted even unto this day. As well as the New Testament itself, these followers bear witness to the faith once delivered to the saints.

Christianity is not books or buildings, but people—people filled with the spirit of Jesus and believing on Him—people who have caught that spirit from other Christians before them.

Polycarp, when a boy, had sat at the feet of the aged John the Beloved Disciple and heard the gospel story from his lips direct, probably about 80 A.D. He may even have heard John on Patmos say:

"And unto the angel of the church in Smyrna write: These things saith the first and the last, which was dead and is alive; . . . Fear none of the things which thou shalt suffer: . . . be thou faithful unto death, and I will give thee a crown of life."

At any rate, the boy disciple of John fulfilled that singular prophecy to the letter.

In the same way, Polycarp passed the torch of truth on in turn to many another youth, including Irenaeus, who became the celebrated Bishop of Lyons. Before his own martyrdom in 202 A.D., Irenaeus wrote in a letter to his friend Florinus how he distinctly remembered having sat at Polycarp's feet and heard the gospel from the old bishop who got it straight from John.

There are other human chains of evidence, one much better known in America and Europe. While the Eastern or Greek Church still emphasizes the John-Polycarp-Irenaeus chain, the Western or Roman church follows the Petrine line, basing its preference on the saying of Jesus, "Thou art Peter, and upon this rock I will build my church."

But the two lines were tangent and supplementary. In fact, the ancient Bishop Polycarp had just returned to Smyrna from Rome the week he was martyred. He had been to Rome to confer with Anicetus, the tenth bishop or pope after Peter, "regarding certain things," so Irenaeus tells us, and especially about the correct date for celebrating Easter. They had agreed about everything else on the agenda, but each decided to retain his own date for Easter.

It is doubtless to be regretted that today, eighteen centuries afterward, the eastern and western churches still disagree on the exact day, but it is much more significant that they both still make Easter their greatest day, the most important in the whole church year.

For what was this "gospel" which Polycarp heard from John the Beloved and told with his own lips to Irenaeus? What was the gospel which Peter had preached?

"Gospel" is the English translation of the Greek word, "Evangelion," meaning good news, or glad tidings.

And the glad tidings that John told Polycarp and that Peter told to hundreds and thousands of eager listeners was the simple "old, old story," old but ever new to each generation, the story of the first wondrous Easter Day.

Both John and Peter told how at dawn there came running to them Mary Magdalene. Breathlessly she told them that the body of Jesus, who had been crucified and buried by the Romans, was no longer in the tomb!

Incredulous, Peter and John had run to the tomb and found Mary's story true. The graveclothes were there, but the body gone. All day the rumors flew thick and fast. That night, by common impulse, the disciples gathered in the secret upper room where they had last supped with their teacher, closed the door carefully for fear of their enemies, and proceeded to exchange their experiences of the day and the stories they had heard.

"And as they spake these things, He himself stood in the midst of them, and saith unto them, 'Shalomka,' 'Peace to you,'" the old familiar greeting. No wonder that

"Then were the disciples glad, when they saw the Lord."

That word "glad" is a masterpiece of understatement on John's part. Glad! They were transported with joy. Their teacher had come back, risen from the tomb to the land of the living! To make doubly sure it was he, they examined his body with its wounds still fresh. And to prove that he was no mere apparition in their excited minds, he took a piece of broiled fish from their interrupted supper and ate it before them.

All these details and many others Peter and John related as long as they lived, and those who heard them caught the fire of the gospel and told others, and so on even to the present day.

And some believed then and some did not, even as today. But to those who really did believe, something strange and beautiful happened. Their whole lives were transformed. The Greeks had a word for it, "metanoia," which meant a change of purpose in life for the better, but the word has unfortunately been translated "repentance." The converts to Christianity were not so much remorseful at their past as they were happy about the future. They began to live as Jesus had lived—selflessly, generously, joyfully, beautifully, like sons and daughters of God. They wished to follow Jesus.

Even when they died by torture at the hands of their persecutors, as they did by thousands for many years, they counted it a special honor to suffer death for their Lord Jesus because He had suffered the shameful death of the cross for them.

Origen, the great Christian scholar of the third century, states that when Peter was crucified in Rome during the persecution of Christians under Nero, the aged apostle insisted that he be placed upon the cross head downward, deeming himself unworthy to die in the exact position in which his Lord had suffered death.

Truly, the blood of the martyrs was the seed of the church, and to the amazement of their enemies and rivals, the Christian communities seemed to grow, decade by decade, not in spite of, but because of persecution.

> Persecute whom you'd make hero:
> What one defends he holds dear;
> Burned not the torches of Nero,
> Christ and his word were not here.

Early Christianity had to contend not only with the Roman emperors who persecuted its leaders, but with jealous, rival religions. The worship of Isis, an Egyptian goddess, who, with her husband-brother Osiris and her son Horus, formed a sort of family trinity, became very popular in Rome, and its priests were hostile to the rising religion of Christianity. The cult of Serapis attracted many. The leaders of Judaism also were naturally very active against this new Jesus-worship which was converting so many Jews away from their ancestral faith.

Mithraism, a religion originating in Persia, was for many years Christianity's most serious rival, partly because it was the favorite faith of the Roman soldiers, whose duties took them into every town of the vast Roman empire, and partly too because Mithra was a young hero-god who helped common people with their troubles, who was translated to heaven where he looked out for the interests of his followers, and whence he was expected to descend at his second coming.

Neoplatonism threatened Christianity for a while. It was a strange mixture of the Greek philosophy of Plato and the Alexandrian mysticism of Plotinus. Its pantheism and mysticism were attractive to Christian mystics. One late Roman emperor, Julian, was an ardent Neoplatonist and sought to restore that faith even after Constantine had officially established Christianity. Julian's death left Neoplatonism leaderless and Christianity triumphant.

There were many other opponents and rivals of the Christian faith, such as Manichaeanism, which rose in the third century A. D. from the teachings of Manes, a Persian who mixed together parts of Zoroastrianism and parts of Christianity. There were also the many gnostic sects who taught salvation by *gnosis*, which is Greek for knowledge, and made inroads on Christianity until there were many who called themselves Christian Gnostics.

But over all these rivals and heresies Christianity rose triumphant, owing largely to faithful Christian evangelists, teachers, missionaries, and bishops, who were true to the teachings of Jesus and his disciples which had been transmitted by word of mouth and by the precious manuscript "epistles," "acts," and "gospels" which later became the New Testament of the Christian Bible.

It is true that there were some compromises. Certain good ideas and customs prevailing in a locality were incorporated gradually into Christianity and usually improved in the process. Scholars allege that our present celebration of Christmas includes such importations as gift-giving, decorated trees, Yule logs, holly and mistletoe, mostly from Druidic and Teutonic religions. They say that our jolly year-end merrymaking resembles more the Saturnalia of the Romans and the wassail of the Norse and Saxons than the quiet adoration of the Christ-child by the shepherds and the magi, and that Mithra's birthday was celebrated on December 25th long before that of Christ.

But these details were unimportant after all. What was important was that Christianity grew and survived, while Mithraism, Gnosticism, Neoplatonism and the rest are now names to look up in encyclopedias. All that has survived of them are the ideas and customs that Christianity took over, sublimated, and wove into its fabric of faith.

One of the great scholars of Christendom, better known to Roman Catholics than to Protestants, although he lived and wrote a thousand years before the Reformation and can be read with great profit by any Christian, was the Bishop of Hippo, the great St. Augustine, whose book, *The City of God*, reconciled differing Christian theologies with each other and with Greek philosophy, and set forth a body of teaching which is accepted in the main even today.

It was Augustine's theology which, to a great extent, enabled the Christian church to survive not only the shock of the fall of the Roman Empire in 476 A. D., but even the tremendous impact of Islam, the conquering religion of Mohammed, which swept the Mediterranean world in the seventh and eighth centuries.

The Christian faith today is divided into many branches, and that fact is often deplored, perhaps too often. It is very unlikely that all the branches will ever be united, for the only basis of unity which any one great branch will accept is that all the others join it in its rules of faith and practice. As a matter of plain historical fact, there never was a united Christian church. The followers of Peter, of Paul, and of James disagreed in Jerusalem when the church was just getting started.

It has been indicated earlier that the Eastern or Greek churches differed greatly from the Western or Roman churches over various details even as early as Polycarp. Inside the Eastern church today there are many divisions into Russian, Greek, Coptic, Armenian, Syriac, and other kinds of Christians, just as Protestant Christianity is divided into

Baptists, Methodists, Presbyterians, Episcopalians and others. And there are several varieties of Baptists and Methodists.

The splits and differences within Christianity, however, are healthy signs that Christianity is still alive and vigorous. Suppress divergent opinions and unite all sects into one authoritarian system, and the Christian religion would die out of inner decay as have other religions.

Christians differ in ritual, in methods of church government, in the importance they give the Bible, and in dogma and theology.

But whether they meet in a bare Puritan meeting-house or an ornate cathedral, whether they kneel in worship or sit erect, whether they sprinkle or immerse, whether they have bishops, elders, or moderators, whatever theories about salvation and immortality they may hold—when they worship, they worship Jesus; when they baptize, they baptize in His name. However they may believe they are saved, they attribute that salvation to their Saviour Jesus; and when they die, they expect to rise to new life with Him because He conquered death that first Easter morning.

Of course all other religions, or almost all of them, celebrate in some form the coming of spring as a symbol of immortality, and the name Easter comes from *Eostre*, the Teutonic goddess of spring. But no religion other than Christianity makes the celebration of the vernal equinox the chief festival of the religious year because it commemorates the central fact of its religion.

For Easter is central and crucial and pivotal in Christianity because that faith is based on belief in the resurrection of Jesus Christ from the dead. Paul wrote to the Christian church in Corinth, "And if Christ be not risen, then is our preaching vain, and your faith is also vain." And from Paul on down to the preachers and priests of today the central emphasis of Christianity has been on the resurrection from the tomb on that first Easter dawn.

All over America on Easter morning, from Central Park in New York across the country to the Hollywood Bowl, rings and reverberates the chant of Christian voices, shouting joyously, "Hallelujah! Christ is risen!" And these cries but echo the voices which a few hours earlier in London and Rome and Jerusalem, each in his own tongue, have proclaimed, "Christ is risen indeed!"

There is something contagious, some spiritual force almost irresistible, in this confident faith in immortality asserted by Christian millions. We may call it wishful thinking, or springtime release of the libido, or an astronomical accident, or merely the shrewd sublimation of a pagan festival by calculating clerics, but at the same time we hope it is true.

Most of us hope that Christians are right when they preach

the gospel, the good news, the evangel that human personality can survive bodily death. We like to think that a laboring man of a little town in Palestine over nineteen centuries ago, filled with a holy spiritual power which he personified and exemplified, could have come back from death and walked for some weeks among his friends to their astonishment and great joy. Therefore, whether Christians or not, we rejoice with them on Easter Day.

Apart from this belief in the resurrection from the dead and the Easter gladness, most of us, whatever our religious background, are Christians to a certain extent and in various ways.

For Christianity is not really one religion, as commonly supposed, but many. It contains within itself, in its many divisions, all the varieties of religious experience that can be found outside it. Whatever your psychological type, whatever your frame of reference, whether you are liberal or conservative, credulous or critical, quiet or excitable, there is some sect of Christendom among whose devotees you will feel at home.

If you like beautiful old chants, processions bearing ancient sacred icons, and lengthy rituals repeated since Byzantine times, you will find all that and much more in the old orthodox Christian churches—Greek, Russian, Armenian, Syrian and Coptic. If, to wonderful music and stately ritual, you would add the voice of authority and world-wide organization, together with an aggressive missionary spirit, you will be happy in the Roman Catholic Church.

On the other hand, if you desire to have more freedom to do your own thinking in important religious matters, if you consider that Christian authority resides in the Bible rather than in the Church and wish to make your own interpretation of the Bible meanings with due regard to the opinions of the best scholars, then it is likely that you will find a welcome in one of the numerous Protestant sects. Which one you select will depend, if you are serious about your belief, upon the various doctrines you consider most important. Otherwise, such matters as accessibility and social friendships may determine your choice.

If you think theological doctrines are most important, you will find congenial friends among the Presbyterians or the Lutherans or the Calvinist branch of the Baptists. Wider intellectual interests will incline you toward the Unitarians or the Episcopalians of the broader school.

The Methodists and some Baptists emphasize the social gospel, and are likely to be active in reform movements, along with Congregationalists, Unitarians and Quakers.

Mystics are welcome in most branches of the Christian church, but are likely to feel more at home in two very widely different communions, the Quakers and the Roman Catholics. Among the Quakers, or Friends as they prefer to be called, the mystic experience may come in the silent meditation of the quiet service waiting with the congregation for the coming of the "inner light," while the Catholic saint frequently attains mystic exaltation of spirit alone at prayer in his chamber or at a shrine.

The more you study Christianity, the more you will be amazed at its infinite variety. There are several hundred different divisions of it represented in America today, the most important of which will be described hereafter in this book.

It would seem that unity among Christians is especially desirable when opposing ideologies are growing so strong. It is true that recently several similar denominations have united, both in the United States and in Canada, but many other attempts have failed, and new sects and cults are constantly arising.

What then, you may well ask, is central and distinctive in Christianity?

Mainly this, that whereas most of its doctrines, customs, practices, liturgies and even its sacred sayings can be found in other and earlier religions, the personality of Jesus is held by Christians of all sects to be unique. He practiced and exemplified what he preached.

He lived as well as taught the Ten Commandments.

His Sermon on the Mount summarized the Jewish teachings he had learned in his youth, but, unlike the scribes and the Pharisees, he "spake with authority" because he lived those precepts, always acting consistently on them, say Christians.

They claim also that Jesus' uniqueness lay in the fact that he acted as God would act if God came down to earth and walked among men. Thus, they say, he was the incarnation of deity, and was God become man, the connecting link between deity and humanity.

But most of all, Christianity holds its Savior-God supreme because, according to the New Testament, Jesus rose from the tomb, triumphantly conquering death itself that first Easter Day.

10

THE ROMAN CATHOLICS

The Church of Authority

THE LITTLE girl was a delicate child, and so very pious and and good that they thought she was not long for this world. Her favorite fun was making small boats out of paper and sailing them down the river with violets as passengers, as any child might play. But what made this girl different was that she said the violets were missionaries she was sending out to convert all the people in the world, and when she grew up, she was going to found a society of missionary sisters.

The strangely romantic part of the story is that, after many years of hardship, self-sacrifice, and superhuman labors, this frail little Italian girl, born a hundred years ago near Milan, really did establish not only the famous order of the Missionary Sisters of the Sacred Heart, but also scores of schools and hospitals on several continents. Moreover, on July 7, 1946, just thirty years after her death in Chicago, she was canonized as a saint, the first citizen of the United States ever to be so honored.

Mother Francesca Cabrini's "violets" are blooming today in both Italy and Little Italy, in Central America and South America, in Spain and in England, in New Orleans, Chicago, Los Angeles, Seattle, and in many another place where she planted and watered them until they were well rooted. The name of the indomitable little nun is especially revered in New York, where the Mother Cabrini Memorial Hospital honors her, as does the Mother Cabrini High School, in which her body, preserved in a glass case, is gazed at reverently by thousands of devout visitors and pilgrims from near and far.

Mother Cabrini's associates, many of them still alive, have told of frequent strange occurrences in the presence of this magnetic woman. When in her convents food or wine was all gone, she would tell the nuns to look again, and they would find plenty where they had previously seen bare shelves. When money was badly needed to pay for work on a building, it would miraculously appear in a drawer to which Mother Francesca pointed. Other nuns could not share her chamber because they were kept awake by unearthly lights which the Mother calmly took for granted and ignored.

But the miracle which American business men most admired was the way in which this modest quiet little woman beat them at their own game. She would come into a strange city, bringing little or no money and usually with a small group of nuns hurrying after her. In a few weeks she would move on quickly to another city, leaving behind her a well-organized school, orphanage, or hospital. In one city she did it in two weeks. She was always having "dreams" of new projects which she would immediately proceed to make come true, with the aid of surprised strangers whom she impressed with the driving force of her creative personality until they too caught her enthusiasm and vision.

Perhaps she succeeded in such marvelous feats of faith

and finally attained sainthood herself because she really believed in miracles and venerated the holy saints. When she became a novice, that is, a sort of apprentice nun or probationer, she chose for her "name in religion" that of a famous male saint, Francis Xavier, a name which became Francesca Saverio when Italianized and feminized. And on her first visit to Rome she promptly went to the Jesuit Church of the Gesù and prayed devoutly in the chapel where the right hand and forearm of St. Francis Xavier was preserved and venerated.

He was her hero because he was the greatest of the lone missionaries of her church since Paul himself, and perhaps also because his great but thwarted ambition had been to become the apostle to China, and she evidently hoped to please her beloved saint by carrying on his work and accomplishing that sacred mission.

Like him, however, she never reached China. But, just as St. Francis Xavier is credited with the conversion of thousands in southern India and, through the seeds he planted in Japan, with 400,000 converts there, so his namesake nun, with equal zeal, accomplished in America some part of what she had hoped to do in China. In all, she founded during her lifetime at least sixty-seven religious institutions, including hospitals, schools and orphanages.

Unlike the various Protestant Christian faiths, the Roman Catholics pay a great deal of attention to the veneration of relics of the saints, claiming that it is a natural human instinct to treat with loving reverence whatever objects our dear ones have left behind. And since the teaching of the Church is that the physical bodies of the saints were "temples of the Holy Ghost" and "will be raised to eternal glory," it is quite consistent that the veneration of a saint's bones, his clothing, or any of his personal belongings is permitted and encouraged. No Catholic is obliged to venerate relics, but he must not say that relics should not be venerated by those who so wish.

Indirectly, however, every Catholic venerates relics, for at the beginning of Mass the officiating priest mounts the steps of the altar and kisses the "sepulchre," the cavity in every altar-stone which must contain the relics of martyrs, and recites:

"Through the merits of thy saints whose relics are here, and of all the saints, we pray thee, O Lord, that thou wouldst deign to pardon us of all our sins."

In the light of this belief, one can understand why Mother Francesca Cabrini paid reverence to the right hand and forearm of St. Francis Xavier.

In December 1949, this same holy relic encased in its gold and crystal reliquary or sacred casket was flown back to

Rome from LaGuardia Airport after a six months' tour. Spanish Jesuit priests had carried it to Japan to commemorate the four hundredth anniversary of the arrival at Kagoshima of the man whose arm and hand were often lifted in that year of 1549 to bless and baptize his converts. Huge crowds, as many as eighty thousand on one occasion, gathered in the great cities of the United States to venerate this sacred limb on its triumphal tour, ending with its five-day exposure in St. Patrick's Cathedral in New York City.

Such a dramatic event naturally raises questions in the minds of those of other faiths which have no such practices, questions which need to be answered for mutual understanding. Non-Catholics ask if this custom is not idolatry, parallel with the worship of the bones, teeth, and even footprints of Gautama the Buddha by his followers. But Catholic teachers are quick to point out first, that Catholic relics are not worshiped: it is the saint from whose body they came who is venerated; and, second, that the veneration given to a saint, either directly or through his relics or his image, is not the same as the worship given to God. They carefully distinguish between *latria,* the Latin word they use for the highest type of worship, that of God himself, and *dulia,* their word for the homage paid to saints and angels. Still another kind is reserved for Mary, who, because of her higher position as the Mother of God, is given the superhomage of *hyperdulia.*

Another question suggested by the exhibition of the hand and forearm of St. Francis Xavier was: where is the rest of the body, and do Catholics believe that the parts will ever be reunited into a living body? In other words, what do they believe about the resurrection of the body and the soul?

At present, the rest of St. Francis' body is in an elaborate reliquary in the Church of the Bom Jesu (Portuguese for Good Jesus) in Old Goa, a city on the west coast of India. Once every ten years it is exhibited to the people. Some of those who have seen the body assert that although the mummified face looks like terra cotta, the body itself is still, four centuries after death, free from corruption. When he died on Sanchian Island in early December 1552, the body was interred in quicklime in order to clean the bones for transfer to Malacca the next summer, but then it was found "perfectly fresh" so it was again buried in Malacca for eighteen months, but remained incorrupt.

The question as to whether or not the parts of the body of this saint, or any saint, or the fragments of the body of anyone killed in an explosion, or the particles of a corpse chemically decomposed in a grave, will ever be reunited and reanimated is not a mere idle inquiry. Men of all races and faiths have wondered about it.

The Catholic answer is that there can be no resurrection of the soul for the simple reason that the soul does not die. Now, according to the great Catholic theologian, St. Thomas Aquinas, "it is contrary to the nature of the soul to be without the body," which requires, of course, the resurrection of the body.

The glorified or risen body which the soul takes on after the resurrection will have identity with the original earthly body, which, however, will be spiritualized to make it immortal and incorruptible. But it is not necessarily the same particles of matter in the body at the moment of death which the soul will reassume at the moment of resurrection. St. Thomas taught that the human nature will be restored in "its state of ultimate perfection, in that youthful age at which the movement of growth has ceased and the movement of decay has not yet begun."

It is also taught that the bodies of the wicked will be resurrected identical, immortal, and incorruptible, but to suffer everlastingly, whereas the just will have "impassable" risen bodies, freed from pain forever.

So the Catholic veneration of the bodies and relics of the saints is not based simply on admiration for an unusual personality, such as the Russian reverence for Lenin's preserved body, or the Hindus' great respect for Gandhi which led them to gather up and treasure the very soil where he fell when assassinated. It is founded on the faith that the very hand and forearm of St. Francis Xavier now preserved in the reliquary will be somehow reunited to the soul of the living saint in heaven.

No wonder that St. Augustine and Pope Gregory the Great, along with many others in the Catholic Church, believed that miracles of healing could be and were wrought through the relics of the saints. There is good Biblical authority for that belief. Under question 219, "Why do we honor relics?" in the latest revised Baltimore Catechism of the Catholic Church, the confirmatory Biblical references are (1) to the story in the Book of Kings recording how a corpse cast into Elisha's grave came to life again when it struck the prophet's bones, and (2) to the account in Acts which asserts:

"God worked more than the usual miracles by the hand of Paul; so that even handkerchiefs and aprons were carried from his body to the sick, and the diseases left them and the evil spirits went out."

The belief that sick people may be tormented or even "possessed" by such evil spirits or demons, and that these demons can be driven out by the rite of "exorcism," is another of the doctrines of the early church still retained by Catholics but abandoned by most Protestants who are apt to employ a physician or psychiatrist rather than an exorcist.

Yet, as recently as 1949, when a fourteen-year-old Maryland boy was afflicted by what some called an evil spirit, and Dr. J. B. Rhine called a "most impressive poltergeist," the youth's non-Catholic parents took him in vain to a Protestant minister, a parapsychology society, and two hospitals where both medical and psychiatric treatments were given. As a last resort, the boy was exorcised more than a score of times by a Catholic priest. In the ancient ritual the climax comes when the priest says to the alleged evil spirit:

"In the name of the Father, and of the Son and of the Holy Ghost, I cast thee out!"

Each time the priest came to these words, the boy cursed, shrieked, and shouted Latin words; but according to Catholic sources reported in the *Baltimore Sun*, the priest finally succeeded in casting out the devil and restoring the boy to normal condition with no further manifestations.

Exorcisms are rarely used, but blessings, another kind of sacramental, are frequent and serve to bring religion close to the daily life of the people. Any priest can give blessings, but the blessing has no effect unless the proper formula is used. Take for instance the Blessing of St. Blaise.

St. Blaise was a physician who became an Armenian bishop and was martyred in 316 A. D. One of the miracles attributed to him in pious legend was his saving the life of a boy who had a fishbone stuck in his throat; so even today he is invoked by the faithful in case of throat trouble, especially on February 3, the day of his martyrdom. The formula is for the priest to touch the throat of the sufferer with two crossed candles which have been properly blessed, saying at the same time:

"May God deliver thee from trouble of the throat and from every other evil through the intercession of St. Blaise, the bishop and martyr. In the name of the Father and of the Son and of the Holy Ghost. Amen."

Not only may persons be blessed, such as a bride and groom, a woman before and after childbirth, a dying person, little children, and people attending a church ceremony; but places and things as well, such as a cemetery, a church, a house, bells, baptismal water, ships, food, bees, animals, railways, bridges, and even in recent years automobiles.

Water blessed by a priest becomes "holy water," the use of which is common in Catholic churches and homes, but unrecognized among Protestant Christians. Every Sunday before the principal Mass holy water is used by the priest to sprinkle the altar, himself, his assistants, and the people. It is used in most blessings and many times a day by devout Catholics in making the sign of the cross.

This making of the sign of the cross, or blessing oneself,

is a distinctively Catholic practice. Upon entering the church, you dip the tips of your fingers and thumb of your right hand in the stoup (vessel) of holy water which must always be handy to the door. With your finger-tips and thumb still held closely together you then touch first your forehead, then your breast, then your left and right shoulders, meanwhile repeating the formula, "In the name of the Father and of the Son and of the Holy Ghost."

The process is often called "crossing oneself" for it is obvious that the motions made do roughly form a cross. Making the sign is considered a symbol of confession of faith in Christ crucified and a prayer for his blessing. Today no magic power is attached to the gesture, but many of the writings of the early and medieval church reveal that it was for centuries popularly believed to be a "seal" against witches, demons and disease.

A good Catholic makes the sign of the cross, with or without water, many times a week, in church and out, before and after prayer, eating or sleeping, and when tempted or in danger.

The Catholic Church, much more than other churches, makes use of material and physical objects to remind its members of spiritual teachings. Among these "blessed objects of devotion" the most frequently used besides the holy water are: candles, palms, ashes, medals, rosaries, crucifixes, scapulars, and images of Christ, Mary his mother, and the saints.

All of these objects are so richly meaningful and burdened with romance and tradition that any one of them would require several pages to be explained and interpreted. The rosary is perhaps the most interesting, and the least understood by non-Catholics.

To a superficial observer a rosary is but a string of beads which the Catholic Christian apparently counts, fingering them as he mutters to himself as a sort of lazy substitute for praying. But in "telling the beads" he is really saying many prayers. In fact, the word "bead" itself, like the word "bid," comes from the old Anglo-Saxon word *bed*, meaning prayer. Each rosary bead represents a prayer.

The word "rosary" means literally a garland or chaplet of roses, and there are many different strings of beads so named, but the commonest is called the Dominican, because of a sweet legend that Mother Mary herself appeared to St. Dominic (1170-1221 A. D.) and revealed the rosary and its use.

But the famous Lady Godiva of Coventry, she who rode through the streets naked, save for her long hair, as a pledge to get her husband the earl to reduce the high taxes, is said by historians to have bequeathed to the monastery she founded "a circlet of gems which she had threaded on a string, in order that by fingering them one by one as she successively recited her prayers she might not fall short of the exact number." And since she died about 1070 A. D., just a hundred years before St. Dominic was born, it would seem that Lady Godiva could claim the credit for originating the rosary.

The Dominican Rosary is so full of meaning, however, and so well established in the affections of Catholics that its place is secure. It consists of one hundred and sixty-five beads, divided into fifteen "decades" of ten small beads each, plus fifteen larger ones between. Beginning with a large bead, the teller says a paternoster (Our Father) and then ten aves (Hail Marys) on the small beads, and a gloria (Glory be to the Father . . .) when the fingers reach the short bit of chain or cord before the next large bead. This makes one decade, and the process is repeated for the other fourteen decades. When, as often, the rosary is the short one of only five decades and five paternosters, the teller can complete the entire fifteen by going around three times.

But the important point about the rosary is that one is supposed to meditate on the fifteen "mysteries" while saying the prayers of the fifteen decades. These mysteries are events in the life of Christ or the Virgin Mary and are, like the rosary beads, divided into three groups of five each.

The Five Joyful Mysteries are (1) the Annunciation of the Angel Gabriel to Mary, (2) the Visitation of Mary to Elizabeth, (3) the Birth of Jesus, (4) the Presentation of Jesus in the Temple, and (5) the Finding of Jesus Talking with the Doctors in the Temple.

The Five Sorrowful Mysteries are (1) the Agony in the Garden, (2) the Scourging, (3) the Crowning with Thorns, (4) Jesus Carrying His Cross, and (5) the Crucifixion.

The Five Glorious Mysteries are (1) the Resurrection, (2) the Ascension, (3) the Descent of the Holy Ghost at Pentecost, (4) the Assumption of Mary, and (5) the Crowning of Mary.

The last two mysteries, based on Catholic tradition rather than the Bible, refer to the belief that at the death of Mary the Mother of Jesus (whom Catholics call the Virgin Mary because they believe she remained a virgin all her life), her body, preserved from corruption, was shortly "assumed" into heaven and there reunited to her soul. Thereupon she was received into the presence of God, and that reception is referred to symbolically as her Coronation or Crowning.

These fifteen mysteries, properly understood, include directly or indirectly the central teachings of the Catholic Church, and there is no doubt that the frequent use of the rosary, with thoughtful meditation on the mysteries, does help Catholics, young and old, to become well versed in their faith.

It was while they were saying their rosary, as they tended the family sheep, that three children, Jacinta and Francisco Marto, aged seven and nine, and their ten-year-old cousin Lucia, noticed the first of the unusual phenomena of the summer of 1917 that led to the establishing of the Portuguese shrine at Fatima, which already rivals as an attraction for pilgrims the older French one at Lourdes and the Canadian shrine of St. Anne de Beaupré.

The three praying children of Fatima were startled that May day in 1917 to see a flash of lightning in a cloudless sky. They were running for shelter when the second flash diverted their course toward a small oak tree on which, to their further great astonishment, there appeared a very beautiful lady clothed in a white gown trimmed with gold. In her clasped hands she held a long and shining rosary.

She spoke to them very briefly, merely assuring them that they need not fear, and asking them to return to the tree the thirteenth of June and monthly until October 13, when, at her sixth and last appearance, there would be a great miracle. Each 13th a larger crowd joined the children and through them the lady counseled the faithful saying of the rosary, attendance at Holy Communion, and strict discipline and penance. She also prophesied the end of World War I, then in progress, and the coming of the more terrible World War II, as well as the Spanish Civil War. Most surprising of all, she predicted: "Russia will be converted and an era of peace will be granted to humanity."

On October 13, 1917, at noon, seventy thousand people had gathered with the children for the promised miracle. The mysterious lady appeared, visible only to the children, and urged again the frequent saying of the rosary and taking of communion, promising those who did so that they would receive special help at the hour of death. She announced herself as Queen of the Holy Rosary, and the children saw with her St. Joseph and the Infant Jesus. Then the rain, which had been falling all morning, stopped; people noticed that their clothing was suddenly dry; and little Lucia, repeating a gesture of the lady, pointed to the sun.

A very strange phenomenon then occurred, according to witnesses, including Portuguese newspaper reporters, among whom were both believers and unbelievers of the Catholic faith. They said they saw the sun grow pale as silver, then begin to revolve like a gigantic colored pinwheel. It stopped and started twice again. The whole crowd of people fell on their knees repeating the phrases of the acts of faith and contrition.

All during the spring of 1950, thousands of Holy Year pilgrims on their way to Rome traveled by special trains and buses from Paris and Lisbon to the shrine at Fatima, where they knelt devoutly, said their rosaries, prayed for forgiveness and grace, and especially for the conversion of Russia and an era of peace for all humanity.

All roads led to Rome that year for the magnificent ceremonies of another "Holy Year," originally proclaimed as a centennial observance by Pope Boniface VIII in 1300 A. D., but changed to a twenty-five year occurrence by Pope Paul II in 1470 A. D. Those pilgrims who visit and worship at certain churches in Rome during Holy Year are granted an extraordinary plenary indulgence, or full pardon, which means, not "permission to sin," but remission of punishment for sin. The pilgrim may transfer this indulgence to someone in purgatory, the place where Catholics believe souls go after death and are "purged" of their sins before they go to heaven.

Rome is to the Catholic what Mecca is to the Moslem— The Holy City, because the Catholic firmly believes that his Church was founded there by Christ himself through St. Peter. St. Thomas Aquinas, the great Catholic theologian, taught:

"To manifest his power still more effectively, [Christ] ordained that the head of his Church should be in Rome itself, the capital of the world, as a sign of his complete victory and that thence faith should spread to the whole world."

It was in Rome that St. Peter, the first pope, according to Catholic history, established his episcopal throne, and was martyred and buried. It is there that his successors in the papacy have sat and ruled until today, save for the seven French popes who pontificated in Avignon from 1305 to 1370 A. D.

In and from the famed Vatican—with its palace, chapels, museums, archives, library, picture galleries, printing-press, and even an astronomical observatory—the pope, or Holy Father, really rules the Catholic world. He is the "Vicar of Jesus Christ," the visible head of the Church, which is the Mystical Body of Christ.

The entire Catholic Church is the Church of Authority because the pope's word is supreme for all Catholics. It is true that he is elected, with much deliberation and ceremonial, by the College of Cardinals, but his power is not derived from them. It is, according to the teaching of the Church, given to him by God directly, and he exercises his powers by divine right as the direct successor of St. Peter. He is infallible in his teaching on matters of faith or morals when speaking *ex cathedra* that is, officially, and then has supreme power of jurisdiction over every individual Catholic and the whole Church.

From Rome the Roman Catholic Church spread westward and soon controlled all Western Europe. As early as 1125 A.D. it came to America, for in that year there was established in Greenland a diocese which had resident bishops until 1377. When Columbus came to this continent, he brought a Catholic bishop-elect with him.

In the United States proper, the first Catholic parish was founded in 1565 in St. Augustine, Florida, over a half-century before the Pilgrim Fathers landed on Plymouth Rock. Maryland was founded in 1634 by Roman Catholics, and vies with Rhode Island for the honor of being known as the first state to have religious freedom protected by law. There has been a rapid growth of the Catholic Church in the United States, especially from 1828 to 1915 when immigration from European countries was highest, and by 1953 reached approximately 30,000,000, with a claimed 330,000,000 throughout the world.

Into whatever part of the world one may go, he will find that, besides the use of the rosary and the making of the sign of the cross, another of the distinguishing practices of the devout Catholic is faithful observance of private or auricular confession, so-called because it is unwritten and told only into the ear of the priest.

Protestants do occasionally confess their sins, publicly in testimony or class meetings and by baptism, and privately in prayer to God. And Jews have their annual Yom Kippur or Day of Atonement. In the very "high church" wings of the Anglican and Episcopal faiths, and in the Eastern or Greek Orthodox Catholic churches, there is confession, but it is not as important or elaborate as in the Roman Catholic system, where it is part of the sacrament of penance and the priest acts as judge, not merely as a spiritual physician as in the Greek or Eastern Church.

Confession, which must be made at least once a year by "all who have come to the age of reason," including priests and even the pope, is essentially telling one's sins to a priest in order to obtain forgiveness. It is believed that the ordained priest has the power both to forgive sins and to judge the sinner because by his ordination he is a direct successor to the apostles to whom Jesus Christ said, "Whose sins you shall forgive, they are forgiven them; and whose sins you shall retain, they are retained."

At confession one enters a little cubicle, somewhat like a phone booth, popularly called "the box," and confesses his wrong-doings to the priest who is behind the screen. Each can hear but not see the other. All mortal sins must be confessed, and although it is not necessary to confess venial sins, it is better to do so because thus strength may be received to resist the temptation of such sins later.

The differences between mortal and venial sins are impossible to explain briefly, especially since a venial sin may, under some circumstances, become a mortal sin. Most Catholics depend upon their priests to clarify this and other matters of faith and practice, and take their word for it, since laymen are trained from childhood to accept without question the authority of the church and its officials.

The main distinction between these two kinds of sin as made in the Baltimore Catechism is that mortal sin is a "grievous offense against the law of God" and "is called mortal, or deadly, because it deprives the sinner of sanctifying grace, makes the soul an enemy of God, takes away the merit of all its good actions, deprives it of the right to everlasting happiness in heaven, and makes it deserving of everlasting punishment in hell." Venial sin, on the other hand, is "a less serious offense against the law of God," and can be pardoned even without confession.

A "good confession" must be humble, sincere, and complete, and must include sins of thought, word, and deed. After confession, the priest gives spiritual advice and absolution (forgiveness) and may assign a penance, which may be an act of devotion, piety, or self-abasement. The purpose of the penance is to make atonement for sin, to get help to avoid future sins, and to satisfy the temporal punishment due.

Another Catholic custom noticed by non-Catholics is the making of genuflections, the quick bending of the right knee in church at various times by both priests and people. It is a form of prayer, and is one of the two "ceremonial reverences," the other being the metanies, or bows and prostrations, still practiced in the eastern churches. The profound bow was the usual reverence in the church until the sixteen century, when it was superseded by the genuflection. Properly made, the right knee should touch the ground, but the body should be held erect, and the sign of the cross should not be made at the same time. Among the many times when the devout Catholic genuflects are when passing before an altar where the Blessed Sacrament (the bread and wine of the Eucharist) is reserved, or where a relic of the true cross is exposed, or to the cross on Good Friday. The clergy genuflect to the altar-cross and to the bishop when on his throne.

Good Friday is of great importance to Catholics who hope to have it made a legal holiday in the states where it is not already so. It is a day of fasting, abstinence, and penitence, and the only day of the year when Mass may not be said, because it is the anniversary of the crucifixion of Jesus Christ, the sacrifice of which all Masses are symbols.

Maundy Thursday is the day before Good Friday, and commemorates the time when Jesus washed the feet of his disciples and instituted the Blessed Sacrament of the Eucharist, or Lord's Supper. The first word of the ceremony in Latin is "Mandatum," which became easily corrupted to Maundy.

Ash Wednesday is the first day of the forty-day fast of Lent which ends as Easter Sunday arrives. It is so named because on that day the officiating priest, after four prayers, sprinkles ashes (made from the palms of the previous year's Palm Sunday) with holy water and incenses and applies them to the foreheads of clergy and people, saying, in Latin, "Remember, man, that thou art dust and to dust thou shalt return."

The word "Mass" was not used in the early church to describe what is now the main ceremony of the Catholic church. Before the sixth century it was variously named The Mystery, The Offering or The Sacrifice, and these are better names for it than Mass, the origin of which is unknown, except it be from *missio*, the Latin word meaning dismissal, used toward the end of the ceremony in the words, *Ite missa est* (Go, the dismissal is made).

The ceremony of the Mass requires for its adequate explanation more space than this entire chapter, but some hints of its importance and significance may be given. In the Mass, which is a symbolic sacrifice, Jesus Christ plays a triple part: He is the priest, offering Himself as the Sacrifice or Victim to God the Father, with Whom He is one. The officiating priest is the visible and secondary minister. The consecration is the most important part of the Mass, the substance of bread and wine is believed to be changed then into the body and blood of Christ. After that, the Host (the transformed bread or wafer) and the Chalice (the cup containing the transformed wine) are elevated by the priest, and a small handbell is rung to notify the people of this most important part of the service.

Then comes the saying or singing of the Our Father by the celebrating priest, who thereupon proceeds to the Fraction of the Host (breaking of the bread), the choir sings the beautiful Agnus Dei (Lamb of God), and there are three prayers preparatory to Communion. If it is High Mass, the Kiss of Peace is given: the priest kisses the altar and then inclines his left cheek close to the left cheek of his assisting deacon, saying *"Pax tecum,"* (Peace be with thee), whereupon the deacon responds: *"Et cum spiritu tuo,"* (And with thy spirit). The same is done to the subdeacon who passes it on to others. This is all preparatory to Communion, which is the receiving of the sacred bread or wafer dipped in the sacred wine (believed to be the veritable flesh and blood of Christ) first by the priest and then given by him to the people kneeling at the altar rail.

The consecration of the bread and wine, followed by the Communion—the receiving of them by priest and people—is the center and core of the Mass. The consecration is, however, preceded, at the very opening of the service, by the Preparation (prayers by the priest at the foot of the altar steps and then at the altar), the incensing of the altar, the Introit (a psalm response), several chants, the reading of a New Testament epistle, the singing of two verses from a psalm, the reading of part of a gospel, the reciting of the Nicene Creed, then more prayers, singing, and ceremonial washing, until the consecration. After the consecration and the communion, there are various ablutions, verses, prayers, blessings, and the last gospel.

There are nearly forty separate actions or items in each High Mass celebration, all of them of great significance and ancient tradition. The liturgy of the Mass is today much as it was at the beginning of the seventh century. Indeed, in outline, it was in existence by the middle of the second century. And no wonder, for its central and most important part, the consecration and communion, is based on the various New Testament descriptions of the Last Supper of Jesus with his disciples.

It should be remembered that this supper, celebrated by Catholics in the Mass and by Protestants in Communion or The Lord's Supper, is based on the old Jewish ritual supper in preparation for the Passover, which, indeed, Jesus was observing with his disciples. The Paschal Lamb sacrifice of the Jewish people is interpreted by Christianity as anticipating the sacrifice of Jesus himself on the cross as the Agnus Dei or Lamb of God. This is one place, as the Ten Commandments is another, where the three religions, Judaism, Catholicism, and Protestantism, have much in common.

Non-Catholics often wonder just what is the difference between High Mass and Low Mass, a question which is apt to make a Catholic theologian smile. For, although there is and can be but one Mass, there are many ways in which it can be celebrated, depending on its function in the life of the Church. There are parochial, requiem, conventual and other occasional Masses, and each of them can be celebrated in any one of the four distinct types: Pontifical (including Papal), High (or Solemn), Sung, and Low.

And a Low Mass is really a High Mass—in modified form. All the important parts of High Mass are retained, but many parts are done differently. The main differences are that the officiating priest is not assisted by a deacon and subdeacon but only by a server or acolyte—often a layman or boy. And

106

since no choir is present, the priest himself says the usually sung prayers, and pronounces them in four tones of voice—clear, medium, low, and inaudible (secretly). For instance, there are parts, like the epistle and gospel, which are said aloud, but the canon (the main part of the Mass) is said silently. And there are usually only two or three candles at the altar.

Catholic children and adult converts are well prepared in the faith by learning the catechism—the question and answer book on the main points of Catholic belief and practice. In England, the Penny Catechism is popular, while the Baltimore Catechism is better known in the United States.

After learning the catechism, the candidate for confirmation—the girls dressed in white with a little crown of flowers and the boys in neat dark suits—presents himself at church where the bishop imposes his hands on the head of the candidate and prays for the gift of the Holy Spirit. The bishop then dips his thumb into chrism (holy oil) and anoints each candidate by making the cross with his thumb on the forehead. Then, addressing him by his newly chosen confirmation name (usually that of a saint), the bishop says: "I sign thee with the sign of the cross and I confirm thee with the Chrism of Salvation. In the name of the Father and of the Son and of the Holy Ghost, Amen." Finally, with a gentle blow on the cheek, the bishop says: "Peace be with thee," the choir sings, and the bishop prays and gives his blessing. The chrism is usually made in the West of olive oil and balsam, but in Constantinople over fifty other ingredients are used, including wine, ginger, and pepper.

One other Catholic custom which puzzles non-Catholics is the matter of fasting and abstinence, which should be carefully distinguished. The latter is stricter, but both have many exceptions. Fasting means, really, taking only one full meal a day, after noon. But two or three ounces of bread may be taken at breakfast, and a light meal, called a collation, of not more than ten ounces, may be taken as luncheon or supper, besides the full meal. Fasting is only for those over twenty-one and under fifty-nine, and even between those ages the parish priest may give a dispensation to the sick and those who do hard work, either physical or mental.

Abstinence, by Catholic definition, is refraining from eating flesh-meat or meat soups. Fish is not considered fleshmeat. All Catholics over seven years old must observe abstinence on Fridays (the day of Christ's crucifixion), Ash Wednesday, and six ember days (the Wednesday, Friday, and Saturday following the first Sunday in Lent, Whitsunday—fiftieth day after Easter, Holy Cross Day—September 14, and St. Lucy's Day—December 13). Included also are the Saturdays of Lent, Holy Saturday (before noon), from midnight before Communion, and the vigils (eves) before Pentecost, Assumption, All Saints, and Christmas. This abstinence is considered an act of penitence and mortification for the health of the soul.

The Catholic church cannot be understood apart from Saint Peter. It is very significant that it is to Peter's great cathedral in Rome that the Catholic pilgrims by hundreds of thousands from all over the world wend their way every Holy Year. For Peter is the connection between the Church and Christ himself. It was to Peter that Jesus said:

"Blessed art thou, Simon Bar-Jona, for flesh and blood has not revealed this to thee, but my Father in heaven. And I say unto thee, thou art Peter, and upon this rock I will build my Church, and the gates of hell shall not prevail against it. And I will give thee the keys of the kingdom of heaven; and whatever thou shalt bind on earth shall be bound in heaven, and whatever thou shalt loose on earth shall be loosed in heaven." (Matthew 16:17–19.)

This is interpreted by the Catholic church as meaning that Christ gave special power in His Church to Peter, making him the head of the apostles, and the chief ruler and teacher of the whole Christian church. This special power and authority of Peter is believed to be transferred to his successors, the popes, down to the present day. This is why the Catholics so firmly believe that they are the only true Church and that if there is to be a great union of all Christendom it must be by other Christians joining the Roman Catholic Church.

Protestants and Eastern Orthodox Catholics, however, interpret the New Testament teachings differently; hence Christendom remains divided.

11

THE ORTHODOX EASTERN CHURCH

IF A ROMAN Catholic or a Protestant should ever have enough curiosity and courage to attend divine service in a church of the third great section of Christianity, he would be in for a surprising and informing experience. This third group, comprising one-fourth of Christendom, is officially called The Holy Orthodox Catholic Apostolic Eastern Church, but its members are often termed Greek Catholics to distinguish from the Roman Catholics. More accurately, and for brevity's sake, they are referred to as the Orthodox Eastern Church, and they shorten it still more, calling themselves simply the Orthodox Church. In New England, that name would mean the Protestant Trinitarian Congregationalists. To be sure, these Eastern Orthodox Christians also believe in the Trinity and are, theoretically, self-governing congregations, but the resemblance goes very little further than that.

The New England Orthodox Church member, probably a direct descendant of the Puritans, is accustomed on Sundays to walk sedately to his oblong high-steepled white meeting house and enter his pew there at 11 A. M., join in the singing of an opening hymn, listen to a short scripture reading, a brief prayer, and a twenty-minute sermon, put his contribution in the collection-plate when it is passed, sing another hymn, and leave promptly at 12 o'clock.

He would find everything different in an Eastern Orthodox Church—building, atmosphere, and service. The building is either equare or round, with a dome, and murals of Bible scenes cover walls and ceiling inside, and sometimes outside. What the western visitor will probably notice first as he enters is a high screen blocking off the whole eastern end of the place from the congregation. The screen is covered with pictures of a peculiar sort, looking like framed portraits elaborately gilded, and has three doors leading to the place behind the screen where the service is apparently going on.

No pulpit is visible, but when the middle door is open he can see an altar. His guide, or nearest worshiper, will tell him the center door is the "Royal" one and that the altar is called the "Throne." There are no pews, save a few chairs around the walls for those who cannot stand, as the rest do when they are not on their knees. The service goes on and on behind the screen and the people come and go as they wish. When they come, they select and light a candle in front of one of the pictures, which apparently represent saints, after which some worshipers kiss the pictures fervently. Then they may start praying.

At first, it seems that the praying and worshiping by the people has very little to do with the service going on behind the screen, but as one becomes accustomed to the confusion, a pattern emerges, for suddenly the people will start singing in response to words of the priests or chants by the hidden choir. Or they may shout a doxology after a litany. Soon the stranger realizes that the priests and deacons behind the screen are really furnishing the proper liturgical atmosphere and background to stimulate and enrich the individual devotions and prayers of lay people, who know perfectly well every step of the performance going on around the altar Throne. This is no one-hour affair, and if the visitor stays long enough he may get the full significance and beauty of the ancient ritual. As responses follow litanies, and prayers are followed by marvellous hymns sung full-throat-ed by musical people who know and love every mounting note, it becomes apparent that here is the masterly rendition of a great liturgical drama, with all the actors knowing and living their parts so well that they need no script. No hymn books or prayer books are visible and western visitors notice that these people have no organ or other musical instrument either for accompaniment, or to keep them on key and cover up weak congregational singing. There are only two other congregations in all Christendom who can come near the Eastern Orthodox for powerful triumphant vocal music, and those are the Lutherans and the Negro Baptists.

Twice a year the liturgical drama, after running along with slight variations from week to week, changes radically. During Lent the services are even longer and take on a penitential aspect, with sad music and many genuflections and prostrations. But since Easter immediately succeeds Lent, there is then a sudden change to notes of praise and triumph over sin and death. For seven days the Royal Door and the others are left wide open, and for six weeks kneeling is actually forbidden.

All worship services in the Eastern Church are dramatic, but the Eucharist or Communion Service is really a sacred play, a cantata or opera, portraying the entire life of Jesus Christ, with the priests, the sub-priests or deacons, and the lay people as actors. Of the three distinct acts, the first is the Childhood and the eighteen Silent Years, as western Christians call them; but to the Orthodox East it is the *Prothesis*, or Preparation of the Gifts. The second act is the *Synaxis*, or Assembly of the Gifts, representing the teaching and healing ministry of Christ; and the final act is the *Anaphora*, or Offering of the Gifts, depicting the Last Supper, the Crucifixion, Resurrection, Ascension, and the gift of the Holy Spirit. During and immediately after this dramatic representation of the Life of Christ, the symbolism of the eucharist is being enacted in a sort of parallel drama—a play within a play. The priests, during the Prothesis, are preparing the elements of bread and wine; during the Synaxis they are assembling them on the Credence beside the Throne (altar); and in the Anaphora the elements are consecrated and distributed.

Westerners of the Catholic faith will notice several differences from their customs. The Eastern Orthodox priests use leavened (raised) bread instead of unleavened, claiming that it has more life in it. The wine is mixed with water, since the Gospel of John states that when the Roman soldier pierced Jesus' side with his spear, there flowed out "blood and water." Into this diluted wine the bread is dipped and thus "both kinds" are spooned to the laity. Even newly baptized infants receive a spoonful that they may be bound to the Church as full communicants as early and strongly as possible.

In several other sacraments and practices the Eastern Church has its different ways of doing things, ways they claim to be according to the apostolic practice of the early church, which is the reason why they call theirs the Apostolic Church.

Baptism in the West, both for Catholic and Protestant, is mainly looked upon as the act by which one is spiritually regenerated and joins the church. In the East, it is all that but has a cosmic meaning as well. Not only another individual is being saved, but the whole cosmos is gradually being redeemed; for an important part of nature—water—is sanctified at every baptism. So the opening and lengthiest section of the baptismal sacrament is the consecration of the water, during which is used the following prayer, quoted here in its entirety because it so well represents the beauty and mysticism of the liturgy of the Eastern Church:

"Great art Thou, O Lord, and marvellous are Thy works, and there is no word which sufficeth to hymn Thy wonders. Before Thee tremble all the powers endowed with intelligence. The sun singeth with Thee; the moon glorifieth Thee; the stars meet together before Thy presence. The light obeyeth Thee; the water-springs are subject unto Thee. Wherefore, O King, who lovest mankind, come Thou now and sanctify this water, by the indwelling of the Holy Spirit, and grant unto it the grace of redemption and the blessing of Jordan. Make it the fountain of incorruption, the gift of sanctification, the remission of sins and the remedy of infirmities."

Instead of pouring or sprinkling, complete immersion is the accepted method of baptism, and is done thrice, once for each Person of the Trinity. And instead of the priest or minister saying , "I baptize thee . . ." the formula is, "The servant of God, John, is baptized in the name of the Father, Amen, and of the Son, Amen, and of the Holy Spirit, Amen." For in the Orthodox Eastern Church it is stressed in all sacraments that they are administered corporately, that is, on behalf of the whole church body.

That idea is emphasized in Confession when the individual goes first to his friends and relatives asking forgiveness, and they say, "God pardons you," and also when he comes to the priest, for the penitent does not kneel, but stands upright, facing eastward, beside the clergyman, who is only a witness, not a judge, but may give advice as a friend and spiritual physician.

Other noticeable differences are that Unction, the anointing with pure olive oil, is not restricted to "Extreme" cases where the person is dying, but is given more frequently to those desiring healing of bodily or spiritual illness, or the purification of their inner life. Sometimes seven priests unite in service, which includes seven scripture lessons about the healing power of Christ. The Eastern Church also rejects belief in purgatory, indulgences, dispensations, and the supremacy and infallibility of the Pope of Rome. Religious pictures called "icons" take the place of holy images and statues.

The Eastern Orthodox people, however, do agree with the Roman Catholics and differ from Protestants in the veneration of the Virgin Mary. They believe in the Virgin Birth of Christ, but reject the doctrine of the Immaculate Conception, proclaimed in 1854 by Pope Pius IX, that the Virgin Mary, "in the first instant of her conception (by her mother Anna) was . . . preserved exempt from all stain of original sin." The Eastern Church, too, holds that Mary was purified from original sin, but not until the angelic Annunciation. Original sin, of course, is the sin inherited from Adam and Eve, according to the belief of most conservative Christians, East or West, Catholic or Protestant.

Marriage (usually called "Crowning") in the Eastern Orthodox Church much resembles a Jewish wedding, for the bride and groom wear crowns and drink wine from the same cup. Divorce is allowed, and remarriage; but in the latter case the ceremony is very apologetic and even penitential, for the priest prays the Lord to "cleanse the iniquities of thy servants because they, being unable to bear the heat and burden of the day and the hot desires of the flesh, are now entering into the bond of the second marriage, as thou didst render lawful by thy chosen vessel the Apostle Paul, saying for the sake of us humble sinners: 'It is better to marry in the Lord than to burn.'"

Orthodox priests and deacons are permitted and expected to marry, and usually have large families. But they may not marry widows, or marry more than once. If a priest's first wife dies, leaving a number of small children, he may marry again and the Church will not condemn him, but he can no longer act as priest, although he is usually given a subordinate position as choir-master or reader.

Monks, however, of whom there are many, are not allowed to marry, and neither are the bishops, who are therefore chosen from the ranks of the monks. Occasionally a widower priest is made a bishop.

The position of both priests and bishops in the East is much less authoritative partly because the church there is not organized or administered so "efficiently" as in the West, and partly also because of the afore-mentioned "corporate" idea of the church and the consequent interpretation of Apostolic Succession.

In Western Catholic Christianity, and in episcopally ruled Protestant churches, the doctrine of Apostolic Succession is very important as the basis of church government, for all these overseers (bishops), however selected or elected, must be ordained by the laying on of hands by similarly ordained bishops and so on back to the apostles. In a sense, it takes a bishop to make a bishop, and bishops tend to become very powerful individuals in all churches which have the Western version of Apostolic Succession and the corresponding episcopal polity or system of ecclesiastical rule.

But the word "bishop" is, after all, only the funny sound which the Anglo-Saxons made back in the fifth and sixth centuries when they came in contact with Christianity and tried to say the tricky tongue-twisting Greek word, *episkopos,* which meant merely overseer, or, to use a Latin derived synonym, inspector.

Now, in the family-type Eastern Church, which is not so much an institution as a living community, the bishop is still a sort of brotherly inspector or representative of the Church, who doesn't so much *rule* the section of the church over which he "sees," as *act for* it. Apostolic Succession is the living chain linking the present generation in the Church with past generations back to the generation of the Apostles. This "succession" the Eastern Orthodox people consider much stronger in faith and spirit and doctrine than a chain of individuals, among whom in any ecclesiastical line, east or west, there are apt to be several rather weak links.

Still further, and here is the greatest distinction in point-of-view, doctrinal set-up, frame-of-reference, or psychological approach, between The Holy Orthodox Catholic Apostolic Eastern Church and all other Christian Churches, with the possible exceptions of the Spiritualists and the Latter-day Saints—these Eastern Orthodox Christians actually believe that their own recently deceased loved ones, the previous generation, and so on back to the first Christian congregations, including all the saints, martyrs, heroes of the faith, church fathers, and Jesus Christ himself, are right there in church with them at the celebration of the Eucharist, as he was with his disciples when he instituted it in the upper room at Jerusalem.

This vital belief in an actual family reunion of the saints should not be confused with the institutionalized and rather faded doctrine in which some other churches *say* they believe, when they recite an ancient creed, the doctrine of the "Communion of Saints." That is the theoretical and rather nebulous unity of church members on earth with the suffering souls in purgatory and the resurrected souls in heaven, plus the angels. There may be such a unity, but these

113

various groups are not conceived of as actually in one place, except perhaps by a rare mystic here and there.

Mystic is the word. The Eastern Catholics are mystics, and their church is full of mysticism, the mysticism of the Greek mysteries, Eleusinian, Orphic, and Delphic, and the deep Persian symbolism of the Mithraic cult to which the early church owed so much. And this mystic reunion with the saints, whose sacred spirits are brought to the eucharistic rendezvous by the Holy Spirit (for this part of Christianity really believes in the third person of the Holy Trinity) is what the Eastern Orthodox folk go to church for, and why they burn candles before the icons, and kiss so rapturously those effigies which represent the saints and martyrs of old. That is why, too, the walls are covered with murals showing pictures of Bible heroes and episodes in the lives of the Saints. By a sort of sympathetic magic or psychic suggestion those icons and frescoes help the saints and martyrs to come back, or at least help the worshipers to see them with the eyes of faith and spiritual intuition. The Western churches, both Catholic and Protestant, can learn much from these Christians in the East, who claim to preserve intact the faith and practice of the Apostolic Age.

Again and again has the question been asked all over Christendom, "Why and how did the rift between the Greek and Roman Catholics ever come about?"

Many books have been written in answer to that question as to why Christianity has so long been split vertically between East and West. There is not room here even to list the reasons which both sides have alleged. But within this century, and even within the last decade, the reasons have been changing, and are likely to continue in flux for several years.

Once all that was heard was the rather silly statement that this great calamity was due solely to a quarrel over one Latin word, *Filioque,* meaning "and from the Son." At the Council of Chalcedon in 451 A. D., Greek and Latin Christians had agreed unanimously that they believed "in the Holy Ghost who proceedeth from the Father." The Western churches, some of them, wished to add that the Holy Ghost proceeded also from the Son. The Popes opposed the idea vigorously until Charlemagne championed it. Some time afterward the leaders of the churches in the East heard of Rome's acceptance of the Filioque, and used that fact later to challenge the orthodoxy of the Pope. The quarrel grew, each side accusing the other of numerous heresies, until the Latin-speaking Christians, comprising the Western Patriarchate, Rome, were arrayed against the Greek-speaking Eastern Patriarchates of Constantinople, Alexandria, Antioch, and Jerusalem. The Filioque phrase was only one of fifty theological and procedural alleged heresies used in mutual accusations and recriminations.

The differences were not merely semantic or dogmatic: they were political, national, racial, temperamental, and psychological. What brought about the deep breach finally was not the Filioque fight, except as the word became a battle-cry, and still is. It was not even the excommunication by the Pope on July 16, 1054, of the Patriarch of Constantinople, spokesman for the whole Eastern Church. That was only one move in a long chess game between the bishops. What did deeply alienate Eastern Christendom at last (as has long been stated in the East and has lately been admitted in Western books and encyclopedias) was the nefarious conduct of the Christian Crusaders from the West on their way to the Holy Land, especially during the Fourth Crusade, when they sacked and plundered Constantinople itself, the Rome of the East, in 1204.

The "heathen pagan" Moslems had always respected Christian houses of worship, but the Western Christian Knights in drunken orgies violated the sacred altars of the Orthodox churches. Constantinople was full of the relics, art treasures, manuscripts, and sacred vessels of the Christian Church, gathered during nearly nine centuries by Christian emperors since Constantine. Most of this important historical collection was looted, plundered, and destroyed. The Holy Altar of the great Church of St. Sophia was broken up and sold. The Crusaders divided the portable treasures with the Venetians (who had provided ships and food for the crusade) and gave them valuable lands besides. For themselves they kept the other half of the plunder and set up the Latin Empire of Constantinople.

Now the Western Pope was not to blame for the sack of Constantinople, although he had started the Fourth Crusade, for its leaders had changed the plans on the way. In a letter to his Cardinal in Constantinople he denounced the sacrileges which the Crusaders had committed. But the damage was done. The common people in the Orthodox churches of the East had paid very little attention to the doctrinal disputes of the bishops or the anathemas and excommunications which popes and patriarchs had hurled at each other. When, however, the citizens of Constantinople and vicinity saw and suffered rape and pillage, desecration and pollution of their most sacred objects, within their own sanctuaries, by Western Christians, their alleged brothers in Christ, they could not forget it, nor let their children's children have religious fellowship with such people.

The leading officials of both branches of the Church eventually got together for talks at the top level and, recognizing that drunken soldiers are likely to do almost anything, and that all the Cross-wearing Crusaders were not necessarily Christians, but included ignorant soldiers of fortune who went along for the ride and the loot, the bishops agreed to a short of armistice. Under the growing danger of being overwhelmed by the powerful Moslems, they tried to bring the two parts of Christianity together for mutual protection. The bishops of Rome and Constantinople met in 1274 at Lyons and in 1439 at Florence, and arranged a reconciliation each time. But it was in vain, for to the Eastern Christian laity, the Moslems were still gentlemen compared with the drunken Western Christians.

The rift is likely to remain until its cause is recognized— until it is admitted that not priestly dogma and doctrine, but the sacrilege and rapine of the Crusaders, concealed till recently under pious legend, romantic ballads, and theological double talk, is what caused the greatest schism of Christendom.

How can the split be healed even if its cause is admitted? The Anglican Church has made a start with meetings designed to let the theologians of the Orthodox Church and the Church of England get acquainted and discuss their differences. A more promising method would seem to be the conferences and camps sponsored by the Fellowship of St. Alban and St. Sergius, bringing together personally the lay people, especially students and other young people, of English and Eastern churches.

The most hopeful portent pointing toward possible future understanding has hardly been noticed in the secular press and magazines, namely, the recent enormous growth of Eastern Orthodox Churches in America. The exact number of their communicants is not known, due to the custom of counting parish membership by adult males only, but current estimates vary from 1,500,000 to over three millions. In 1910, when the population was ninety-two million, they numbered only 385,000. If they had grown only with the population, they would now number 675,000. So they have increased probably about three times as fast as the population.

They are of at least fifteen denominations, but they are divided nationally rather than doctrinally; e. g., Albanian, Bulgarian, and Greek Orthodox Churches. Four of them, the Romanian, Russian, Syrian, and Ukranian Orthodox Churches, are Constituent Bodies of the National Council of the Churches of Christ in the United States of America. In spite of their national names, however, they now pray for and give full loyalty to the President, Congress, and armed forces of the United States, and all those in places of lawful civil authority.

These Eastern Orthodox Churches in the United States

contain a surprising proportion of children and young people. They are in our schools and colleges with splendid scholastic records and keen participation in community activities. The same is true of the ones in our offices and industries. They are loyal both to their ancient Apostolic faith and to American democracy, for their churches have taught them the "corporate" idea in human religious relationships, which is only another version of the republican democratic principle.

The very fact that they have such a large representation in the National Council, which is, after all, an organization of Western Christians, is indicative of a beginning of the healing of the old breach, for the Eastern Orthodox Christians in Europe, North Africa, and Western Asia, when they condemned Western Christianity, not only considered the Roman Catholics idolatrous pope-worshipers, but thought the Protestants were even worse for putting the Bible in the place which belonged to God alone. Some of the misunderstandings are evidently being cleared up in this country and in certain quarters.

The Eastern Orthodox Christians in this country themselves may furnish, in a generation or two, the intelligent democratic leadership which is necessary to bring about friendly cooperation and an eventual gradual healing of the old wound in the Church of Christ, the Christ who prayed so earnestly for his disciples, "that they all may be one."

In Russia, the Eastern Orthodox Church was severely treated by the Communist government for years. Church lands and schools were confiscated; state support of the churches was terminated; and a determined anti-religious campaign conducted. In 1917 there were over 40,000 churches and nearly 51,000 priests; in 1941, only 4,255 churches and 5,665 priests. But in 1942-43 a milder policy was adopted by the government, apparently because of the war with Germany. An agreement of some sort resulted in the present compromise arrangement of toleration of the church at the price of subordination to and control by the government. The same status exists in general in the satellite countries.

12

THE LUTHERANS

The Church of the Reformation

THE LUTHERAN Church is the only major Protestant denomination named for a man. The Episcopal, Presbyterian, and Congregational churches take their names from the way they are governed—whether by a bishop (*episcopus*), elders (*presbyters*) or by the local church members themselves (congregation). Baptists are so called because of their emphasis on the rite of immersion, and Methodists were nicknamed from the strict methodical habits of study and prayer practiced by the founding Wesleys and their early followers.

The church is named Lutheran simply because there is so much of Luther in it. One cannot fully understand the faith and practice of this church unless he knows about the man whose life and thought are back of it all. The first thing to learn, however, is never to call this faith "Lutheranism." Just as the Moslems who follow the teachings of Mohammed resent non-Moslems calling their religion "Mohammedanism" instead of Islam, in like fashion the members of the Lutheran Church object to having their beliefs thoughtlessly mislabeled Lutheranism. Neither Mohammed nor Luther wished to be worshiped.

And if you ask your Lutheran neighbor what you shall call his religion if not Lutheranism, he will reply, "Christianity," for he claims that his faith is simply the pure original apostolic Christianity of the early church, which Luther restored by freeing it from the errors which had crept into it during fifteen centuries.

The followers of Luther are not very keen on being called Protestants, either, for they disagree in both doctrine and worship with the other Protestant sects, who Lutherans think, go too far. Usually the Lutheran pastors refer to the other non-Roman and non-Greek Christian churches as the Reformed.

So, with the followers of Luther differing strongly from the Roman Catholics in some respects and from the other Protestants in other respects, they have kept very much to themselves through the centuries, and are consequently little known to other Christians, and therefore, of course, somewhat misunderstood. The Catholics have naturally attributed to Lutherans the beliefs of other more radical Protestants, and the latter have looked on Lutherans as only slightly disguised Catholics.

It is important that the Lutherans should be understood by those of other religions in this country, for they are the third largest Protestant group here, with their approximately six and a half million members as compared with nearly eighteen million Baptists and over eleven million Methodists. In the world, they are the largest Protestant denomination by far, even though it is estimated that their prewar eighty million has been reduced to sixty million. It has been said that the Lutheran church was the first casualty in World War II. Since their largest membership was in the Baltic countries and the Scandinavian peninsula, their losses were very heavy.

But if this still large Christian communion is to be understood by the other communions, an understanding which is certainly imperative if Christendom is ever to reach any form or pattern of unity at all, then the beliefs Lutherans hold and the services and ceremonies which they conduct should be described and explained, and the reasons for the differences given. And that cannot be done except against the background of the life story and beliefs of the very remarkable man, Martin Luther.

Even in so doing, one must tread carefully. In reading several Lives of Luther, written by friends, enemies and neutrals, it would be difficult at times for one to realize that the various authors were talking about the same person. Here the facts will be presented as impartially as possible; for the purpose in this study of many religions is always to illuminate the subject and appreciate the religion, while pointing out what in each religion is interesting and helpful to those of other faiths.

When one studies the accounts of Luther's childhood, for instance, there is a clue to the origin of one of his outstanding virtues which was reflected in his doctrines and is seen today among the members and leaders of the Lutheran Church. That prominent trait or characteristic is called steadfastness, firmness and constancy by his admirers and stubbornness by his foes.

According to Luther's own statements he was the victim of severe beatings throughout his childhood and early youth. He says:

"My father once whipped me so severely that I fled from him and it was hard for him to win me back . . . . My mother once beat me until the blood flowed, for having stolen a miserable nut."

In the Mansfeld school, which he described later as "hell and purgatory," the boy Martin, not yet in his teens, once got fifteen whippings in one forenoon.

Now, allowing for the fact that educators from Bible times until quite recently have held that to spare the rod is to spoil the child, it must be admitted that young Luther seems to have had more than his share of that kind of physical education. The question is whether the beatings were what made him so tough and resolute later or whether he was beaten so often because he was such a stubborn child anyway. Probably he was naturally somewhat timid and fearful, but even so would take a beating rather than yield to authority when he thought he was in the right, and that punishment only made him more determined to stand by his guns.

Like most of the people of his time, young Luther was in

real terror of evil spirits, witches, and devils. He feared his parents' beatings but he feared even more the goblins and devils of the night when he crept up to his attic room. And that very real fear stayed with him. He wrote:

"Where such a fear enters a man in childhood, it can hardly be rooted out again as long as he lives. As he once trembled at every word of his father and mother, to the end of his life he is afraid of a falling leaf."

That was probably a dramatized exaggeration, but emphasized a personal problem he had always to face. In spite of his primitive fears, however, he courageously stood by and fought for the truth as he saw it.

When in later years (1521) the Pope called on the Emperor Charles V to condemn Luther to death as a heretic, and the Emperor summoned the monk to appear before the court at the city of Worms, the friends of Luther advised him not to go, although he had been sent an imperial safe conduct, a guarantee that he would not be seized at the hearing. These friends reminded Luther of what had happened a century before, when the reformer of Prague, John Huss, had been taken and burned at the stake in spite of the then Emperor's "safe conduct." But Martin Luther replied:

"Though there were as many devils in Worms as tiles on the roofs, yet would I go." And when he appeared before the Diet, or Council, and was given a chance to recant, he asked for time to prepare his answer. After a night of prayer and conference with his friends he gave his famous answer, call it courageous and resolute or stubborn and obstinate, according to your point of view:

Unless I am convinced by Scripture or by right reason, for I trust neither in popes nor in councils since they have often erred and contradicted themselves—unless I am thus convinced, I am bound by the texts of the Bible. My conscience is captive to the Word of God. I neither can nor will recant anything, since it is neither right nor safe to act against conscience. I reiterate everything I have ever preached or published. Here I stand! I cannot do otherwise! God help me! Amen!

That same firmness has been a mark of Lutherans for four hundred years since. They stand firmly where Luther stood. Because Luther thought and said that the other reformers, especially Zwingli, the leader of the Swiss Protestants, went too far away from the Roman church, so far that he was guilty of "mad and furious blasphemies," the followers of Luther have often since refused to have fellowship with the followers of Zwingli, Calvin, Knox, and other reformers.

The Lutherans also stand firmly, as Luther did, against any overtures from the Roman Catholic Church. In reply to the address of Pope Pius XII, opening the Holy Year of 1950 and inviting all Protestants to come back to what is often called the Mother Church of Christendom, the following official answer was given by Dr. John W. Behnken, president of the Lutheran Church Missouri Synod, one of the largest divisions of American Lutheran faith. That answer clarifies the present Lutheran position on several points, and also shows how faithfully the spirit and attitude and even the views of Martin Luther still obtain today among his American followers. Dr. Behnken stated (December 23, 1949):

"The Lutheran Church looks upon every year as a holy year—a year for repentance of men and for the grace of God, who freely forgives sins in Christ Jesus.

"In his Christmas message calling for the return of Protestants to the Roman Catholic fold, Pope Pius XII has re-iterated all the claims with which the Roman Church has placed itself between God and men. We Lutherans recognize only one Mediator between God and man—the man Christ Jesus. For us, therefore, there can be no return to a church which claims to take the place of Christ and whose leader claims to be the vicar of Christ.

"It saddens us that the Pope refers to believing Protestants as 'children who abandoned us, offended us, made us and are making us suffer.' It saddens us, too, that the Roman Church has maintained and even augmented the abuses of Christ's teaching which forced Martin Luther to protest in his day, and forces us to protest in ours.

"More than the outward organizational unity under one head for which the Pope has appealed, the Christian Church today needs men and women who believe in Jesus Christ with a whole heart, and recognize Him alone as Lord and Savior."

Since the Lutheran Church is just about halfway between the Roman Catholic Church and the other Protestant bodies, it would seem to be strategically located doctrinally to lead a movement for uniting Western Christendom, but it is plain to be seen that such an event is extremely unlikely for some time to come.

On the other and more hopeful side, it can be truly said that there is noticeable today a trend in some Lutheran circles toward less sequestration. Dean Sperry of Harvard Divinity School wrote in his recent book *Religion in America* (page 232):

"American Lutherans are finding it more and more difficult to keep apart and aloof from our Protestantism as a whole, and even at the cost of some modification of its premises, Lutheranism is now beginning to move toward the other churches."

A leading Lutheran, too, the president of an important theological seminary, recently admitted that the time has come for Lutherans to be less exclusive. He said:

"Other Christians don't know us and we don't know them. The Lutheran Church of America cannot for our own good maintain the traditional point of view and say, 'We will have nothing to do with other Christians.' . . . I think we Lutherans will have to act differently in the future than in the past."

Another heritage from Luther is evident in the Lutheran Church of today, a legacy of great virtue, namely, a body of clergymen with high educational standards. This tradition goes back to Martin Luther, who, contrary to rumor and stories circulated by prejudice, was not a poor ignorant renegade priest who gave up his vows to indulge his vices. The Lutheran Church has pastors of excellent education because Martin Luther was himself well educated and realized the importance of a literate and well-trained ministry.

After a very desperate time at several preparatory schools, during which he had to beg his food on the streets, Luther was finally able to eat regularly when the generous Frau Cotta heard him singing, literally for his supper. He was then fourteen and she took him into her home and enabled him to show at school what he could really do. In his eighteenth year he entered Erfurt University and proved such a brilliant scholar that he had his Bachelor of Arts degree at nineteen and his master's degree, second in the class, when but twenty-one. At twenty-six he received his Bachelor's degree in Theology, and his doctorate at twenty-nine.

When twenty-eight, Luther was sent to Rome to transact important business for the Augustinian order of monks, of which he was by this time an important member, and he was so successful in that mission that he was rapidly promoted, and lectured in philosophy, theology, and the Bible. In the year 1515, when but thirty-two years of age, he was appointed Vicar, with the oversight of eleven monasteries.

So Doctor Martin Luther was far from being an ignorant monk, even before he left his church. He could have gone along with the crowd of clergy of his day and might have done very well for himself had he stayed in the church where he already had a good start.

But, like many other monks and priests and scholars, Luther was getting worried about his church, the Roman Catholic Church, of which he was a loyal and hard-working teacher, official, and progressive minded leader.

Whatever be anyone's opinion of Luther's later actions, there can be no doubt that up to the autumn of 1517, he was an honored and respected Roman Catholic. The pope knew him and, as the records show, admired him.

One reason for Doctor Luther's worry was that when he, an eager and devout young monk, had at last been able to visit the Sacred City of Rome in 1511, he had been shocked by the unholiness of the Holy City. The Rome of Pope Julius II and his predecessor Alexander VI was glorious in its art treasures but decadent in other ways, as its own scholars knew and deplored.

Erasmus, the great Roman Catholic scholar, who remained in the church even after Luther was excommunicated, wrote caustic criticisms of the abuses within the church, which had a wide circulation throughout Europe in the form of books and pamphlets and which Luther and many others were reading. In fact, it has been said of the Reformation that Erasmus laid the egg that Luther hatched. In this connection, it is very significant that Erasmus's popular little book, *A Handbook for the Christian Soldier,* published in Antwerp as early as 1504, thirteen years before Luther broke with the church, advocated a return to primitive simple Christianity, leaving aside the complicated ritual and ceremonials of the church, and interpreting Christian doctrine and duty by the teachings of the early church fathers and the Bible itself.

This is exactly what Luther tried to do, and what he and his followers claimed he did do. So the main point at issue between Erasmus and Luther, as between the Roman Catholic Church and the Lutheran Church, was not whether the church needed to be purged of abuses and bad personnel that had crept in, but rather whether this purifying could be done within the church.

Erasmus chose to stay, and Luther chose to leave.

The dramatic story of how Luther nailed his challenging ninety-five theses, or propositions for debate, on the church door at Wittenberg, how all Europe was stirred and took sides in the controversy, how Luther was called before church and civil authorities and excommunicated and his books burned, how he escaped by hiding in a friend's house at Wartburg where he wrote pamphlets and translated the Bible into German, and finally how he established the church which bears his name—all this is in the history books.

The key to understanding Lutheran faith and practice is to remember that it is halfway between Roman Catholicism and the more liberal types of Protestantism, such as the Congregationalists, Baptists and Methodists, in architecture, liturgy, form of services, and articles of faith.

A neutral observer would think, most likely, that as far as appearance goes, Lutheran churches, outside and in, are more Catholic than Protestant. As with Catholic churches, there is always a cross on top of a Lutheran Church, but not often on other Protestant churches.

The interior of a Lutheran church building, although very simple in appearance in comparison with a Roman Catholic church, is full of meaning to its communicants. There is apparently nothing but chancel and nave, or auditorium, once the narthex or entrance anteroom is passed. But to the Lutheran the nave means ship, the ark which Noah was commanded by God to build so that he would be safe when the flood came. Thus the Christian finds refuge in the church of Christ from the floods of sin and death.

In the nave are the benches or pews (sometimes with kneelers) arranged on both sides of the center aisle. It is very important to Lutherans that this aisle be left open, for it leads to the altar, which is the symbol of the Presence of God, and nothing should be permitted to stand between the people and the altar. This open center aisle, to Lutherans, teaches the "universal priesthood of all believers." Lutherans say:

"This is one of the great truths that Martin Luther rediscovered in the Bible: that each person may come to God by himself. He does not need a priest or a saint to intercede for him, that is, to speak to God for him. Jesus' death on the cross reconciled us to God and made any other go-between unnecessary."

Here Lutherans part company very definitely from the Roman Catholics and agree with other Protestants, especially Baptists, who emphasize the priesthood of believers even more than do the Lutherans.

The chancel, or front part of the church, is toward the east whenever possible in the Lutheran arrangement and for two reasons, just as in the early church. First because the sun rises in the east and early Christians called Jesus the Sun of Righteousness, and second because they expected that at the second coming Jesus would come from that direction.

The Lutheran baptismal font is not in the chancel, but in the nave, as in the early church. Infants are baptized as well as adults, by the pastor making the sign of the cross on the forehead and the breast and by applying water three times upon the head, naming each Person of the Holy Trinity. Any lay Lutheran can perform a baptism in an emergency.

The chancel is usually three steps higher than the nave, and contains the lectern, the pulpit, the altar, often a kneeling rail and sometimes a choir.

To Lutherans the pulpit is very important because from it the Word of God is preached, and the Word of God, the Bible, is, according to Luther's teaching, the only rule and source of faith. For he held that the Scriptures are the sole authority for the Christian, and rejected not only the special priesthood, but also the whole sacramental system of salvation as held by Roman Catholics. To be sure, the Lutheran Church exalts the value of the sacraments, but Luther held that the only value of any sacrament is as a witness to the divine promise in the Bible.

Although important, the pulpit is not placed in the center of the chancel, which is reserved for the most important of all objects, the altar, which symbolizes the Presence of God. And yet, even here, the Lutheran emphasis on the Bible is apparent, for it said:

"At the altar we receive the Word of God, through the reading of the Gospel and the Epistle, and through the Holy Communion."

Standing on the mensa, or top of the altar, or on a retable or gradin, two kinds of elevated shelves, is the cross, "to remind us again of the priceless gift of salvation." When a crucifix, with the figure of Jesus on it, is used, it symbolizes the death of Christ, whereas the plain or "empty" cross signifies the resurrection. On the mensa also is a missal stand, on which the service book rests, and, on Holy Communion days, the sacramental vessels for the bread and wine. The bread is in a paten or plate or a cuplike dish called a ciborium, while the wine is served from a large cup or chalice or, more recently, from trays of more sanitary individual cups. Thus, standing symbolically on the mensa or altartop, is the Word in both missal and Sacraments, representing the two means through which Christ comes to the Lutheran worshiper, when he participates in the service of worship.

There is no sepulchre of relics cut into the mensa, without which in the Roman Catholic Church no Mass can be celebrated. This is one of the several practices which Luther omitted.

Lutheran churches may have a large candle on either side of the altar, or a single candle only, or a group of candles, all typifying the Living Light of the World.

Usually too, there are flowers in a vase on the retable or gradin to symbolize new life. Lutherans believe that "as the seed dies in the ground and grows into a green living plant, so we, too, through death, shall come to a new eternal life with Jesus Christ."

It is the custom in some Lutheran churches, after the money collection is taken, for the offering plates to be placed on the altar "to symbolize the dedication of our gifts, indeed, of our lives to God."

Lutherans have a Church Year, or Calendar, much resembling both the Roman Catholic and the Anglican or Episcopal churches, except that the Sunday nearest October 31 is celebrated as Reformation Day. Considerable emphasis is laid on liturgical colors. For instance Christmas vestments are white; on Ash Wednesday they are violet; on Reformation Day, red. Pastors, when officiating, wear special robes or gowns, as do Roman Catholics, Anglicans, but very few other Protestants, although the practice is becoming the vogue in city churches. Outside the church, some Lutheran pastors wear clerical collars; many do not.

Those who attend a church service of a Sunday morning will note resemblance to the Roman Catholic Mass in a few respects; but in certain others, perhaps more, it is like a regular service in the more formal of the other Protestant churches.

Lutherans usually bow their heads in silent prayer as they take their places in the church pew while the organ prelude is being played. During the singing of the first hymn, the minister goes to the altar and kneels in prayer, but at its conclusion turns to the congregation and says (or sings, or the choir sings)

Holy, Holy, Holy is the Lord of Hosts!
The whole earth is full of His glory.

Then the minister calls the people to confession just before he turns and faces the altar and leads the people as all in unison recite the rather lengthy Confession of Sins, after which they sing the Kyrie Eleison (Lord, have mercy) and the minister replies with Gloria in Excelsis (Glory be to God on high).

The congregation then sings a hymn. The minister says "The Lord be with you," and after the response "And with thy spirit" he reads the Collect (Prayer) for the Day and the people respond with the Amen. The Epistle for the Day is then read from the lectern or from the epistle (south) side of the altar and, after either an ancient Gradual sung by the choir or a Gradual Hymn by the congregation, the Gospel for the Day is read on the gospel side or from the pulpit, followed by the recitation by all of either the Apostles' Creed or the lengthier Nicene Creed as a Confession of Faith.

An anthem and then a hymn precede the sermon, a very important part of the Lutheran service, for this is not a mere talk by a trained speaker but a message by an ambassador through whom God speaks His Living Word.

After the sermon there come in quick succession a short prayer by the minister, a brief benediction, various announcements, then the weekly offering and the Offering Prayer as the plates are placed on the altar. Another hymn follows and a Salutation; then, with the minister facing the altar, the congregation unites with him in reciting the long

126

Great or General Prayer, followed by The Lord's Prayer, the Benedicamus and the Response. The service ends with the minister giving the Aaronic Benediction to which the people reply with the Three-fold Amen.

In place of the Roman Catholic Mass, the Lutherans celebrate Holy Communion or The Lord's Supper. The frequency of its observance varies in branches of the denomination, but a common practice is to observe it once a month and seven other special times of the church year. The opening liturgy for the communion service is much like the morning service just described, but it may be shortened. The Holy Communion itself is simple, consisting mainly of hymns, prayers and the reading of the passages of scripture referring to the institution of the Lord's Supper by Jesus Christ, then the distribution of the bread and wine after they are consecrated. The Sanctus, the Pax, and the Agnus Dei are sung just before and during the administration of the Blessed Sacrament (consecrated bread and wine).

The Lutheran Communion differs from the Roman Catholic Mass in that *both* bread and wine are given the communicant, as in all Protestant churches, whereas the Catholic communicant is given only the wafer or bread, the priest having partaken of the wine.

As to the relation of the bread and wine to the body and blood of Christ, there is great difference of doctrinal opinion among Christians, the Lutherans disagreeing with both Roman Catholics and the rest of the Protestants. The great question is "What do you believe you receive in the Lord's Supper?"

Roman Catholics believe that the substance of bread and wine is changed into the body and blood of Christ, so that only the outward appearance of bread and wine remains. This is called "transubstantiation."

Practically all Protestants except the Lutherans hold that when Jesus Christ said at the Last Supper, "This is my body" and "This is my blood," he meant that the bread and wine represented his body and blood. So they consider the ordinance of the Lord's Supper symbolical and celebrate it as a memorial.

Lutherans, like the Roman Catholics, believe in the "real presence" of the body and blood of Christ in the bread and wine, but teach that the communicant receives the true body and blood of Christ "in, along with and under the bread and wine."

This theory is sometimes called "consubstantiation" by non-Lutherans, but Lutherans object to that word which they claim means the uniting of the bread and wine with the body and blood of Christ into a third substance differing from both. This the Lutherans do not believe, maintain-

127

ing the doctrine of the "real presence" as a *fact*, but not presuming to explain the *method* by which Christ is present.

These distinctions may seem hair-splitting to non-Christians or even to Christians who are not theologians, but they are very important for every well-informed person to know about, for they are the doctrinal points which are keeping Christianity divided.

Lutherans have baptisms and confirmations much resembling the Roman Catholic ceremonies, but their confessions are public and a part of the service of worship; although the layman may consult his pastor privately for advice in personal matters. Lutherans use the Catechism, especially Luther's Smaller Catechism of 1529. So do Roman Catholics use catechisms, but this is one thing they took over from him, not he from them.

The beliefs of Martin Luther, accepted by the Lutheran Church, may be summarized as follows:

The sole authority of the Scriptures. This means rejection of the special priesthood and the elaborate sacramental system of the Roman Catholic Church.

The old creeds and all their main teachings have been retained.

Baptism, including infant baptism and baptismal regeneration, has been retained.

The Lord's Supper, including the doctrine of the Real Presence, has been retained.

Belief in both heaven and hell has been kept, but the doctrine of purgatory is rejected.

Justification by faith alone is central. Good works do not save a man, but are a necessary fruit of faith.

Luther insisted that only those matters of Roman Catholic faith and practice which were contrary to or not included among Bible teachings should be changed or eliminated. His most notable exclusions are compulsory confession, compulsory celibacy of the clergy, monastic vows, and the teaching that the Mass is a sacrifice.

One thing Luther added to the services of the church was the singing of the people. For, in the churches he established, the people no longer sat through a service and listened to Gregorian chants sung by a trained choir while they themselves sat mute for the most part. Luther's hymnbook, of hymns which he and his friends composed, introduced congregational singing into the churches, and the faith of Luther spread so rapidly because it was not only preached, but sung itself into the hearts of the people. His great hymn "A Mighty Fortress Is Our God" has been called "The Battle Hymn of Protestantism." To this day a stranger coming into a Lutheran church from almost any other Christian communion is at first startled and then thrilled and invigorated by the hearty congregational singing, so much a part of the spirit of this great denomination.

Not only through music did the new faith reach the people. There were three great painters who became friends of Martin Luther and contributed their talent to spread the Reformation. Lucas Cranach illustrated Bible stories and painted pictures of Luther, his wife, and Melanchthon, Luther's great friend. Albrecht Dürer made drawings and woodcuts; his "Praying Hands" are well known everywhere. And Hans Holbein illustrated Lutheran pamphlets and caricatured current evils.

The new faith spread rapidly not only in all Germany but also throughout Denmark, Norway, Iceland, Sweden, Finland, Lapland, and the Baltic Provinces. In all these lands it became the state or official religion. It even spread to parts of France. It also came to America.

French Huguenot Lutherans set up a colony in Florida as early as 1564, but the Spanish there beheaded them and put a sign on their graves: "We slew them not as Frenchmen, but as Lutherans."

In 1619, one year before the *Mayflower* brought the Pilgrims to Plymouth, the first Protestant Christmas service in America was held on the bleak shores of Hudson Bay by Danish Lutheran sailors who presented their pastor, Rasmus Jensen, with fine white foxskins to line his gown.

There were Lutherans among the Dutch who settled New Amsterdam, but the followers of John Calvin among the Dutch were stronger and fined the Lutherans whenever they held services. When the English conquered New Amsterdam and renamed it New York, they instituted religious liberty, and the Lutherans built a church near Bowling Green. The first library in New York, brought from Europe by Jonas Bronck, the Dane for whom Bronx Borough and Park are named, contained both Luther's German Bible and his Catechism.

In 1638 and 1639, boatloads of Swedish Lutherans came to this country with their pastor, Reorus Torkillus, and settled in what is now Delaware and southern Pennsylvania. Peter Minuit, the German who bought Manhattan Island for the Dutch from the Indians for twenty-four dollars' worth of beads and ribbons, bought the west bank of the Delaware for the Lutheran Swedes from the Indians for a brass kettle and a few trinkets.

German Lutherans seeking religious freedom came to Pennsylvania with Penn's Quakers, and the first German Lutheran service in America was conducted by Rev. Heinrich Koester in 1694 in Germantown, near the new Quaker town of Philadelphia, then only a decade old.

Successive waves of Lutheran immigrants from Germany and the Scandinavian and Baltic countries settled in all parts of the United States and have always shown themselves good substantial citizens. Because of their native reticence they have not until lately advertised their religion very much, with the result that their faith is the one about which other Christians here know the least.

Particularly, Americans should become aware that the Lutherans have played a large part in our national history. For three interesting but little-known instances among many:

It was a Lutheran boy who called a Lutheran sexton to ring the Liberty Bell, July 4, 1776, to proclaim the signing of the Declaration of Independence.

The first president of the Continental Congress was the Lutheran, John Hanson, who had the National Seal designed, organized the first Cabinet, and issued the first national Thanksgiving Proclamation.

The first Speaker of the House of Representatives, who with John Adams, signed the Bill of Rights, was a Lutheran pastor, Frederick Augustus Muhlenberg.

This Faith of the Reformation, founded by Martin Luther, is interwoven in all our history, and flourishes here today partly at least because of its emphasis on freedom and liberty.

13

THE PRESBYTERIANS

The Church of the Elders

MEMBERS OF THIS denomination are sometimes referred to as "Scotch Presbyterians," because the first ones arriving in America in any great numbers were refugees from Scotland fleeing the terrible persecutions—"the killing times"—during the reign of Britain's Charles II. From 1660 to 1668 the Scotch and Scotch-Irish came by shiploads and settled in Pennsylvania and New Jersey.

But Presbyterians from several other countries were already here, worshiping in churches which were not called Presbyterian, yet had practically the same beliefs. For instance, there were many of them among the English Puritans who settled Massachusetts and Connecticut. Cotton Mather, the eminent Boston divine, estimated that of the 21,000 Puritans emigrating from England to New England between 1620 and 1640, over four thousand held Presbyterian views.

The majority of the Puritans were known as Congregationalists because the individual congregation or church governed itself. The Presbyterians had a slightly different idea of church government, but they heartily agreed with the

Congregationalists in repudiating the system of the established Episcopal Church in England in which the bishops held the authority.

Both Congregational and Presbyterian Puritans agreed in theology also, following the teachings of John Calvin of Geneva. So they all worshiped together in the white New England meeting-houses, feeling there was no need of separate Presbyterian churches.

France, the birthplace of Calvin, had its quota of refugee Presbyterians in America, too. After their many persecutions, of which the Massacre of St. Bartholomew had been only the beginning, companies of them emigrated to South Carolina, Virginia, Florida, and the vicinity of New York City, settling mostly in Staten Island and a place they named New Rochelle in 1688, after the French Protestant city La Rochelle from which they had come. These French Presbyterians were often called Huguenots, said to be a slight misspelling of the nickname Hugonots given them in France because some of them had held conventicles or camp meetings near the King Hugo gate of the city of Tours. Another explanation more generally accepted derives the name from Bezanson Hugues, a Genevan reformer.

Besides the Scottish, English and French Presbyterians there came to this country from Switzerland, Germany, and Holland many Calvinists who established here the churches known as Swiss, German, and Dutch Reformed, all governed in the Presbyterian way.

What manner of man could this John Calvin have been, whose religion could stir the heart so deeply and convince the mind so logically that men and women of six European nations left their homeland at great personal sacrifice, and came in a great mass migration to America that they might worship God and run their churches according to the teachings of this powerful and persuasive new prophet of Protestantism!

Calvin was undoubtedly one of the greatest intellects the world has ever known. By the time he was twenty-two he had mastered most of the knowledge of his day in theology, law, and literature. At the age of twenty-six he had written his great work *The Institutes of the Christian Religion,* one of the most important and influential books of the last one thousand years.

His greatness cannot be credited to ancestry or family, for he came of no line of geniuses. His mother was an innkeeper's daughter and his father a combination of lawyer, business manager, and secretary to the Lord Bishop of the cathedral of Noyon.

But the boy did have educational advantages due to his father's position. Shortly before he was twelve, he was tonsured (given the clerical haircut symbolizing Christ's crown of thorns) and made a chaplain of the cathedral. This position paid a salary but required no work; it was a form of subsidy which enabled him to go to college in Paris and study for the Catholic priesthood. At eighteen he became a curate and was already attracting attention as a debater.

Here the father Gérard Cauvin or Calvin, stepped in and advised his son to change from the field of theology to that of law. Before John was nineteen, he was studying in Orleans under one of the best legal minds of France, de l'Étoile. The quick transfer was probably not due entirely to filial obedience, for there is evidence that the young man was already becoming dissatisfied with the religious faith of his father. Indeed, he was looking with interest upon the faith of his cousin, the scholar Olivetan, a disciple of Lefèvre, a greater scholar who was even then revising the classical French version of the Latin Bible and laying the groundwork of scholarship for the French Reformation. After a year and a half of intensive study of law in Orleans, young Calvin continued it with other teachers in Bourges for the same length of time, accomplishing in those three years the incredible feat of acquiring a thorough acquaintance with the theory and practice of the legal profession.

This drilling in basic law and logical argumentation by the time he was twenty-one years of age accounted for the clearness and strength of his thinking later.

Suddenly, with the death of his father in May, 1531, young Calvin's life changed again. He had studied first theology and then law at his father's wish. Now, free to make his own choice, he decided to become a man of letters, and returned to Paris to profit by the teachings of the great humanists there. In less than a year he published a Latin commentary on Seneca's book *De Clementia*—Concerning Mercy.

More important, however, for his own life and for the history of the Christian Church, he began the study of Hebrew and continued the study of Greek which he had begun in Bourges. These languages he mastered with his customary ease, and found himself face to face with the scriptures in their original tongues. Doubtless he read also the writings of Erasmus and Luther. The result was that, somewhat to his own surprise, he began defending the new theology then rising in Paris.

The die was cast for him on All Saints' Day, 1533, exactly sixteen years after Luther had nailed his theses on the church door at Wittenberg. But although Luther had been thirty-four, Calvin was only twenty-four when he uttered his challenge. It came about in a rather unusual way, and the details will probably never be known.

Calvin's boyhood friend of undergraduate days in the University of Paris, Nicholas Cop, had risen in prominence until he had just been elected, in spite of his youth, to the position of Rector of the University of Paris. According to custom he had therefore to deliver an oration on All Saints' Day. Some authorities say that the new rector prevailed upon his old friend Calvin to write the oration for him; others assert that Calvin delivered it. All agree, however, that Calvin was to some degree responsible for it.

At any rate, the bold championship of the new theology, the demand for church reform, the challenge to return to the evangelical gospel of the New Testament, all later became familiar to Calvin's listeners. But on All Saints' Day 1533, in the Church of the Mathurins, Paris, those sentiments produced a sensation, and the authorities summoned Cop to appear before the *parlement* of Paris. They tried to seize Calvin also, but got neither, for the discreet young rector was in Basle by then, and the other young scholar was back home in Noyon.

For three years Calvin traveled rapidly about, seldom staying long in one town, unwelcome in most places, and always pursued by the authorities. He gave up his chaplaincy and a rectorship, thinking it only fair to relinquish any income from the church whose tenets he could no longer believe. We know that he was imprisoned at least twice, for short terms, and that sometime in 1534, in a grotto near Poitiers, he officiated at a communion service of the Evangelical Church of France, with a piece of rock serving as the sacred table for the bread and wine.

By this act, dramatic and decisive, he all unconsciously assumed the leadership of the scattered and persecuted Protestants of France, himself the most harried heretic of all. Those who leaned to the reformed doctrines, especially those who knew the real author of Cop's brilliant oration, by common consent sought out Calvin for advice and instruction.

Now he found himself doubly pursued, by both foes and friends. He later remarked wryly concerning this time: "all my retreats were like public schools." In this austere and apparently cold young man, so severe and strict in conduct that legend says his Latin classmates had nicknamed him "The Accusative Case," there was some dynamic and magnetic quality of character which drew and held people. Renan, over three centuries later, said Calvin's success as a leader of men was due to his being "the most Christian man of his time."

During these three years of retreats, 1533-1536, he managed to find an occasional chance to write. People were asking for doctrinal guidance in the new religion. He sensed that this was no mere local or temporary need. All Europe had long been looking for a restatement of Christian theology. And he gave it to them.

For when his foes were closing in on him and his life was in danger everywhere in France, he escaped to Basle, Switzerland, in 1536, and published there the precious manuscript he had been secretly working on, *The Institutes of the Christian Religion,* destined to become the Magna Charta of Protestantism.

The book, an immediate sensation and best-seller, was translated into all European languages and passed through many editions. Even today, well over four centuries later, it is to be found in a number of versions including English, German, Dutch, Spanish, Italian, Magyar, Greek, and Arabic. It has been necessary to translate it into modern French, for few Frenchmen today can read the language of Calvin's time.

The publicity was distasteful to the retiring scholar: he hoped to have time for peaceful study in Strasbourg, but it was not to be. That same year, 1536, as he detoured through Geneva to avoid a war-zone, he was commandeered by Guillaume Farel, and in the city where he had planned to spend but the night, he spent practically the rest of his life.

Farel first asked, then begged, then adjured Calvin to remain in the city and help the Protestants there, actually threatening him with a curse if he did not. Calvin later referred to it as a "formidable obtestation." Today is would probably be called a powerful sales talk.

It seems that the people of Geneva had revolted against their bishop, and, politically, against the Duke of Savoy. Farel, a disciple of the pioneer French reformer Lefèvre, had persuaded the Genevans to accept the Reformation, but the people really did not know what they believed. They only knew what they did not believe, and the city was full of false prophets and fanatical preachers offering peculiar remedies for sin.

In August 1536 Calvin began lecturing on Paul's Epistles in St. Pierre's church, and people flocked to hear him. His choice of subject was doubtless due to the fact that the great crucial doctrinal point on which the Protestants in Germany, France and Switzerland differed from Catholic teaching was Paul's emphasis on "justification by faith alone." By Catholic doctrine, a man's works as well as his faith counted for his salvation. But the average layman of the time had no idea what Paul taught. Even if he could read, a very rare accomplishment outside the ranks of the clergy, he probably did not have a Bible. And if he could read and had a Bible, he would have difficulty in understanding Paul's Epistles until they were explained. That is why the reformers laid such emphasis on translation of the Scriptures and the education of the common peole.

So Calvin expounded Paul's letters for a year, without pay, and was so helpful thereby that with the consent of the people, the magistrates elected him preacher. That is all he and Farel were waiting for. They had drawn up a statement of Christian belief in twenty-one articles, and called in the citizens of Geneva, in groups of ten, to swear to it as citizens under oath. This was Calvin's rather autocratic scheme to make Geneva Christian. He went on to establish schools, enforce attendance, and require the new Protestant catechism as part of the course. At the same time he tried to keep the new church free from state control. But it was when he sought to become dictator of public morals, that the growing opposition to his reform came to a head. He refused to let persons of whose method of living he disapproved come to the communion table. Thereupon the people of Geneva through their magistrates banished Calvin and his associates from the city, shortly after Easter in 1538.

The setback proved an actual blessing to John Calvin. It wakened him to reality. He had known books, theories, doctrines, and theology, but he had not known people. That Easter morning in 1538 when he had refused the communion bread to all the people of Geneva because he had seen them celebrating their annual spring festival in their customary hilarious fashion the day before, he deserved the prompt banishment he got.

During his three years' exile he learned about people. For one thing, he got married to a charming young widow who contributed much to his humanization. Idelette de Bure deserves more credit than she has ever received, for she taught John Calvin more than his professors. In that three years he also attended conferences where he met other reformers, like Melanchthon, Luther's lieutenant, who opened Calvin's eyes to certain practical aspects of the reforming business. Before his return to Geneva, he took time to re-examine his ideas, and that process resulted in a revision and enlargement of his *Institutes*, as well as two new works, a *Commentary on the Epistle of Paul to the Romans* and a *Tract on the Lord's Supper*.

While Calvin was away, Geneva had its troubles. A cardinal tried to restore Catholicism, but a single letter from Calvin stopped him, though Calvin was still in exile. For the letter was a simply stated summary of what the Reformation was all about, and it convinced the people of Geneva that Calvin's side was the right one. They begged him to come back to them.

On September 13, 1541, he returned in triumph, and took advantage of their welcoming enthusiasm to set up the form of church government which he had thought out during his exile, the very system of rule by presbyters which gave the name to Presbyterianism itself.

Calvin had come to realize that his new type of church needed more than a new theology; it must have a new polity (form of government) as well. When he began his work in Geneva, he had unconsciously assumed the role of dictator, but he had been forcibly reminded that the people of the new religion had no more use for a Protestant pope than for the older Catholic kind. The laymen of the churches of the Reformation wanted a say in the government of their own churches, locally and nationally.

That voice must include the privilege of choosing their own spiritual leaders. Instead of letting the bishop choose the local priest or minister and his assistant deacons, these new laymen wished to "hire and fire" their ministers and themselves elect the deacons in the local church. And although Calvin had himself been "fired" by these same citizens of Geneva and had not particularly relished the experience, he realized that the spirit of the new religion, with its emphasis on the freedom of the Christian man, demanded some measure, at least, of lay participation in all church government.

The polity which Calvin devised and established in Geneva a little over four hundred years ago was such a wise one that it is used today, with few changes, in the many thousands of Presbyterian churches throughout the world. But Calvin's modern followers would prefer to say that he "rediscovered" Presbyterianism, believing that the first Christian churches were thus governed. They point out that in the early Christian church presbyters are many times more often referred to as church officers than are bishops. They claim that at first a bishop was the same as an elder or presbyter, and that the later rise of bishops to higher authority, first in the individual church, then in groups of churches, then in large dioceses and archdioceses until the bishop in Rome (the pope) was over all the clergy, is not justifiable by Scripture and leads to religious tyranny.

On this point Episcopalians and both Greek and Roman Catholics disagree with the Presbyterians and quote other scripture on their side, holding that bishops are just as scripturally justified as presbyters.

The best way to understand the Presbyterian system is to think of it as practically the same as the government of the United States—a republic in which representatives are elected by the people to rule for them.. Such representatives are naturally selected from the older and more experienced members of the group, and since the Greek word for elder is *presbuteros*, the reason for the name of the church is obvious.

In the individual church the group of elders is known as

the *session*. In an average size church there are likely to be five elders; four ruling elders who are laymen and one teaching elder, the minister. The ruling elders assist in many ways in running the church—caring for the church property, arranging for meetings, admitting new members, keeping the membership roll up to date, supervising the details of worship, including the music, overseeing the young people and the church school—in fact, doing anything they can to promote the spiritual and temporal affairs of the church. On Sundays the ruling elders are on hand to welcome strangers, act as ushers, take the collection, and, on Communion Sundays, prepare and distribute the bread and wine. They also help in the pastoral work of visitation of the sick and care of the poor in the parish.

Now, other Protestant churches have laymen who function in many of these capacities. The ones who attend to the spiritual affairs are usually called deacons; the ones in charge of money and property matters are often termed Trustees, or members of the Board of Directors or of the Prudential Committee. But the Presbyterians consider their ruling elders as equal in rank to their minister or teaching elder. Both kinds of elders are elected by the people of the church, and both kinds are solemnly ordained. The result is that the Presbyterian ruling elders usually take their position more seriously than is sometimes the case with deacons and trusteees in other churches. They usually hold office for life, but since that frequently means that the affairs of the church are left in charge of very old men out of touch with the thought-world of the young people of the church whom they are supposed to guide and supervise, a number of Presbyterian churches today have three-year terms for their ruling elders, and no re-election until after one year.

Although the word presbyter means an older man, the Presbyterians are not a church of old people only. Far from it. In any Presbyterian church today there are plenty of lively young people, and the official "elders" themselves are by no means all old men.

The most important unit of government in the Calvinistic system is the *presbytery,* which unites the "particular" (individual) churches of a district, and supervises and controls them. It consists of all the ministers in the district and one ruling elder for each settled minister. One unusual feature is that the teaching elder or minister is not a member of any church, but is a member of presbytery; he is responsible only to, and can be removed only by, his presbytery. The presbytery examines, licenses, and ordains candidates for the ministry, installs them in churches, and permits, or does not permit them to change churches.

Whereas the local Baptist and other churches having a

congregational polity "hire and fire" their ministers, the Presbyterian churches can hire but not fire theirs.

Above the presbytery is the *synod,* which must include at least three presbyteries and usually covers the churches of a state or perhaps two. There are forty synods in America. They meet once a year, mostly to hear and adjust complaints and appeals from the presbyteries.

The *General Assembly* is the national governing body, the highest executive, legislative and judicial authority. It meets for a week once a year, each time in a different city. Each presbytery is represented by at least two commissioners, and there are usually a thousand commissioners present. This great annual meeting is one of the features of American religious life. Somehow these people can make even "annual reports" thrillingly interesting, reports from "the four boards"—Christian Education, Pensions, National Missions, and especially Foreign Missions with stories of devoted workers in thirty foreign countries, including chronicles of Christian heroism coming from Korean Presbyterian mission churches.

The first Presbyterian General Assembly held in the United States was convened in Philadelphia in May 1789 at the very hour that the first United States Congress, under the new Constitution, was held in New York, and one of the acts of the Assembly was to appoint a committee to draft an address to President George Washington.

This was no mere coincidence. If a Presbyterian elder were told that his church government with its sessions, presbyteries, synods, and General Assembly seems to have been patterned after the form of the American government of towns, counties, states, and the nation, he would smile knowingly, and might reply that this suggestion placed the cart before the horse.

Between 1705 and 1775 a good half-million "Scotch Presbyterians" migrated to this country and joined their predecessors who had settled in the middle colonies after the migration of 1660-1688. They felt very resentful toward England because of the persecutions and hardships they had suffered there, and so it was natural that they should be in the forefront of the leaders of the Revolution.

John Witherspoon, who had come from Scotland only eight years before, but was already the leading Presbyterian teaching elder in America, was the only clergyman in the Continental Congress of 1776 and so the only minister to sign the Declaration of Independence. He said then:

"That noble instrument upon your table, which ensures immortality to its author, should be subscribed this very morning by every pen in this house. . . . To hesitate is to consent to our own slavery."

So ardent and devoted to the patriot side were the Presbyterians, that in England the Revolution was referred to as "The Presbyterian Rebellion," while in Parliament Horace Walpole said whimsically that Cousin America had run off with a Presbyterian parson. And the Tory rector of Trinity Church in New York lamented in 1776:

"I do not know one Presbyterian minister, nor have I been able, after strict inquiry, to hear of any, who did not by preaching and every effort in their power promote all the measures of the Continental Congress, however extravagant."

One Presbyterian minister, James Caldwell, pastor at Elizabethtown and chaplain of a New Jersey regiment, was the spiritual ancestor of the more recent chaplain of "Praise the Lord and pass the ammunition" fame, for at one critical skirmish when his fellow-patriots were running out of wadding for their muskets, Caldwell ran into the church, came out with an armful of Watts' Psalm-Hymn Books, and yelled:

"Now, boys, give 'em Watts!"

A little later the brave parson and his wife were both killed by the British and his church edifice burned, but his spirit lived on in both his republican church and his republican nation.

Scotch Presbyterianism, indeed all Presbyterianism, owes much to another man besides Calvin, the intrepid John Knox, who preached in Scotland what he had heard Calvin teach in Geneva, and who was responsible more than any other man for the final success of the Reformation in Scotland. In his boldness and his eloquent and compelling sermons, Knox was much like Luther. Both men were very vigorous and excitable. Luther is said to have thrown his inkstand, contents and all, at some apparition he took to be the devil. And Knox was so violent that a fellow Scot who heard him preach said:

"He was lyke to ding the pulpit in blads and flie out of it."

His verbal battles with Mary Queen of Scots, with the domination of Scotland's religion for the prize, rank among the great theological debates of the world. Her power, wit, and beauty were pitted against his eloquence and logic, and he won. In his colorful career he had been, in turn, a priest, a Protestant preacher, a galley slave in the French navy, and a royal chaplain to the king of England. He refused a bishopric, helped Calvin translate the Geneva edition of the Bible, and finally led the Scottish Reformation.

Knox's proposed system of schools for Scotland was similar to Calvin's comprehensive scheme of education. In the twenty-three years between his return to Geneva in 1541 and his death in 1564, Calvin was a sort of combination of City Father and City Manager, for he practically controlled the life of the city, morally, spiritually, politically, and educationally. He established not only the University of Geneva, but also an

139

academy and the first free public schools of Europe. His training of young clergymen who went out to many countries made possible the rapid spread of Presbyterian and other Calvinistic churches.

That emphasis on the proper education of the clergy is still a characteristic of Presbyterian churches today. There is also, in line with the tradition of Calvin and Knox, a strong emphasis on education for the laity. Of the American Presbyterian young church members of college age, 85% are in some college or university.

Calvin and Knox, especially the latter who taught that rebellion against tyranny is a duty of Christians, had much to do with establishing the spirit of republican democracy which made possible our American free institutions, both political and educational. But it is now apparent that those institutions have, in turn, had a beneficial humanizing effect on the stern teachings of Presbyterian doctrine. No Calvinist today would attempt to defend the 1553 buring of Servetus the Unitarian in Geneva.

Historically, the famous "Five Points of Calvinism" have been (1) Election or Predestination, (2) Limited Atonement, (3) Total Depravity, (4) Irresistibility of Grace, and (5) the Perseverance of the Saints. It is impossible to explain fully here these theological doctrines; it took Calvin himself a whole book to do so, and hundreds of books have since been written to explain his book. But since all five points are based on the idea of the absolute sovereignty (overruling power) of God, it is possible to get a general idea, which can be roughly stated as follows:

Men are born in sin, totally depraved. Christ died to save men from that sin, but his atonement is limited because God predestined some men, the elect, to be saved unto everlasting bliss, and foreordained others to be damned unto everlasting punishment. The elect cannot resist this saving grace of God and will persevere in that state of grace until they reach the state of glory.

This stern Calvinism, with its emphasis on the power and arbitrary rule of God, may once have nerved the Puritans and Huguenots to fight and die for their religion, but modern men are inclined to reject such an arbitrary and apparently capricious God. If the non-elect cannot be saved, no matter how hard they try to do right, and if even infants, when non-elect, are precondemned by God to eternal damnation in hell, that doctrine is unacceptable to the majority of American Presbyterians themselves.

Thus, in 1903, the Westminister Confession of Faith was amended by a Declaratory Statement by the northern "Presbyterian Church in the United States of America," the largest Presbyterian body (2,526,172 members), to read:

140

"—the doctrine of God's eternal decree (predestination) is held in harmony with the doctrine of his love to all mankind, his gift of his Son to be the propitiation for the sins of the whole world, and his readiness to bestow his saving grace on all who seek it . . . a salvation sufficient for all, adapted to all, and freely offered in the gospel to all; that his decree hinders no man from accepting that offer; and that no man is condemned except on the ground of his sin." And a second section of the Declaratory Statement includes the sentence: "We believe that all dying in infancy are included in the election of grace, and are regenerated and saved by Christ through the Spirit. . . ."

So the old idea that God did the electing or choosing has been changed, in the case of adults, to the new interpretation that man himself can choose whether or not to accept salvation, and the new doctrine has been somewhat humorously put: "The elect are the whosoever-wills; the non-elect, the whosoever won'ts."

The revised catechism of the northern Presbyterian Church in the United States of America includes various statements concerning religious matters that would have displeased sixteenth century Presbyterians but are much more acceptable today than the doctrines they displace. The Bible is "where we learn how God wants us to live." As for prayer, "There is no such thing as unanswered prayer. God may answer a prayer with 'Yes,' 'No,' or 'Wait'—but always He answers." Instead of the old-time thought that men's bodies are carnal and lustful and to be "kept down," there is now the positive teaching that "We should value our bodies . . . to be kept pure and in health." The "resurrection of the body" no longer means just that, but the emergence of a "spiritual body" which will "be perfectly suited to our celestial existence." Heaven is simply the place Christ has gone to prepare for the saved, and as for hell, "The punishment of the wicked is eternal separation from the favor and fellowship of God and His people. . . . Left alone, man is indeed in hell."

The liberal amendment of the Westminster Confession and the revision of the catechism by the northern division of Presbyterianism was followed in 1925 by a similar liberalized confessional statement of the third-largest body, the "United Presbyterian Church of North America" (222,200 members), clearly denying infant damnation and welcoming to the sacraments all professing Christians who practice what they profess.

The southern Presbyterian synods which split off in Civil War days or shortly thereafter are now known as the "Presbyterian Church in the United States," and number 744,901 members. This second-largest division has long since resolved the original wartime differences with other American Pres-

141

byterians, but, along with several smaller branches of the faith, still adheres in general to the more conservative type of Calvinism.

A friendly relationship prevails among all nine divisions of Presbyterians in America and between them and other Reformed churches here and abroad of Calvinistic origin and governed by a presbyterian polity. Since 1876 these have all been organized into a Pan-Presbyterian Alliance, meeting every four years. This is likely to promote the eventual federal union of all these bodies.

Modern Presbyterian church edifices and the meetings held in them do not show any notable differences from other Protestant denominations such as Baptists, Congregationalists, or Methodists. There is no required order or ritual or liturgy. But any local congregation is free to adopt a ritual or liturgy if the majority so desire. There is a denominational Directory of Worship, but the variety of forms permissible is very wide. As long as the service is orderly and dignified and pleases the people of the congregation, no one else can officially object.

There are only two sacraments, baptism and the Lord's Supper, and there is a wide range of practice even in these. The usual baptism is by sprinkling, but pouring or immersion may be used if the candidate or the church desires. Infant baptism is practiced as an expression of the covenant relation of parents to God in behalf of their children.

As for the Lord's Supper, or Communion, the particular church determines how often and under what circumstances it shall be observed. Whereas the Roman Catholic Church and the Lutheran faith believe that the bread and wine are transubstantiated into the very body and blood of Christ and that both Christ's body and the bread are partaken; Congregationalists and Baptists hold that the supper is simply symbolical; and Calvin taught that Christ is spiritually present in the bread and wine—modern Presbyterians either follow Calvin's theory and find the ordinance a distinctive channel of grace or, like the Congregationalists, recognize its symbological character.

In other words, the Presbyterian Church today, with its three and a half million members in the United States, allows more choice of beliefs and practices than most other Protestants. While the creed is the revised Westminster Confession, it is not required that one should accept even that in order to join the church. "Anyone who can be a Christian can be a full member of the Presbyterian church." In permitting such a wide range of faith and practice Presbyterians believe they are faithfully reproducing the early Christian church of the apostles and presbyters.

THE EVANGELICAL AND REFORMED CHURCH

This church of modified Presbyterian form of government and similarly or more modified Calvinistic doctrine, now numbering 751,956 members, belongs therefore in the Presbyterian orbit. It requires no expanded description to a reader who has read the preceding pages, but deserves his attention because of the way it illustrates how several smaller denominational groups can come together and then attract still others into the union.

Six missionaries, ministers of Lutheran and Reformed churches, were sent to this country by the Evangelical United Church of Prussia, and formed in 1840, near St. Louis, the Evangelical Union of the West, which grew rapidly among German-speaking folk into the German Evangelical Synod of North America. That synod amalgamated with four others whose members had the same beliefs, and the new combination used the same name without the word, German. By June 26, 1934, when it united with the Reformed Church in the United States it had 281,598 members to join with the 348,189 of the latter, making 629,787.

The Reformed Church of the merger came from the followers of the great reformers, Zwingli, Calvin, and Melanchthon, of Switzerland, when the great German wave of immigration invaded Pennsylvania and spread to Ohio and North Carolina. They gradually permitted the formation of English-speaking churches, and soon developed missionary enterprises in the United States and abroad. The united church has continued and expanded the missions, both home and foreign, and supports or sponsors eight colleges and three theological seminaries. In 1949, the Evangelical and Reformed Church was ready to unite with the Congregational Christian Churches, but the merger was temporarily blocked in 1950 by a court decision. In late 1953, however, the New York State Court of Appeals cleared the way for renewing negotiations, and the merger is imminent. The next logical step would be for the new Evangelical-Reformed-Congregational-Christian group to merge with the Presbyterians.

14

THE EPISCOPALIANS

The Church of Beauty

WHETHER YOU LOOK AT their churches, their rituals, their religion, or their lives, you can't help noticing that the Episcopalians are lovers of beauty.

They believe that the source and meaning of all beauty are in the Lord Jesus Christ whom they worship; therefore in honor of their Lord they use every art to make their church and its services as beautiful as they can.

When you approach an Episcopal church, either a cathedral or a small village house of worship, and whether that church be in this country, in England where it is known as the Anglican Church or the Established Church, or in some distant mission station in Africa or the Orient, you will be impressed by the architecture of the building and the attractive setting and landscaping. Just to look at the church as you pass by will give you a benediction of beauty and peace.

If you enter the church—and unlike most other Protestant churches the Episcopal ones are kept open every day for anyone to rest, pray, or meditate—you will find quiet beauty there. You may be the only one in the building, but the very design of the interior and the sacred symbols and objects there displayed will silently bring you a message of the beauty of holiness and the holiness of beauty. Everything about the church, outside and in, has been dedicated to the glory of God, and has been carefully planned to indicate it by every possible means. Design and adornment, shape, position, and color—all have meaning.

As you enter the church your eye looks straight up the center aisle to the altar, the central and most important object because it is the symbol of God's presence, without which the building would not be a church. Nothing stands between you and the altar; nothing obscures it, for that center aisle symbolizes the pathway of life leading directly to God.

At one side of that aisle, near the entrance, is the baptismal font, signifying the entrance to the Christian life, just as the altar represents God, the goal of life.

If you walk up the aisle closer to the altar, you will note more symbolism. There are three levels on which the church is built—the nave or main body of the church, then an elevated platform for the choir stalls, and highest of all the sanctuary where is the altar. These levels have been interpreted by one of the Episcopal bishops as follows: the nave representing life in this world, the choir meaning paradise, and the sanctuary symbolizing heaven in the presence of God.

In the center of the altar stands the cross, representing Christ and symbolizing everything Christian. On either side of the cross, candles signify that Christ is the light of the world, just as the flowers beside the cross remind us of the resurrection.

Before you reach the altar, however, you pass several other objects on the side—the lectern, the pulpit, and the choir stalls. The lectern, or reading desk, holds the Bible. You pass it, on your right, as you approach the altar. This is to signify that the Bible is a guide book on our way to

God, a help in the Christian life, but not its end or aim. This location of the Bible is more important than it may seem to a casual observer, for in the Lutheran Church the Bible is on the altar, since Lutherans claim we know God through the Bible.

On the other side is the pulpit, for Episcopalians regard preaching as not central but intended for encouragement and instruction on the Christian way. They say they come to church to worship and not to hear sermons. In many other Protestant churches, however, the pulpit is placed in a central position because the sermon is regarded as the most important part of the service, as the prophetic preaching is supposed to be inspired by God and to lead men to God.

In the Episcopal church the choir and organ are divided, half on each side, so as to keep the altar clear. In most other Protestant churches, the choir and organ are centrally placed, directly behind the pulpit, but the Episcopalians say they do not worship the organ; they worship God. The choir sits sidewise to the congregation, as they are not there to give a concert or to entertain the audience; their purpose is to lead the people in singing praises to God.

If you look around the interior of an Episcopal church, you are likely to see in carved wood or stained glass many other symbols depicted. The most frequently used ones are the dove as a sign of the Holy Spirit which descended on Jesus at his baptism, the triangle for the Holy Trinity, the hand which symbolizes God's loving Providence (or, if it is shown emerging from a cloud, God the Creator) and the letters I H S. These initials are often seen, but seldom correctly interpreted. Some will tell you they mean "I Have Suffered." Others derive them from the Latin *Iesus Hominum Salvator*, meaning "Jesus, Savior of Men." Another Latin interpretation is *In Hoc Signo (vinces)*, meaning "In This Sign Thou Shalt Conquer." But the best scholarship derives them from the early Christian abbreviation of Jesus' name in Greek, which was IH(SOY)S.

Many Episcopal churches have very beautiful stained glass windows depicting biblical characters and scenes. If you look closely, you will find in the corners and among the ornamental flowers and scrolls of these colored windows a number of other symbols, such as the keys, the lily, the crown, the palm, the phoenix, the fish, the anchor, the circle, the star, the three nails, the vine, and the *agnus dei* or Lamb of God, a haloed lamb carrying a bannered cross. All these designs have important meaning for the Christian, and most of them are very ancient.

There are various colors to be seen about the altar and chancel, typifying the great truths of Christianity and, as in the Catholic and Lutheran churches, the tints are changed with the seasons of the Christian year. Green is used for the long Trinity season and also for Epiphany; it is the universal color, that of nature itself. White is used for Christmas, Easter, Ascensiontide, Transfiguration, All Saints' Day; also for baptisms, marriages, and confirmations. All these are occasions of rejoicing. For the somber seasons of Advent, Lent, Rogation and Ember Days, the penitential color of violet or purple is dominant. Red is for the days of martyred saints, and at Whitsuntide to recall the tongues of fire which the Book of Acts says descended upon the disciples at Pentecost.

The beauty of the architecture and furnishings of the Episcopal Church is consonant with the beautiful service and liturgy itself. From Processional to Recessional of the choir, the whole program moves in simple stately majesty. In various churches the service may be changed; some are more elaborate than others. But the general plan is the same. A good idea of the average "Morning Prayer and Sermon" may be had from the order of service used at Calvary Church in New York City.

The Processional Hymn is followed by the General Confessional, the Venite, a Psalm, the First Lesson, the Te Deum Laudamus, and the Second Lesson. Then comes the Jubilate Deo, the Creed, Versicles, Collects and Grace. There is a hymn then before the Sermon, and the Offertory Anthem afterward. The service closes with the Presentation and Dedication of Pledges and Offerings, the Doxology and the Recessional Hymn.

To explain these terms further—the Processional Hymn is sung by the robed choir as the singers march slowly from an inner room to the back of the church and then down the center aisle with the congregation joining in the singing. The Recessional at the end of the service simply reverses the route.

The General Confession is a prayer offered by the minister and whole congregation, all kneeling. The Venite, beginning, "O come, let us sing unto the Lord," is a chant composed of verses from the 95th and 96th Psalms. The Te Deum Laudamus ("We praise Thee, O God") is an ancient Christian hymn of unknown authorship, and the Jubilate Deo ("O be joyful in the Lord") is the chant of the 100th Psalm. The First Lesson is read by the minister from the Old Testament part of the Bible, and the Second Lesson from the New Testament.

The Creed is a short statement of belief, a confession of faith, and either the Apostles' Creed (the most popular of all Western Christendom) may be used, or the longer Nicene Creed, so named for the Council of Nicaea of 325 A.D. where it was formulated and authorized. The Apostles' Creed, which was once thought to have come from the Twelve Apostles themselves but is probably in its present form later in origin than the Nicene, runs as follows:

"I believe in God the Father Almighty, Maker of heaven and earth:

"And in Jesus Christ his only Son our Lord: Who was conceived by the Holy Ghost, Born of the Virgin Mary: Suffered under Pontius Pilate, Was crucified, dead, and buried: He descended into hell; The third day he rose again from the dead: He ascended into heaven, And sitteth on the right hand of God the Father Almighty: From thence he shall come to judge the quick and the dead.

"I believe in the Holy Ghost: The holy Catholic Church: The Communion of Saints: The Forgiveness of sins: The Resurrection of the body: And the Life everlasting. Amen."

In modern times, as a concession to those who cannot honestly say that they believe that Jesus Christ "descended into hell," it is permitted to substitute the phrase, "He went into the place of departed spirits." The Nicene Creed simply says on that point: "He suffered and was buried: And the third day he rose again."

The Creed is recited standing: then the Versicles are said:

Minister: "The Lord be with you."
People: "And with thy spirit."
Minister: "Let us pray. O Lord, show thy mercy upon us."
People: "And grant us thy salvation."
Minister: "O God, make clean our hearts within us."
People: "And take not thy Holy Spirit from us."

The people then kneel for the Collects (Short prayers) and longer prayers, which are sometimes omitted, and then the Order of Morning Prayer ends with the Grace, or benediction taken from Second Corinthians 13:14:

"The grace of our Lord Jesus Christ, and the love of God, and the fellowship of the Holy Ghost, be with us all evermore. Amen."

A visitor unfamiliar with the Episcopal form of service of worship will be somewhat surprised at the number of times the congregation changes position. The people kneel to pray, stand to sing or recite God's praises, and sit to listen to the minister's words of instruction. These changes are made rapidly, and a stranger will find himself "out of step" if he tries to keep up with the regular attendants. Besides these major activities, some worshipers add the making of the sign of the cross, genuflecting (bending the knee) and bowing the head. All in all, Episcopal church-goers are more often in motion than those of any other church. This they explain on the ground that they are participators in the service and not mere spectators or listeners. They go to church neither to be lectured nor entertained, but to worship God. They show through physical acts and attitudes the outward observance of an inward devotion.

A visitor to an Episcopal church service who is familiar with other Christian churches is likely to remark on how similar the Episcopal service is to that of the Roman Catholic Mass. He will perhaps be puzzled by this coincidence when he notes that, nevertheless, the church he is visiting is called a *"Protestant* Episcopal" church.

As you examine this unusual church further, you will find it quite true that Episcopalians are, in a strange way, both Catholic and Protestant. Their church is like the Catholic, not only in its church interiors and its liturgy, but in other ways as well. One is the matter of polity, or church government, for both churches are ruled by their bishops, instead of by presbyters (elders) as in the Presbyterian Church, or by the congregation itself as in the Congregational and Baptist Churches.

Another way in which Episcopalians resemble Catholics is their insistence on apostolic succession; that is, no priest is considered properly ordained unless by a bishop who has been ordained by another in a long unbroken line back to the Apostles themselves. Part of the ordination ceremony consists of the bishop and other priests and bishops present laying their hands on the head of the man to be ordained, who thus receives a transmitted contact from the Apostles, referred to by the bishop's words: "Receive the Holy Ghost for the Office and Work of a Priest in the Church of God, now committed unto thee by the Imposition of our hands."

There is a historic reason for these resemblances to Roman Catholicism in "The Protestant Episcopal Church of the United States of America" (to give it its full official name) for it claims direct descent, through its parent Anglican Church or Church of England, from the first Christian church founded when Jesus Christ commissioned the apostles to Christianize the world. By the third century A. D., and perhaps before, Christianity existed in Britain where it has continued ever since, although it was nearly extinguished by the invading Angles and Saxons.

In the sixteenth century the Christian Church *in* England became the Christian Church *of* England; that is, it became nationalized. There were bitter years of quarrels and even wars before the breach was finally made when England refused any longer to accept the supremacy of the Pope. There

148

were political, economic, and even personal reasons for the separation. But the important point for the present study is the fact that the very Parliament which legislated the separation also stated that the English people had no intention to "decline or vary from . . . the ancient Catholic faith of Christendom."

King Henry VIII's unsavory marital tangle was for a while one of the factors in the movement toward separation, but during the many years before the break was complete, such other long-range factors as the invention of the printing press and the growth of nationalism had a powerful influence. The movement on the continent known as the Protestant Reformation also had a tremendous effect on England.

For you will find upon examining the Thirty-nine Articles, which state the cardinal tenets of both the Anglican and Episcopal Churches, a number of reasons why, in spite of the resemblance to Catholicism, the American Episcopalians call their church *"Protestant Episcopal."*

The main differences between the Episcopalians and the Catholics are these: the Episcopalians reject the supremacy of the Pope, the doctrine of purgatory, the use in worship of images and relics, the celibacy of bishops, priests, and deacons, the sacrifice of the Mass, the saying of Masses for the dead, the use in church of "a tongue not understanded of the people" (Latin), and the use of the books of The Apocrypha (1st and 2nd Maccabees, etc.) as Holy Scripture "to establish any doctrine."

Of the seven recognized by the Roman Catholic Church, the Thirty-nine Articles accept only two sacraments, Baptism and the Lord's Supper. Episcopalians reject also the doctrine of transubstantiation (that the bread and wine become the actual body and blood of Christ) and teach that "The Body of Christ is given, taken, and eaten, in the Supper, only after an heavenly and spiritual manner."

Even the Thirty-nine Articles are not to be taken strictly. Much mental reservation is allowed. You can attach your own meaning to the words. The result is that there is a wide variance of opinion inside the Episcopal Church itself. Three distinct parties are recognized, Low Church, Broad Church, and High Church. The Low Church Party emphasizes the more distinctly Protestant point of view and is largely evangelical, likely to be strong for personal experience and direct immediate faith in Christ. The Broad Church people are the Modernists, emphasizing reason and character as more important than faith or sacraments. The High Church Party stresses tradition, history, and authority. They are the nearest to Catholicism and are often called the Anglo-Catholics. They value all seven sacraments, sometimes use a rosary, call Holy Communion "Mass" and seem to be approaching belief in the doctrine of transubstantiation. As a matter of fact and practice, neither laymen nor the clergy are required to assent to the Thirty-nine Articles either at confirmation or ordination.

This wide variation in belief which is permitted and even encouraged within the Episcopal ranks is by them called "comprehensiveness." The differences of opinion have sometimes caused high tension, such as the dispute in 1923 between the high church and broad church parties in New York City over the doctrine of the virgin birth of Christ, but the church has held together.

Episcopalians claim to contain in their church the best of Catholicism and the best of Protestantism, allowing fellowship between higher critics and evangelicals, between prophets and priests; and because of their ability to keep people of such diverse opinions working together in one church, they maintain that theirs is the best equipped and experienced of all churches to bring about the unity of Christendom.

To the Episcopal Church, through its parent Church of England, we are indebted for a contribution of beauty of another sort than architecture, art, and ritual—the King James version of the Bible and the Book of Common Prayer, "the greatest book in English excepting only the Bible." It should never be forgotten that it was the Anglican Communion which contended for and won the great victory for free religion of having the Bible printed in English, open in the churches, and available for the common people to read.

The Prayer Book makes the Bible still more available and easy to understand, for it contains the heart of the New Testament. Evolved through many centuries, it includes many ancient Christian prayers and even "elements from the Jewish service books used in the Temple at the time of our Lord." It voices in time-hallowed phrases the prayers and aspirations of mankind seeking the truth and struggling toward the light, and it expresses confidence in man's final happiness in the triumph of right over wrong.

The Book of *Common* Prayer consists of prayers and statements of faith to be used "in common" with others assembled for worship, but it is used also as a devotional manual and guide for private prayer by millions of Christians, including many who are not of the Episcopal household of faith.

Revisions in England and in this country have kept the Prayer Book adequate for the evolving needs of thinking people. Besides the English editions of 1549, 1552, 1559, and 1660, there have been the American revisions of 1789, 1892, and 1928. In the latest edition, a number of improvements have been made, including changes in the Communion, Baptismal, and Burial services, besides the widely discussed omission of the woman's promise to "obey" in the Marriage Service.

Over a hunderd new prayers were added in 1928, including a particularly beautiful one to be said "At Night" which might well be used even by non-Christians:

"O Lord, support us all the day long, until the shadows lengthen and the evening comes, and the busy world is hushed, and the fever of life is over, and our work is done. Then in thy mercy grant us a safe lodging, and a holy rest, and peace at the last. Amen."

There are new prayers "For a Sick Child," "For a Birthday," For Quiet Confidence," "For Those in Mental Darkness." "For One About to Undergo an Operation," and a wonderful one "For all Poor, Homeless, and Neglected Folk." This last one has been popularly called "The Forgotten Man's Prayer."

It may well be that the alertness of the Episcopalians in responding to the spiritual needs of modern people is responsible for their growth in church membership, from 2,160,207 in 1949 to 2,790,935 in 1953, a gain of nearly 30 percent in four years.

15

THE CONGREGATIONALISTS

The Church That Came Over in the Mayflower

IF A CHURCH is a body of believers rather than the building in which they hold their meetings, as most people agree, then the first Congregational church in America arrived here in the square-rigged 180-ton *Mayflower* in December 1620.

In one sense, it was less than a church, for the majority of the members had remained behind in Leyden, Holland, with their beloved pastor, Rev. John Robinson; and only forty (thirteen of them young children), under the leadership of Elder Brewster, had sailed to the new world.

In another sense, however, it was more than a church; it was the first unit in the American democracy-to-be, the germ of the future republic of the United States. For in the cabin of that little ship the epochal "Mayflower Compact" was signed, one of the most important documents not only of American history but of the long struggle of mankind toward free institutions.

"In ye name of God, Amen," it begins. "We whose names are underwriten, the loyall subjects of our dread soveraigne lord King James, . . . having undertaken for ye glorie of God, and advancemente of ye Christian faith, and honour of our king & countrie, a voyage to plant ye first colonie in ye Northerne parts of Virginia, doe by these presents solemnly &

mutually in ye presence of God, and one of another, covenant & combine ourselves togeather into a civill body politick for our better ordering & preservation & furtherance of ye ends aforesaid; and by vertue hereof to enacte, constitute, and frame such just & equall lawes, ordinances, Acts, constitutions, & offices, from time to time, as shall be thought most meete & convenient for ye generall good of ye Colonie, unto which we promise all due submission and obedience. In witnes whereof we have hereunder subscribed our names at Cap-Codd ye 11 of November, . . . Ano Dom. 1620."

The word "covenant" was very significant, for it heralded a new order in both church and state. Here the "congregation" was covenanting or agreeing together to make its own laws, civil and religious. For the first time a group of men and women were to be governed by a compact drawn up and signed by themselves entirely of their own volition.

Whether or not the Pilgrims ever "landed on" the particular boulder now enshrined as "Plymouth Rock," will probably never be ascertained. On Forefathers' Day, December 22, the day celebrated as the landing date, most of them were still in the *Mayflower*, anchored off what is now Provincetown. But—something vastly more important—the Mayflower Compact was the cornerstone of American democracy. Not only did the first Congregational church come over in the *Mayflower;* so did the New England Town Meeting, and the Declaration of Independence, and the United States Constitution and Bill of Rights.

The "Association and Agreement," as the Pilgrims first called their Compact, was obviously modeled on the covenants of their Scrooby-Leyden group and a few other somewhat similar independent churches which had recently been evolving in England.

When the invention of the printing press made Bibles available to the working people of England, they discovered to their surprise that the early Christian churches had been much more simple and more democratic than was their Anglican Church, which they were forced by law to attend. Into that church they had been born and baptized. The King of England was its head, and not to attend that church and faithfully observe its rules and customs, whether one believed its theology or not, was regarded as treason, and treason was punishable by death.

So, when the new Bible readers of England sought to be what they called "True Christians," like the early followers of Jesus in Bible times, and left the regular churches and met secretly (in each other's homes or in old gravel pits) for simple services of worship and fellowship, they ran into serious trouble.

At that time (the sixteenth and early seventeenth centuries) the still medieval theology of the state church was so far behind the progressive thought of the awakening intelligence and growing education of the people of England that the clergy were openly satirized. Manners and morals were corrupt, both outside the church and within, as many of the more devout ecclesiastics themselves realized and deplored. For many years a growing group of sincere religious people had desired to purify the church from within, both morally and spiritually, and were therefore called "Puritans."

The task proved difficult, however, for the old order was strongly entrenched and reluctant to give place to new. The best efforts of the Puritans were making such exasperatingly slow headway that little bands of the reform-minded, tired of waiting, decided the time had come for "Reformation Without Tarying for Anie," as one of their earliest leaders, Robert Browne, entitled his famous tract-sermon, published in 1582.

The Puritans of the new left wing went so far as to urge separation from the state church, and were therefore dubbed "Separatists." These people, however, much preferred to be known as the "gathered" church, and that revolutionary name and idea they owed largely to Browne. In England, then, it was taken for granted that the way a person got into the church was by being born and baptized into it as a child. Browne, however, believed that one should enter a church by deliberate act of solemn conviction and choice, resolving to live a pure Christian life with a gathered church of the like-minded. In Norwich a company of people secretly "gathered" together in church fellowship on the basis of Browne's teaching and by means of a covenant.

This occurred early in 1581 and was the first Congregational church in England. Although the word "congregational" was not used to describe such churches until the middle of the next century, the entire significance of this revolutionary change in the base of church membership lay in the fact that the Norwich church was a congregation rather than a parish.

Instead of their pastor being chosen by a bishop (usually at the suggestion of the man who practically owned the church because he had inherited or purchased the "benefice" or "living," and without the people of the parish even being consulted), the new Separatist churches chose their own pastor, ordained him themselves, and supported him, financially and morally. In time the gathered groups became self-governing and self-sustaining. They made their own local church laws and enforced them. They erected their own church buildings and kept them in repair. And to a great extent, they chose even their own theology, for they would not "call" a minister until they had heard and approved his sermons, and they even asked for his resignation later on if the majority of the congregation decided that he had departed from the faith. They were truly "independent" churches, and were so called in England for many years, more often than "congregational" as in America.

All this did not happen at once in Browne's Norwich church, or in the other Separatist churches, but the germ of democracy in religion was in Browne's early teaching, even if somewhat vague and blurred as he felt his way on a strange path, and it later evolved naturally into the great Congregational and Baptist denominations in both England and the United States.

These pioneer Congregationalists were nearly exterminated at the very beginning by ruthless persecution and imprisonment of the laymen and women, and more particularly by the systematic execution of their leaders. Twenty-five Separatists, jailed in notorious Newgate, died there from the intolerable conditions.

But the followers of the martyrs were far from extinguished. They simply went underground temporarily in England, or slipped away to Holland or America seeking freedom to worship God in the way that seemed best to them. As had happened so often before, the blood of the martyrs became the seed of the church. There were then in England over twenty thousand Separatists, so Sir Walter Raleigh stated, and the death of a few leaders and the imprisonment of others merely meant that their places were soon filled by equally earnest and determined believers in the new faith. And in spite of the law against conventicles, secret meetings of the new congregational order were being held, as in the early Christian church, which knew very similar persecutions.

William Brewster was postmaster of Scrooby, a little town on the main road north from London into Yorkshire. He was a thoughtful Cambridge University man, and a citizen of importance. A number of other educated men and people of prominence in Gainsborough and other nearby towns used to drop in to visit him in his spacious old Manor House. Craftsmen also, like Francis Cooke, a wool comber of Blyth, came a dozen miles of a Sunday. Young Bradford, twelve years old when Brewster adopted him in 1602, helped greet and serve the guests, and listened carefully to the conversation then and long afterward, in Holland and in the Plymouth colony. For the orphan boy whom Brewster adopted became the narrator of the whole exciting Pilgrim story and was the governor of Plymouth for thirty-six years.

In his history Bradford tells of the secret Sunday services Brewster held for some years unsuspected in the manor house "by procuring of good preachers . . . and drawing on of others to assist & help forward in such a worke, he himself being most commonly deepest in ye charge . . ." For Brewster,

154

it seems, "had a singular good gift in prayer, both publick & private, in ripping up ye hart & conscience before God . . ."

Two clergymen, Richard Clyfton and John Robinson, both Cambridge men like Brewster, left the Anglican church and "prophesied" in the Separatist "gatherings" at Scrooby. The illegal conventicle meetings flourished until neighboring Church of England people became suspicious of the Sunday Psalm-singing coming from the tap room of the former Manor House of the bishops. Soon it became wise to hold the meetings at night in the woods. Spies found them even there, and many of them were fined and the leaders jailed.

But persecution only confirmed them in their faith, and as soon as Robinson and Brewster were released, plans were made to find some place where they could worship like "True Christians." By stealth and devious ways many of them managed to assemble by 1609 in Leyden, "a fair & bewtifull citie," and resume their meetings, with John Robinson as pastor and William Brewster as Elder. For over a decade they were comparatively peaceful and happy there, and the congregation grew to three hundred souls.

Yet for several reasons they decided to leave Holland and voyage to America. One reason was that Pastor Robinson had heard many complaints, according to Bradford, that the young people were "getting ye raines off their neks & departing from their parents. . . ."

It is likely, though, that it was not what they wished to escape from, but what they wished to go to, that became the deciding factor. They were among the first of the thousands of Englishmen who began hearing the call of the New World. Dutch and English sailors and fishermen described it as a land rich in natural fruits and game, bordered by seas full of fish, where anyone could get wealthy without hard work. These rumors were spread by several English companies organized for colonizing purposes, and the Leyden church folk thought it might be wise to sail to the new country called Virginia where, though far from England, they would still be Englishmen on English soil. Besides, war between Holland and Spain was looming, and they did not want to serve in the Dutch army.

"Lastly, and which was not least, a great hope & inward zeal they had of laying some good foundation . . . for ye propagating & advancing ye gospell of ye kingdom of God in those remote parts of ye world. . . . So they lefte that goodly & pleasante citie which had been their resting place near twelve years. But they knew they were pilgrimes & looked not much on those things, but lift up their eyes to ye heavens, their dearest countrie, and quieted their spirits."

Pastor John Robinson, who wished to go with the "Pilgrims," (as they were thereafter called from Bradford's above remarks based on Hebrews 11:13) but chose to remain behind with the great majority of the Leyden church, preached a farewell sermon to his tearful flock, one sentence of which has become immortal in Congregationalism, "The Lord hath more truth and light yet to break forth out of his Holy Word."

After many difficulties, one hundred and two persons left Plymouth, England, on the Mayflower on September 16, 1620. Of the one hundred and two, fifty were men, twenty women, and thirty-two children! Contrary to popular tradition down through the years, only forty of the one hundred and two were the Scrooby-Leyden Pilgrims, and of the forty, only seventeen were men, ten women, and thirteen children. And of these forty from Leyden, only four adults were from the original Scrooby church, William and Mary Brewster, William Bradford, and Francis Cooke.

The forty from Leyden called themselves "Saints" and the rest of the freemen who boarded the ship in England they called "Strangers." These latter, families not particularly interested in religion but in bettering their condition in the New World, included seventeen men, nine women, and thirteen children. Besides, there were five "hired men," eleven men servants and bonded men, one woman servant, and six orphan or servant children. The bonded or "indentured" men were sort of unpaid adult apprentices, working several years for their keep and passage.

It comes as a surprise to learn that Captain Myles Standish and Priscilla Mullins were not of the Saints, but Strangers; while John Alden who later married Priscilla, was one of the hired men who joined the company in London as a cooper.

There was a rough voyage of two months until the *Mayflower* reached Cape Cod in mid-November, and it was another month before they began disembarking at what is now Plymouth. During that month they lived on the ship while some of the men explored the coast to find the best place for a settlement. It was on the ship also, on November 21 (November 11, old style calendar) that the Mayflower Compact was signed. Of the fifty men aboard, forty-one signed the Compact, of whom only seventeen were of the Leyden Saints. Nevertheless, all who disembarked from the *Mayflower* and settled in Plymouth were thereafter known as Pilgrims, and the Saint and Stranger discrimination soon died a proper death.

Undoubtedly, one reason why the rather mixed company which built New Plymouth on the site of an abandoned Indian village became so soon unified into the famous colony of the Pilgrim Fathers and Mothers was the suffering they endured together. That first winter half of them died from "the sickness," which some termed "galloping consumption" and others blamed on the scurvy due to the long voyage without fresh vegetables, but it may have been caused by their building little huts on the site which the Indians had recently deserted, perhaps because of deaths from the same disease, probably a form of virulent influenza.

But when the *Mayflower* sailed back to England in the spring of 1621, not one of the remaining Pilgrims returned with her. And before the end of 1621 the little ship *Fortune* brought "35 persons to remaine & live in ye plantation," and in 1623 the *Anne* delivered sixty more.

The hope of doing missionary work among the Indians was an important motive for going to the new world, and the Pilgrims were soon at it very zealously, teaching the "salvages" to say grace before meals. The red men enjoyed hearing the Genesis story of Creation, and even approved highly of the Ten Commandments, except the seventh, the one against adultery. They said it would be too inconvenient for a man to be tied to one woman. They returned the courtesy of being taught the Bible by teaching the missionaries how to "drink" tobacco.

The Pilgrims had come to the new country, however, primarily for freedom to worship God as they wished. But they had left their pastor, John Robinson, behind in Leyden. Until he should come (which he never did) Elder Brewster was to lead their meetings of worship. Thereafter at Plymouth he also served as Elder until Ralph Smith, the first pastor, arrived in 1629. As an Elder Brewster could do almost anything but administer the sacraments. He talked twice every Sabbath, "and that both powerful and profitable." As for performing marriages, it was decided that should be done by a civil magistrate anyway, for it is "nowhere found in the gospel to be laid on the minister as part of his office."

In their revolt against the established ritualistic Church of England, the Pilgrims used no Prayer Book, celebrated no saints' days, not even Christmas and Easter. For nine years they did not commemorate the Lord's Supper. But in every home, morning and evening prayers and grace before meals were strictly observed, and every man was expected to instruct and discipline the other members of his family, including his wife, according to the stern code of Calvinism.

There must have been occasional trouble there. It has been facetiously said that the Pilgrim Fathers had to endure the hardships of the terrible winters on that stern and rockbound shore, but the Pilgrim Mothers had to stand all that and the Pilgrim Fathers too.

For about eight years, the Pilgrims of Plymouth were the only non-conformists in New England, but then the rush started. In 1629, nine hundred arrived; in 1630, two thousand, and after ten years twenty thousand English colonists had settled around Massachusetts Bay. These were not all non-conformists; many were Anglicans; and a surprising number were not even professing Christians.

The first of the new settlers established themselves in Salem in 1628 and 1629. They and many who came during the next decade were Puritans who still wished to purify it of its defects and abuses. They had not come to America like the Separatist Pilgrims to set up a new kind of church, but to establish a revised version of the English church. And in other ways they differed from the Plymouth people: a considerable number of them were well-to-do, and many were aristocrats of the English nobility.

Yet in a very short time, the Puritans of Massachusetts Bay became congregational Separatists themselves. What caused the apparently sudden change? Crossing the Atlantic may have had something to do with it, but the precipitating agent seems to have been a physician. Called from Plymouth to treat the sick of Salem, Dr. Samuel Fuller, who was really more deacon than physician, preached Separatism by bedsides and everywhere else so effectively that he influenced the Salem Puritans, including their doughty leader John Endicott, and they soon decided they would have a free church of their own.

On August 6, 1629, the Salem Puritans took the momentous step of creating a church by a one-sentence agreement:

"We covenant with the Lord and with one another and do bind ourselves in the plans of God to work together in all his ways according as he is pleased to reveal himself unto us in his blessed word of truth."

They further separated themselves from the Anglican church by disregarding the bishops and apostolic succession and choosing for themselves a pastor, Samuel Skelton, and a teacher, Francis Higginson, and then ordaining the two men, after hearing sermons and prayers by both, a sort of hurried "candidating."

They had given "notice to the church at Plimouth, that being the only church that was in the Country before them." And a delegation led by Governor Bradford, "coming by sea, . . . hindered by cross winds, . . . came into the assembly afterward and gave them the right hand of fellowship . . ."

Thus was established the congregational "polity" or system of government still obtaining in Congregational, Baptist, and many other American churches today. The local church "calls" and, with the counsel of delegations from neighboring churches of the same faith, ordains its minister. It depends upon no outside authority and accepts no dictation. Associations of churches in the same district are usually formed, and national conferences are convened, but neither has jurisdiction over the local church.

In June of the next year 1630, seventeen shiploads of settlers led by John Winthrop arrived in what was soon called Boston Harbor. From the start, the Boston or Massachusetts Bay Colony prospered; there were people enough and resources enough, whether of money, adaptability or ingenuity. In July 1630, covenant-based churches were established and ministers elected and ordained in settlements which became Watertown and Charlestown, and several others soon followed, including Boston, Newtown (Cambridge), and Matapan (Dorchester).

In October 1632, Governor Winthrop and a company from Boston, including Pastor John Wilson, visited Plymouth, where, wrote Winthrop in his famous journal:

" . . . they were very kindly entertained and feasted every day at several houses. On the Lord's Day [Sunday] there was a sacrament [observance of the Lord's Supper] which they did partake in. And in the afternoon, Mr. Roger Williams, [then assistant pastor at Plymouth and soon thereafter founder of the Baptist settlement at Providence, Rhode Island] according to their custom, propounded a question, to which the pastor, Mr. Smith spake briefly: then Mr. Williams prophesied [preached]: and after, the Governor of Plymouth spake to the question; after him, the elder [Brewster]; then some two or three more of the congregation. Then the elder desired the Governor of Massachusetts and Mr. Wilson to speak to it, which they did. When this was ended, the deacon, Mr. Fuller, put the congregation in mind of their duty of contribution; whereupon the governor and all the rest went down to the deacon's seat and put into the box, and then returned . . ."

The democratic character of the meeting is apparent. The order of service in Congregational Church services has changed somewhat in the centuries since, but the people still "put into the box."

In ten years from its settlement, Boston was the hub of colonial activities. Soon those who had fled from the state church in England had one of their own in Massachusetts, and the Puritans became so "puritanical" that they passed and enforced laws so strict as to be ludicrous. Persons were fined for serving cakes or sweets except at weddings and funerals. Any observer of Christmas—anyone who even quit work on that day—was "amerced" (fined) five shillings. Any woman who scolded was compelled to wear all day in her doorway a large sign reading "Scold." Until 1870 smoking was prohibited in public except in a small part of Boston Common.

The pastor of the Cambridge church, Thomas Hooker, did not like the Boston system of control of the state by what he called the "high church," and in 1636 led his own flock in search of more freedom to the Connecticut valley where they founded Hartford. While Hooker was famous for his advocacy of civil rights, and preached that with the people lies all civil authority, he meant by the people, the members of the church. By 1676 Hartford had laws against Quakers, Priests, and "dissenters from the established worship of this Dominion," and interfered in the private lives of its citizens by such statutes as:

"Married persons must live together, or be imprisoned."

"No one shall travel, cook victuals, make beds, sweep house, cut hair or shave, and no woman shall kiss her child, on the sabbath day."

"No one shall . . . keep Christmas, or Saints days, make minced pies, dance, play cards, or play on any instrument of music, except the drum, trumpet, and jews harp."

The attempts of the Puritan church authorities to keep the church "pure" from any practice or person of whom the pastors disapproved led to repeated instances of rebellion by such outstanding individuals as John Davenport, who founded New Haven in 1638; Roger Williams; and the intellectually brilliant nurse, Mistress Anne Hutchinson, whose crime was apparently that of being a mystic.

The Puritans had their worst troubles with Quakers and witches. The Quakers, followers of George Fox who was winning many Separatists to his Society of Friends in England, rejected all rites and ceremonies including baptism and the Lord's Supper, and broke many civil laws. When the exasperated Puritan authorities tried to discourage the persistent law-breaking by hanging four Quakers on Boston Common, a revulsion of feeling set in, and the common sense of the common people demanded that such persecution cease. The final Puritan hysterical outbreak was the witchcraft delusion; at its peak in 1692 nineteen men and women were hanged in Salem for having traffic with the devil.

In the remorse over these excesses, the Puritans turned over a new leaf, and in the 18th and 19th centuries the Congregational Churches gradually assumed the leadership in liberal, tolerant, progressive religion. They have always been strong for education, for they were the founders and supporters of Harvard, Yale, Dartmouth, Williams, Middlebury, Amherst and Oberlin colleges, and of Mount Holyoke, Smith, and Wellesley for women.

They have produced such theological giants as Jonathan Edwards, who led the revival known as "The Great Awakening," Timothy Dwight, Horace Bushnell, Henry Ward Beecher, Washington Gladden, Dwight L. Moody, George A. Gordon, and Lyman Abbott. For leaders in social reform, they point to Dr. Graham Taylor, Dr. Josiah Strong, and that modern Deborah, Jane Addams of Chicago.

Foreign missionary work started in 1806 when five young Williams College students under a haystack in a storm dedicated their lives to taking the gospel to distant lands. From their resolve grew the great American Board of Commissioners for Foreign Missions.

Home mission work had started even earlier, for the rather clumsy attempts to save the souls of the "salvages" by teaching them to say grace before meals were succeeded by more effective methods. John Eliot became teacher of the Roxbury church in 1632 and soon made himself the Apostle to the Indians by studying their language, translating the Bible into Algonquian, and converted many of the natives to Christianity. His success with his "Praying Indians" led to the establishing in England of the Society for the Propagation of the Gospel in New England. By 1670 there were four thousand praying Indians, but some of them later joined hostile tribesmen fighting the colonists. Afterward, however, such great preachers as Jonathan Edwards and David Brainerd renewed the missionary efforts, one notable result of which was the establishing at Lebanon, New Hampshire, of "Dr. Wheelock's Academy for the Promotion of Christianity and Civility among the Savage Indians of This Continent," which later was moved to Hanover and became Darthmouth College, whose football players today are consequently called the "Indians."

There has been considerable change in the form of worship and order of service in Congregational churches since the early Pilgrim days. Then they "eschewed" and discarded anything reminding them of the Roman Catholic or Anglican Episcopal churches. The churches of the seventeenth and eighteenth and for the first half of the nineteenth century were ultra-plain inside and out, practically "barnlike," and the meetings matched the buildings in simplicity, for they consisted of long sermons and prayers and the reading of Scripture. The only music was the singing of Psalms from the *Bay Psalm Book*, which John Eliot had helped prepare. Organs were forbidden, but since the Bible did mention "horns and trumpets," horns were permitted.

But people, especially young people, began to demand and get other hymns, less doleful and of not such slow tempo. Recognition of Christmas and Easter, which had been forbidden, crept back in, and later the whole Christian year. Sermons and prayers were shortened and the entire service brightened. By the end of the nineteenth cenutry, Congregational services, like those in other churches of evangelical Protestantism, began with an organ prelude, then in order, the Doxology sung by all, the Invocation Prayer by the minister, Scripture Reading, a hymn, Responsive Reading, an anthem by the choir, the Long Prayer, another hymn, the Sermon, prayer, announcements, the collection, another hymn or anthem, and finally the benediction. The once three-hour service had been shortened to one hour. But by mid-twentieth century a strong trend toward a more elaborate liturgical service, with processional and recessional, has become popular, and the service is growing longer although the sermons have became very brief.

The theology, too, has changed several times since the days of Cotton Mather, Thomas Hooker, and Jonathan Edwards. In the early nineteenth century, Horace Bushnell occupied the pulpit of the Hartford North Congregational Church all his life and by his preaching and his book *Christian Nurture* so greatly humanized the previous harsh Calvinism by emphasizing the more loving aspects of the religion of Jesus and by stressing the natural nurture of children through the educative process rather than salvation by sudden catastrophic conversion that Congregational theology took on new life. Almost a century later, George A. Gordon of Old South Church, Boston, built upon Bushnell's foundation a more mystic faith which still further softened and modified the old Calvinism.

Of recent years, Congregationalists have grown increasingly interested in the unifying of similar denominations. The chain fission which shattered Calvinism into dozens of sects has been halted by some alchemy of the human spirit, and the trend toward unity is abroad. In 1886 the Congregationalists tried to unite with the Free Baptists, but unsuccessfully. In 1892 a partial merger with Congregational Methodists was achieved. Other attempts at mergers, concordats, and unions with such varied groups as the United Brethren, the Methodist Protestants, the Disciples of Christ, the Presbyterians, and the Universalists met with failure, perhaps because the time was not ripe.

But in 1929 full unified fellowship was attained with the denomination known as the Christian Church. This denomination was also a protest against ecclesiastical domination of various sorts and was itself a union of three smaller groups originally led by James O'Kelley, a former Virginia Methodist; Abner Jones, a Vermont Baptist; and Barton W. Stone, a former Kentucky Presbyterian. They had united on a Biblical, evangelical platform emphasizing Christian character as the basis of membership rather than theological creed, so there was no difficulty in their forming a democratic union with the Congregational Church.

The two denominations are now one, called the Congregational Christian Churches, numbering, by the 1953 *Yearbook of American Churches*, 5,597 local churches, 5,760 ordained clergy, 668,702 Sunday School scholars, and 1,269,466 church members.

16

THE BAPTISTS

The Church of Freedom

TEN YEARS AFTER *The Mayflower* brought the Pilgrim Fathers to America, another ship, also small but important, cast anchor in Boston Harbor after a stormy voyage from England. Among *The Lyon's* twenty passengers there arrived, with his charming youthful wife, Roger Williams, "a young minister, godly and zealous, having precious gifts."

The young couple had looked forward eagerly to their new life in the new world after their sufferings for their faith in old England, but they were sadly disappointed. It is one of the paradoxes of history that the really splendid people who had themselves previously come to America seeking freedom to worship God in their own way, blindly refused to grant the same freedom to other newcomers whose way of worship was somewhat different.

The colonists did not realize at first that the views of the young preacher differed from theirs, and they gladly let him preach in Salem for a while, since his "precious gifts" included eloquence and great learning. He knew several languages, as well as the amazing new invention called shorthand, and had taught Dutch to his young contemporary, John Milton.

The new young preacher, however, kept asking publicly two very embarrassing questions: what right had the King of England to give to the settlers in America the lands owned by the Indians, and what right had the civil rulers to force a man to attend and support a church in whose religion he did not believe?

It is always easier to punish a thinker than to answer him. So, in 1636, five years after he had come to America, the young heretic, Roger Williams, was condemned for "broaching and divulging new and dangerous opinions," and banished from the colony. For fourteen weeks he wandered in the winter wilderness, knowing not, as he later wrote, "what bread or bed did mean," for although he had money, there was no food or shelter for sale in the forest. Finally he found shelter with the Indians in what is now Rhode Island.

There he bought land from the red men, which was then a novel idea, very pleasing to the surprised Indians but very irritating to the other white settlers. Williams always got along well with the Indians for he treated them like human beings, as William Penn did later, and several years before had already paid them the courtesy of learning their language.

The Massachusetts colonists were still further disturbed when the heretic preacher established on his new-bought land a town of refuge which he significantly called "Providence," announcing that all the people who were having a hard time in Boston or elsewhere on account of their religion would be welcome in Providence, whether Separatists, Quakers, Jews, Turks, or anybody, and that everyone could worship God as he pleased, or even not go to church at all.

Over two hundred years later, in 1872, the Congress of the United States, recognizing that this principle of religious freedom, or "soul liberty," as Williams called it, was what had made American democracy possible, rather belatedly placed in our national capitol a memorial to him, and paid him this official tribute:

"In all our history no name shines with a purer light."

Word about the invitation to Providence spread at once and people flocked there, even many from his Salem church, including his brave young wife who had given her child, born while Williams was wandering in the wilderness, the challenging name, "Freeborn Williams."

Now Roger Williams had recently become convinced that a church should be made up of adult believers only, and so he established such a church in Providence in 1638. He asked a man named Ezekiel Holliman from Salem to rebaptize him, and he then rebaptized Holliman and ten others.

Meanwhile the Indians had planned to surprise and exterminate the Massachusetts colonists. Williams heard about the plot and went "alone in a poor canoe, scarce acquainting my wife, through a stormy wind, with great seas, every minute in hazard of life" to the Indian headquarters where, after a powwow of three days and nights, he persuaded the sachems to give up their plans for the massacre.

Some years later, in 1663, when Williams sailed into Boston harbor from England with letters from members of Parliament commending him to the Massachusetts governor, he expected to be warmly welcomed in recognition of his former great services to the colony. Nevertheless, he was not permitted to land because the authorities feared that they might thereby "condemn themselves for their former proceedings against Mr. Williams."

Roger Williams, one of the most forgiving men who ever lived, bore them no resentment. He could afford to overlook their ingratitude for he had already bypassed them. As he sailed quietly away home to Providence, he carried in his trunk very carefully a royal charter for Rhode Island, granted by King Charles II, establishing in that independent little colony "the first government in the world whose cornerstone was absolute religious liberty."

It is to this great statesman-prophet-preacher, Roger Williams of Rhode Island, that the principal credit belongs for the founding of the Baptist faith, essentially American in origin, as it is now organized throughout the world.

The Methodist faith came here from England, where John and Charles Wesley had founded it. The Lutheran faith came here via Holland and Sweden from Germany, where Martin Luther had set it up. Presbyterianism came to America largely from Scotland, whither John Knox had taken it after learning its Calvinism from John Calvin himself in Geneva.

But Roger Williams, so far as can be discovered, had worked out his faith almost alone, and reached his Baptist conclusions after entering this country. He has been called "the most provocative figure thrown up on the Massachusetts shores by the upheaval in England, the one original thinker among a number of capable social architects."

There had been reformers and forerunners of the faith in England and on the continent, like Hubmaier in Austria (who deserves a place alongside Luther, Calvin, and Zwingli), like Menno Simon in Holland, from whom came the Mennonites, and like the English divines, Smyth and Helwys. But these brave pioneers had only parts of the beliefs which Williams put together into a unified whole. They had other ideas also, which he rejected, such as the refusal to swear an oath in court and refusal to do military service. And there is no record of his having had any contact with them or their disciples. John Bunyan, the greatest English Baptist, was only a boy of ten when Williams founded Providence.

For his little church in the new City of Refuge Roger Williams did not insist on an iron-bound creed, but a few basic principles which Baptists still maintain today. Some of these are now held by other denominations, but the following exact combination of principles is held only by the Baptists, although today the denomination of the Disciples of Christ differs but slightly.

Williams had his Bible with him during his weeks in the wilderness, and very evidently read and pondered it much. Baptists are fond of saying that anyone who reads his Bible carefully is sure to become a Baptist. And they say, too, that they need no creed, since they find the Book a sufficient guide to conduct. At any rate, one cardinal Baptist tenet has always been:

(1) THE BIBLE IS THE SOLE RULE OF FAITH AND PRACTICE

Growing out of this is the second Baptist principle:

(2) ONLY BELIEVERS SHOULD BE BAPTIZED INTO CHURCH MEMBERSHIP

After baptism, the candidate is for the first time permitted to partake of the Lord's Supper, a simple crumb of bread and a sip of grape juice in commemoration of Jesus' last meal with his disciples. It is held that these two ordinances, both established by Christ himself, are sufficient. They are looked upon as symbols only however, symbols of religious truths, but of no efficacy in themselves. The reason why Baptists baptize only those "old enough to know their own minds,' refusing to baptize infants, is that in the 8th chapter of The Acts of the Apostles, when the Ethiopian was converted by Philip, the former said, "See, here is water: what doth hinder me to be baptized?"

And Philip replied: "If thou believest . . . thou mayest."

And the Baptists, following the Bible, insist that merely sprinkling water on the candidate, or pouring water over his head, is not what was done in Bible times. Only immersion will do, for the Greek word in the New Testament is *baptizo*, the word used for immersing a piece of cloth in dye. Furthermore, anything but immersion spoils the symbolism of the rite, for, as Paul maintains in his Epistle to the Romans 6:4, the little drama of baptism portrays death and burial to sin, and resurrection to a new life. As a matter of history, immersion was the custom of the whole Christian church until the eleventh century, when Pope Gregory VII decreed sprinkling to be the proper method.

There are varieties of immersion, both as to place and procedure. In country places a pond or river is used, preferably the latter, since Jesus himself was baptized by John the Baptist in the River Jordan. In cities, Baptist churches have large tanks, usually concealed under the floor of the pulpit platform, but sometimes behind the rostrum in a niche decorated to represent the Jordan River. Indeed, a small amount of water from that river, brought from Palestine in bottles, is sometimes poured into the waters of the baptistry, but that is rather "special."

Down the steps into the tank descends the robed candidate, to be met by the minister who, garbed in a robe over breast-high rubber boots, is already there. He guides the convert to the proper place in the tank, places one hand over the folded hands of the candidate and with his other hand takes a firm grip on the collar at the back of the neck. He then asks:

"Do you, Samuel Jones, take the Lord Jesus Christ as your personal Savior?"

"I do," is the answer.

"Upon this public profession of your faith, I now baptize you in the name of the Father, and of the Son, and of the Holy Ghost."

With the last word the minister tips the candidate backward until his face and body are completely submerged, then lifts him up again, wipes his face with a handkerchief, and guides him to the steps, where the deacons help him out, and blanket him. Thus, symbolically, he "dies to sin and is raised to newness of life." The formula varies somewhat, for the minister may change it at will. Some Baptist churches have practiced triune immersion, dipping once for each person in the Trinity. Usually a choir or quartet sings "Just as I am, without one plea," as the candidate enters the pool, and "Jesus, Lover of my soul," or some similar hymn as he emerges from the water. When all are baptized, the minister, still in the water, raises his hands, as in prayer, and quotes the Gospel of Luke 14:22:

"Lord, it is done as thou hast commanded, and yet there is room."

So, as a third principle of the Baptists, although they maintain that baptism is not requisite for salvation, they hold:

(3) BAPTISM SHOULD BE ONLY BY IMMERSION

The fourth principle, sometimes referred to as "the priesthood of the believer," is perhaps better stated:

(4) ALL SOULS HAVE DIRECT ACCESS TO GOD

This means that men may come in contact with God through prayer, meditation and Bible reading without needing any mediator, ritual, priest, or advocate.

Parallel to the independence of the believer is the independence of the individual church. Baptists have no bishops or official overseers. The local congregation "hires and fires" the minister, elects its own officers, and owns and administers all its property. Therefore, Baptists affirm:

(5) THE LOCAL CHURCH IS AN INDEPENDENT DEMOCRACY

The sixth and final principle which Baptists particularly emphasize, following Roger Williams, is:

(6) CHURCH AND STATE MUST BE KEPT SEPARATE

Williams had seen the evils of a state church in both England and New England. In Virginia, where the English state church still was in control a century after Williams, three Baptist ministers were arrested for preaching their faith. In defending them, Patrick Henry, the great orator, shouted in court:

"Good God! you are charging them with the awful crime of preaching the gospel of our Lord Jesus Christ!"

A little later, when the Constitution of the United States was drawn up and published, the Virginia Baptists noticed that it contained no guarantee of religious liberty. They agitated for such a guarantee and interested George Washington, James Madison and Thomas Jefferson in the project. The result was the first amendment to the Constitution, granting religious freedom.

Thus, out of the wintry wilderness meditations and Bible reading of Roger Williams, founder of the Baptist faith, came a great advance in human progress toward freedom and democracy.

These six great principles are often set before the thousands of Baptist congregations. What reward is offered to the faithful who keep them? Exactly what the Bible offers—salvation from sin, and eternal life. But the interpretation of both salvation and immortality differs greatly in various Baptist churches. Much latitude is allowed; the six principles demand it. There is a vast difference between the theology of a Fundamentalist Baptist preacher in the South and that of Dr. Harry Emerson Fosdick. Yet both hold unquestioned places in the Baptist fold.

Orthodox or liberal, Baptist churches usually follow this simple order of service. The congregation rises and sings the Doxology, "Praise God from Whom all blessings flow." Then comes the Invocation, in which the minister calls God's blessing on the meeting. Then he reads a passage of Scripture from the Bible, and makes a longer prayer. A hymn or anthem is sung. The sermon comes next and varies greatly in length. Some congregations demand forty-five minutes, but the trend is toward shorter discourses. The deacons are likely to remind the pastor that "No souls are saved after the first twenty minutes." After the sermon come the parish announcements, formerly a lengthy procedure, but now much shortened by the use of mimeographed sheets distributed before or after the service. Then the collection is taken up; there is a hymn, and finally the benediction. Some churches have more music, but modern congregations grow restless if the service lasts more than an hour.

As for discipline, since there is no set creed, Baptists have no written laws of conduct for members on such matters as gambling, drinking, smoking, card playing, dancing, and theater going. All these are usually frowned upon, however, and sermons are preached against them. There are great differences in discipline between city and country, south and north. In some localities tobacco is taboo; in others cuspidors are provided in all pews. The custom of attending the movies has rather upset the former taboo on theater going. Generally speaking, Baptist churches are much more lenient today than they were a generation or two ago.

A writer who remembers having been severely reproved for whistling on Sunday in his Baptist youth has lived to hear (and be rather shocked by) a large Baptist revival audience whistling lustily "When the roll is called up yonder."

For a century after the death of Roger Williams, the Baptists in this country were a small sect of misunderstood and persecuted outcasts whose ministers were frequently arrested for daring to preach their "peculiar" faith.

Today, however, the nearly eighteen million members of Baptist churches compose the largest Protestant denomination in America, boasting many leaders in education, industry, and public life. If the Baptists christened babes in arms and Sunday School children and counted them as members, as many churches do, they would probably nearly equal in number the Roman Catholics, usually reckoned our largest church.

As an indication of the way the once-despised Baptist church is growing throughout the world, it is a fact that during the year 1948, in Burma alone, 27,000 natives were immersed as a public testimony to their new-found Baptist faith. Among the seven and a half million Negro Baptists in the United States is the largest Protestant congregation in the world, the Abyssinian Baptist Church in Harlem, New York City, with 12,000 members.

What do these Baptists have that they have grown so great? The dramatic stories of typical Baptists provide the answer.

From Burma, for instance, came the true story of the intrepid Adoniram Judson and the three unusual women who loved him and shared his missionary adventures from Malden, Massachusetts, to Madras and Mandalay. Miss Ann Hasseltine of Bradford, Massachusetts, an attractive schoolteacher of twenty, was rather excited as she waited on table in her father's house, full of guests that day in 1810. It was an important meeting of Congregational churchmen to whom young Mr. Judson had just announced his great wish to go to the Far East as a missionary. She hovered near to anticipate any request for service the young man might make, but he seemed unaware of her marked interest. As she discovered later, he was actually then composing a flattering poem in her honor. There still exists the letter he wrote her father asking for her hand; it is something of a love classic in its way, for he wrote:

"I have now to ask whether you can consent to part with your daughter early next spring, to see her no more in this world; whether you can consent to her departure for a heathen land, and her subjection to . . . the dangers of the ocean, the fatal climate of India, to degradation, insult, persecution, and perhaps a violent death? . . ."

There was much more, and today it would seem far more likely to have received a negative answer rather than the consent which the conscientious suitor actually won. As a matter of fact, his apprehensions were mild compared with the reality which the young couple faced when they reached Burma after a trip of a year and a half.

Learning the difficult Burmese language was the first task. Mrs. Judson managed all the family affairs herself so that her husband could conserve his time and energy for studying the strange tongue; but because she had to pick up a few Burmese words and use them in her contacts with servants and shopkeepers, she actually learned the language before he did, to the surprise of both of them.

On board ship they had spent much time in Bible study, which led them to become Baptists, and so their little boy, born four years after they left home, was named Roger Williams Judson.

When war broke out with England, the Burmese promptly threw Mr. Judson into jail, saying that anyone who wore a hat must be an Englishman. Ann brought to the wretched prison clean linen and food for her husband, but the New England mince pie she lovingly concocted from buffalo meat and plantains so affected him emotionally that he had to give it to a fellow-prisoner. A lion was caged nearby, and when it died after days and nights of roaring, Ann Judson begged to have her husband transferred to the empty cage—it was cleaner and better. After much sickness and further imprisonment, the courageous couple began mission work in a new station, and Mrs. Judson was starting a girls' school during her husband's absence when she was stricken with fever and died, surrounded by weeping Burmans mourning "the White Mamma."

Eight years later, in 1834, Mr. Judson married Sarah Hall Boardman, the widow of another Burman missionary, who was a tower of strength in the work, for she spoke and wrote Burmese fluently, and translated hymns, a catechism, and part of Bunyan's *Pilgrim's Progress*. As with Ann Hasseltine, the hard work of the mission field broke down Sarah's strength, and she died in the harbor of the famous island of St. Helena on board the ship which was taking her home to recover her health.

Back in America on furlough, Judson read with interest a story written by Fanny Forrester in the *New York Mirror,* a magazine which was the forerunner of the love story publications of today, and expressed a wish to meet the writer.

Miss Forrester was undergoing the then (1845) novel operation called vaccination. Perhaps she had an extrasensory premonition that she would soon be traveling in the tropics! With his usual rather tactless directness, Mr. Judson rebuked her for wasting her literary talents writing magazine love stories.

Smarting from the irritation of both vaccination and re-proof, she replied rather shortly that her real name was plain Emily Chubbuck, that she wrote on light themes because she had to make a living, and as Fanny Forrester writing for the *Mirror,* she could at least eat.

Judson was delighted with her spirit and explained smil-ingly that he had been only leading up to a request that she write a biography, in fact, the life of his recently deceased second wife. And, with his usual direct action, he soon mar-ried her and took her to India.

So, just a year after Sarah Judson died, Emily Judson, while in the good ship *Faneuil Hall,* composed the very un-usual poem which she called "Lines Written Off St. Helena," ending:

> Blow, blow, ye gales! wild billows roll!
> Unfurl the canvas wide!
> O! where she labored lies our goal:
> Weak, timid, frail, yet would my soul
> Fain be to hers allied.

For three years Emily worked with her husband in Burma, near the old Moulmein pagoda; then bade him a last goodbye as, broken in health at last, he sailed for the home he never reached. She herself, sick unto death, soon followed him. Adoniram Judson and his three valiant wives literally gave themselves, body, mind, and soul, to plant the Baptist faith in the land of Burma, where now it flourishes.

When Ann Judson named her child Roger Williams Jud-son, she was commemorating a great Baptist leader, and so was Sarah Judson when she translated *Pilgrim's Progress* into Burmese. Nearly every American Baptist home places next to the Bible a copy of Bunyan's immortal classic, written by that Baptist hero for his fellow-prisoners in Bedford Jail. For twelve long years he was kept in that jail because every time he was freed, within a few hours he was preaching his Bap-tist faith to great crowds. And he said when the authorities urged him to give up his beliefs:

"I have determined, the Almighty God being my helper and shield, yet to suffer if frail life may continue so long, even till the moss shall grow on mine eyebrows, rather than thus to violate my faith and principles."

The list of Baptist martyrs is long, and we can mention but two or three. Balthasar Hubmaier, the noblest of the Swiss Baptists, was burned at the stake in Vienna in 1528. His brave wife stood near him in his last hour, urging him to remain firm until the end. Three days later, she was taken to the Danube and flung from a bridge into the river, a heavy stone tied round her neck. In England, the last execution for heresy was the burning at the stake of the Baptist Edward Wightman at Lichfield, in 1612.

In spite of these burnings, and the drownings which their enemies, with a malicious irony, referred to as "the third baptism," their numbers grew. The blood of the martyrs is the seed of the church, and by the light of burning heretics Christ's bleeding feet we track.

One reason why the Baptists are the largest of the denominations and are growing the fastest is that they have caught much of the spirit of the early disciples. There is a sort of divine urgency and a missionary earnestness about them. Whether one agrees with them or not, he must listen to them and respect their spirit and devotion. Their faith and optimism are sublime. The chain of Jessie Burrall Baptist Bible classes for young women has for its motto: "We specialize in the impossible!"

Another reason for Baptist growth is that this church has ever been the meeting-place of the common people. Like the Roman Catholics, the Baptists have two-thirds of their membership today in the lower economic stratum. Roger Williams was the son of a tailor; Bunyan was a tinker; and in any community in our country, many of the working people are Baptists.

A few years ago, when Dr. Green of Calvary Baptist Church in Washington, D. C., gave the right hand of fellowship into church membership to Charles Evans Hughes, Chief Justice of the Supreme Court, he gave it at the same time and in the same way to a humble but earnest laundryman. Said Dr. Green: "The ground is level at the foot of the cross."

THE DISCIPLES OF CHRIST

So much resembling the Baptists in doctrine and polity as to need only a brief historical explanation, the Disciples of Christ are often called the Campbellites after their founder, Thomas Campbell, a dynamic Irish Presbyterian of progressive views. Subsequent to his being censured by his western Pennsylvania Presbytery for preaching unorthodox doctrine, he withdrew and founded, with his son Alexander, the Christian Association of Washington, Pennsylvania. He did not wish to set up a new denomination; like many reformers, he wished only to restore the faith and polity of the original apostolic Christian Church.

His earnestness and simple faith drew many followers, and he soon had a big proposition on his hands. He tried to get the Pittsburgh Synod to take his group into fellowship, but in vain, for he kept insisting that neither the Calvinist Presbyterian creed nor any other should be required for church communion. He did get a working agreement with an association of Baptists, but after a few years that too failed. Afterward, about 1830, people called his followers simply Disciples of Christ, or just Christians. Other ministers and their followers who had left the Presbyterian and other churches because they found them too rigid had also adopted the name Christian. Many of these joined Campbell's growing church. Other "Christians" formed a separate denomination of that name which in 1931 united with the Congregationalists. Campbell himself preferred the name Disciples, and that is what his followers are called today. They grew rapidly, but in 1906 a conservative section split off and became the Churches of Christ, with over a million members now. The main body, still progressive and democratic, is almost two million today. There has been talk of a union with the Baptists, which is overdue, but a few minor matters still keep them apart.

17

THE LIBERAL CHURCHES
AND RELIGIOUS SOCIETIES

Universalists and Unitarians

THESE TWO denominations have long been considering the federal union recently accomplished. A joint Universalist-Unitarian Commission arranged a referendum and announced in the summer of 1953 that, with 84% of the accredited Universalist churches voting and 86% of the Unitarian, the former approved the proposed union by 79% and the latter by 94%. On August 21-24, 1953, at Andover, Mass. (famous for the "Andover Creed" called "the quintessence of New England Calvinism"), these two denominational protests against Calvinism approved the by-laws and authorized the necessary legal steps for their federal union, entitled "The Council of Liberal Churches (Universalist-Unitarian)."

The unification was long overdue, but New Englanders believe in long courtships, and liberals in theology are often conservatively cautious in everything else. Unitarians have had as their chief doctrinal emphasis since William Ellery Channing the belief, contrary to the Calvinist teaching of man's total depravity, that a spark, at least, of divinity exists in every man; and Universalists since John Murray have maintained, contrary to Calvin, that all mankind will eventually be saved since God is Love. Consequently, around Boston, where the two denominations have long occupied national headquarters opposite each other—Unitarians at 25 Beacon Street and Universalists at 16—both in the shadow of the golden-domed Massachusetts Statehouse, the observation has often been made that the two churches have been flirting long enough and should in all decency "get hitched."

The Universalists and Unitarians have been, for many

years, very close in theology, both groups having rejected long since not only belief in eternal punishment and in original sin and its corollary, total depravity, but also in the doctrine of the Trinity—that God is three persons in one: Father, Son, and Holy Spirit. That rejection of belief in the Trinity gave the Unitarians their name when early in the nineteenth century the Pilgrim-Puritan Congregationalists split on the issue into the Trinitarian Congregationalists and Unitarian Congregationalists. The former kept the second word of the name and are now known as The Congregationalists, and the latter retained the first part of theirs and formed in Boston The American Unitarian Association on May 25, 1825, the very day on which, unknown to the Americans, The British and Foreign Unitarian Association was formed in England, by a liberal group there unaware of the Boston movement. It was one of the most surprising of historical coincidences.

Disbelief in the Trinity was what the Trinitarians called it, but to the Unitarians it was a return to monotheism (belief in one God the Father Almighty) which they considered was the faith of the early church, for the doctrine of the Holy Trinity is nowhere stated in the oldest and best Greek manuscripts of the Bible. It is true that the King James Version of I John 5:7 states: "For there are three that bear record in heaven, the Father, the Word, and the Holy Ghost: and these three are one." Together with the first chapter of John's Gospel, where Jesus, although not mentioned by name, is obviously identified as "the Word," that verse gives Biblical testimony to the doctrine of the Trinity. But the "heavenly witnesses" verse is not in modern revised versions of the original Greek New Testament. It was not in the first or second editions of Erasmus' famous Greek-Latin translation in the early sixteenth century. But he put it into the third edition, as he had promised to do if anyone would show him a Greek manuscript containing it. The one they showed him was a sixteenth century copy, but he kept his word, against his own better scholarly judgment. The King James translators used the third Erasmian edition, and the "heavenly witnesses" remained in edition after edition until the English revisers in 1881, and subsequent translators, had the moral courage to remove the verse.

Trinitarians today base their belief either on the Latin translations of the Greek text, such as Jerome's Vulgate, which contain the heavenly witnesses, or on inferential evidence by combining several passages which, taken together, apparently imply the doctrine of the Trinity; or, as another type of evidence, Trinitarians fall back on ecclesiastical tradition.

To modern Unitarians and Universalists, however, the old Trinity-Unity debate is thrice-threshed straw. The issue with them is no longer whether God is Three Persons in One God-head or just one indivisible God, but whether either such a mathematical or metaphysical deity exists at all! The issue is Theism vs. Humanism, as will be further explained in the discussion of Humanists later in this chapter.

The Universalists (a name abbreviated from the clumsy term, Universal Salvationists) had been more or less organized and functioning in local groups in Germany, England, and Scotland in the 17th and early 18th centuries, and their echoes had been heard in America. But the organization of the first Universalist societies in this country must be credited to the intrepid John Murray, a convert of James Relly in London, in turn a convert of Whitefield, the Calvinistic Methodist revivalist. Relly had developed the idea of "finished salvation" in Christ, which really amounted to universal salvation, and he and Murray were therefore outcasts from Whitefield's Connexion. (See Chapter 18, The Methodists, p. 197)

Murray migrated to America in 1770, and then occurred another of those coincidences which make religious history so interesting and tend to confirm belief in Providence. He had expected to land in New York, but the ship, storm-driven, ran aground on the New Jersey coast. Left in charge of the part of the cargo beached to lighten the ship, Murray visited a nearby small village named Good Luck, founded by Thomas Potter, by then an old man, who had been waiting for the Lord to send him a preacher for the meeting-house he had built. Obviously Murray, whatever his theology, was God-sent. September 30, 1770, is the date on the boulder marking the preacher's first sermon in America. In 1774 he settled in Gloucester, Mass., where there were Rellyites already, and they drew up in 1779 a covenant for the first American Universalist organized church. Articles of Faith and a plan of church government, drawn up in Philadelphia in 1790 by the followers of Elhanan Winchester, known at first as Universal Baptists, were adopted by Murray and his group in 1791.

In 1803 thirty-eight New England Universalist churches held a convention in Winchester, New Hampshire, and approved the Winchester Profession, still used today, which affirmed belief in the Bible, "one God whose nature is Love," and in final restoration of "the whole family of mankind to holiness and happiness."

Murray was a Trinitarian, but with the vigorous leadership from 1800 to 1850 of Hosea Ballou, who flatly rejected the deity of Christ, the movement became Unitarian, although the Unitarians, particularly Channing, objected to some of Ballou's other ideas.

It was Channing who had most to do with formulating the early theology of Unitarianism in this country, but he owed much to his predecessors. The three Johns—Biddle, Milton, and Locke—together with Joseph Priestly and Thomas Belsham—had already spread rather widely in England the principles of Unitarianism, or Socinianism, as it was often called, after the 16th century Italian reformers, Lelius and Faustus Socinus, who had taught that "The essence of God is one, not in kind but in number."

Priestly, the great scientist who discovered oxygen, which he called "dephlogisticated air," brought Unitarianism with him in 1794 when he came to America, and established The First Unitarian Church of Philadelphia in 1796. King's Chapel, Boston, under James Freeman, had in 1785 deleted all traces of Trinitarianism from its Episcopalian liturgy, and the induction of the very liberal Henry Ware as Professor of Divinity at Harvard College in 1805 indicated that the growing Unitarian wing of Congregationalism had captured a key position. The Trinitarians retaliated by establishing Andover Theological Seminary, where every professor had to sign the famous Andover Creed, a theological Loyalty Oath so heresy-tight it would make present-day deviation hunters envious.

By the time Channing preached his famous sermon at the ordination of Jared Sparks in the Unitarian Church in Baltimore in 1819, the movement of protest against Calvinism had reached the stage of development where it needed a positive and constructive declaration of faith, and that was what Channing supplied, then and for some time thereafter. He defined his "one sublime idea" as "the greatness of the soul, its divinity, its union with God by spiritual likeness, its receptivity of his Spirit, its self-forming power, its destination to ineffable glory, its immortality." He was more convinced that man's rational nature came from God than that any book did, so he found the final authority in reason and conscience.

This sort of religion was, of course, pretty close to what might be termed Proto-Humanism, with a few gestures toward Theism. But Channing still held on to a few orthodox tenets, such as belief in Christ's miracles and even his pre-existence; and modern Unitarianism, having passed through its Emerson, Theodore Parker, Minot Savage, and Charles W. Eliot stages has broadened and deepened considerably since Channing.

Never a very numerous denomination, it has made up in quality for any lack in quantity, having a thousand times as many representatives in the Hall of Fame at New York University and in *Who's Who in America* as it is numerically entitled to. Of late, however, Unitarians have sufficiently overcome their apathy toward missionary activity to establish group fellowships in outposts of liberalism—over a hundred in the last four years—and a Church of the Larger Fellowship, with rather surprising results in expansion. From 61,600 in

1941 they have increased to 88,420 in 1953. With the 75,982 Universalists the new merger starts with 164,402 adult members.

There has also been a change in the distribution of Unitarians, for whereas once there was some considerable truth in the allegation that they claimed to believe in "The Fatherhood of God, the Brotherhood of Man, the Leadership of Jesus, Salvation by Character, and the Progress of Mankind Onward and Upward Forever," but really believed only in "The Fatherhood of God, the Brotherhood of Man and the Neighborhood of Boston," neither of those attributed creeds is now accepted by Unitarians.

In the first place, they have no official creed whatever, and theists who personally believe the first phrase, the Fatherhood of God, and humanists who do not, work together in the same denomination and the same local church to help bring in the Brotherhood of Man and the Progress of Mankind, although the latter may not be as automatic and inevitable as earlier more optimistic liberals had expected. And the Unitarian advance has spread far beyond the Neighborhood of Boston, geographically and theologically. Of the 115 new fellowships, only two are in New England, seven are in Texas, and seventeen in California. The Western Unitarian Conference, with headquarters in Chicago, has always been more leftish in theology than the national organization, and the majority of its ministers are now Humanists in religion.

The National (formerly Federal) Council of the Churches of Christ in the United States of America, comprising nearly thirty-four million of the fifty-two million Protestants in the United States, excludes Unitarians and Universalists from membership. So does the World Council of Churches, representing one hundred and fifty denominational bodies, Protestant and Orthodox, which had its first Assembly at Amsterdam, Holland, in 1948. Why? Because both these "councils" are preponderantly "orthodox" in the sense that the churches represented hold that all "right thinking" people calling themselves Christians must believe in such doctrines as Christ's vicarious atonement for man's sin by his death on the cross, his deity, the Holy Trinity, the inspiration of the Bible, the just retribution for sin, and some sort of personal immortality. It is doubtful if these doctrines are by either Council held to be all of equal importance. The first seems to be considered the crucial one, and Universalist-Unitarians certainly do not believe in that one.

Unitarians cannot imagine Jesus Christ barring from any church or fellowship of churches anyone who "accepts his name and sign," as their president, Dr. F. W. Eliot, has said. And another Unitarian has condemned the kind of liberals who "give the creeds an interpretation which historically is dishonest, and with tongue in cheek link themselves with orthodox and traditional Christianity to 'get in on the big game' and be on the popular side."

One can understand the embarrassing position of the National Council officials, however, one of whom is reported to have said that if either of the "Unies" were admitted, the Lutherans would stay out. Inasmuch as there are over six million Lutherans in the United States and only 164,402 Universalist-Unitarians, the answer is obvious.

Unitarians and Universalist lay-people have not been very much disturbed by their exclusion from the Councils, as most of them are more interested in practical social-service work locally and in national and international social reform movements than they are in theology. The splendid international work of the Unitarian Service Committee in recent years, especially the sending of teams of physicians and surgeons abroad to bring knowledge of the latest techniques to doctors in less developed areas, seems to most liberals to be one modern interpretation of Christianity, carrying out the spirit of the healing miracles of Jesus.

Because of their interest in democracy and social progress, Unitarians have considered it a duty to take an active interest in political issues. Out of the thirty-four Presidents of the United States, five have been Unitarians (Jefferson, the two Adamses, Fillmore, and Taft); and Washington and Lincoln, known as Deist and Freethinker respectively, were closer to Unitarianism in belief than to any orthodox church. And Adlai Stevenson, long an active Unitarian, got a few million votes in the 1952 Presidential election from Christians whom he surprised by his knowledge and admiration of the Bible. He is a splendid example of the average Unitarian—intelligent, socially conscious and informed, humor-loving, and literate.

When the new federal union of Universalists, who believe in salvation by love, and Unitarians, who emphasize reason in religion, begins functioning smoothly, it will be well worth the attention of all students of religion.

ETHICAL CULTURISTS

The American Ethical Union, of about 5,000 members, composed of twelve Ethical Societies, from New York (the parent society) to Los Angeles, has many of the emphases of the Unitarians just mentioned, in particular, the intellectualism, the insistence upon moral character above theology, the absence of an official creed, the stress on education, and a large engagement in social service and reforms. In fact, in many communities the local Unitarians and Ethicalists work together for the same ends and greatly resemble each other.

Historically, as well as to a large extent ideologically, Ethical Culture lies midway between Unitarianism and

Humanism. The Amercan Unitarian Association was founded in 1825, The First Humanist Society of New York in 1929, and the Society for Ethical Culture in the City of New York halfway between, in 1876. Its original and general character are closely associated with Felix Adler.

Born in Germany in 1851, emigrating to America with his rabbi father in 1857, Adler was graduated from Columbia University at the age of nineteen, went back to Berlin and Heidelberg for graduate work, and was Professor of Hebrew and Oriental Languages at Cornell at the incredibly early age of twenty-three. Two years later he founded the New York Ethical Society, disappointing his family, who had expected him to enter the rabbinate. He had little use for the formalism and ancient theology of orthodox Judaism.

In Germany he had come in contact with the teachings of the philosopher, Immanuel Kant, and was so deeply impressed that even today a knowledge of the Kantian philosophy is very helpful in understanding the lectures of the older Ethical leaders.

There was more than Kantianism, however, in the back of Adler's young mind when he founded, to use his own words, "among men of my own age, or nearly my own age (24 years, 9 mos.) a little society, which we ambitiously called a Union for the Higher Life, based upon three tacit assumptions: sex purity, the principle of devoting the surplus of one's income beyond that required for one's own genuine needs to the elevation of the working classes, and, finally, continued intellectual development."

Another account states that "At the urgent request of a number of persons who had become acquainted with his point of view, which assigned the supreme place to right conduct and proclaimed that the good life is not necessarily dependent upon theological beliefs, he inaugurated, in 1876, the New York Society for Ethical Culture, which soon counted considerably over a thousand members. 'Deed, not Creed' was his motto."

A number of wealthy men were glad to back young Adler's movement financially, and soon it began spreading to the larger cities. These local societies were federated into the American Ethical Union and by 1906 an International Conference was formed with the announced object: "To assert the supreme importance of the ethical factor in all the relations of life, personal, social, national and international, apart from any theological or metaphysical considerations."

The movement had spread to England by 1888, and thirty societies were formed there. The English meetings are more like a church service than are those in America, but the latter are more so than they were, although the Sunday Morning addresses, as in most Unitarian churches, are more like lectures than sermons. There is a great variety in the different societies, some with very simple programs, others with an almost liturgical quality. The music is usually of a higher grade, artistically, than that in most churches. There may be hymn-singing; the Christian visitor will recognize the tunes, but not the words, and may be shocked at the alterations. Prayers will be conspicuous by their absence, but there may be a Silence for Meditation, and there will probably be a reading of inspirational scripture, but not always from the Judeo-Christian sacred writings, as the Bible may be called. In some foreign societies, meeting weekdays, there is simply a lecture followed by a discussion. In any meeting one is apt to hear Felix Adler's version of the Golden Rule quoted: "So act as to elicit the best in others, and you will thereby release the best that is in yourself."

The very progressive Ethical Culture schools are world famous. Adler established the first free kindergarten in New York, and helped establish the Workingmen's School and the Manhattan Trade School for Girls. In 1883 he founded the first Child Study society in this country, and was for many years the chairman of the National Child Labor Committee. Samuel Gompers was one of the earliest members of the Ethical Society of New York.

The characteristic Ethical Culture emphasis on the pragmatic rather than the metaphysical is illustrated by the story told of Dr. Abraham Jacobi, the great pediatrician. A mother had lost her child and was bewailing God's cruelty in thus bereaving her. Said Jacobi, with surgical kindness, "Don't blame God, madam. It was dirty milk."

THE HUMANISTS

The question of what is the difference if any between Ethical Culture and Humanism is often asked. The answer is that once there was a vital difference, but now it has largely disappeared. The First Humanist Society of New York was founded in 1929, four years before Dr. Adler's death; and he and Dr. Alfred W. Martin, his immediate successor, were not Humanists and not favorably impressed with its philosophy. This was a natural attitude, for Adler and his contemporary disciples were Ethical Idealists, and Ethical Idealism is an absolutist (nonrelative) philosophy, while Humanism is empiricist in its philosophy, ever seeking new truth by experiment and observation. Dr. Adler believed in an ultimate reality in or behind or above our human finite experience. For him this ultimate reality, infinite, absolute and eternal, was a sublime moral order, a sort of spiritual universe, already perfect and complete, attracting upward to itself the moral and ethical in us. Catholics and followers of Spinoza are also on the absolutist side of the fence: for Catholics the ultimate reality is a personal God; for Spinozists it is a mathematical universe. For Adler it was a moral order, absolute and eternally the same.

The Humanist, in line with the empiricism of modern natural science, accepts the tentative character of all knowledge, ceases to seek certainty, and, as Dr. E.A. Burtt, Professor of Philosophy at Cornell, states on page 467 in *Types of Religious Philosophy*, "is satisfied instead with the prospect of the progressive correction of knowledge through continued inquiry and novel discovery." The Humanist believes in moral obligation, but to him it is a social ideal, rather than dutiful obedience to an ultimate law, whether that absolute law has been revealed to or by Moses, Maimonides, Spinoza, or Adler; or whether, by another apostolic succession, the alleged absolute gospel once and for all delivered to the saints has come down through Paul, Augustine, Calvin, and Jonathan Edwards. The Humanist recognizes the attraction of the "absolute" in philosophy and religion; it has all the seductiveness of the idea of complete "social security" in an economic system; but he knows that any absolute prevents the free pursuit of empiric science in any field, and that he cannot have freedom who chooses security. Therefore he prefers to continue to take chances on human intelligence, roving and experimental, mistakes and all, rather than trust the most beautifully decorated and widely honored religious tradition which has anything or anybody ultimate or absolute concealed therein.

Dr. Adler had come a long way from the faith of his fathers, and must certainly be honored for his splendid contribution to religious and social progress. But he had not come quite so far as he and his followers long believed; for his ultimate reality, his absolute moral law or order, was only his father's Torah, the Divine Law, handed down by Yahweh to Mosheh on the Mount, the eternal unchangeable Torah, sublimated in Adler's Ethical Idealism into a mystic ineffable infinite Moral Order.

The great man has been gone only twenty years, but the Humanism he distrusted is now the accepted philosophy and religion of the majority of Ethical Culture "Leaders," as their ministers are termed. And although Ethicalism has no creed, it does have trends and emphases, and the trend may certainly be said to have swung away from the absolutist philosophy of Adler's day, still held by some Ethicalists, toward the empiricism of Humanism since in August 1952 there was held in Amsterdam, Holland, the First International Congress on Humanism and Ethical Culture.

Delegates were present from The American Humanist Association, The American Ethical Union, The English Ethical Union, The Humanist Association of Holland, and the Vienna Ethical Society, as well as representatives from The First Humanist Society of New York, the Belgian Humanist Association, two Humanist groups each from Holland and India, and one from Germany. Greetings were read from The Chinese Humanist Association in Formosa. And on August 26 this international assembly officially established The International Humanist and Ethical Union "in response to the widespread demand for an alternative to the religions which claim to be based on revelation on the one hand and to totalitarian systems on the other . . . Ethical Humanism unites all those who cannot any longer believe the various creeds and are willing to base their convictions on respect for man as a spiritual and moral being. The fundamentals of modern, ethical Humanism are as follows:

"1. It is democratic. . . .
"2. It seeks to use science creatively, not destructively. . . .
"3. Humanism is ethical. It affirms the dignity of man and the right of the individual to the greatest possible freedom of development compatible with the rights of others. . . .
"4. It insists that personal liberty is an end that must be combined with social responsibility in order that it shall not be sacrificed to the improvement of material conditions. . . .
"5. It is a way of life, aiming at the maximum possible fulfillment through the cultivation of ethical and creative living. . . ."

The Presidential Address by Julian Huxley, printed in full in the Ethical Culture *Standard* and the Humanist bi-monthly, *The Humanist* in the 1952 fall issues, is a remarkably cogent and complete presentation of the religion of Humanism. Huxley stresses the fact that Humanism is a new religion, and forever answers those who call it merely a philosophy, defining religion, whether theistic or non-theistic, as "an organized system of ideas and emotion which relates man to his destiny."

Dr. Huxley especially emphasized the fact that a new recognition of the importance of religion "has emerged from the comparative study of religions, that new branch of anthropological science which has done so much in the last fifty years to clarify our understanding of the role that religion has actually played in human life."

The Humanist movement in America had its rise, however, among Unitarian ministers, of whom probably half the five hundred are now Humanists, at least to a considerable extent, although even thirty-five years ago there were not more than four or five. Yet the advent of Humanism in Unitarianism was almost inevitable. Dean Sperry of Harvard Divinity School once said something to the effect that the logical evolution of Christianity was toward Protestantism, of Protestantism toward Unitarianism, and of Unitarianism toward Humanism. Certainly Channing laid the foundation for it.

Dr. John Dietrich of Minneapolis and Dr. Curtis Reese of Chicago in 1919 and 1920 preached at Unitarian conferences sermons which brought a latent Humanism to the surface and into public attention. It was at once attacked by the Theists in the denomination, but gained adherents among both clergy and laity. The First Humanist Society of New York was founded on September 29, 1929. Its purposes, principles, and activities, including the Humanistic new type weddings, funerals, and recognition services, are described in *Humanism, A New Religion* (Simon & Schuster, 1930); *Humanizing Religion* (Harper & Bros., 1933); and in more detail in *The Preacher and I* (Crown Publishers, 1951).

The historic Humanist Manifesto appeared in the spring of 1933 in the magazine, *The New Humanist* (now *The Humanist* edited by Dr. E.H. Wilson), under the auspices of the American Humanist Association, whose headquarters are now in Yellow Springs, Ohio, where copies of the Manifesto are available. It set forth the principles of Humanism as then conceived by the thirty-four signers, including eleven eminent college professors and fourteen Unitarian ministers, as well as two Ethical Culturists, one Universalist and one liberal rabbi.

The movement has been spreading quietly but rapidly, especially in colleges. One university philosophy faculty of twenty members is reported by one of its number to be all Humanists. Among the signers of the 1933 Manifesto were Harry Elmer Barnes, Edwin Arthur Burtt, John Herman Randall, Jr., Roy Wood Sellars, and John Dewey. On the Advisory Board of The First Humanist Society, besides the professors just mentioned, are Will Durant, Thomas Mann, Albert Einstein, and Julian Huxley.

In a book, *Religion and Our Divided Denominations* published in 1945 by Harvard University Press, Dean Sperry, the editor, gave one chapter each to the four divisions of American Religion—Roman Catholicism, Protestantism, Judaism, and Humanism; and in his Introduction he quotes Bishop Barry of England as having said that "fifty per cent of the intelligent people of the modern world are humanists." That is, of course, an exaggeration, and Dean Sperry points out that these persons are "ecclesiastically unorganized," but he adds that they "deserve recognition." With several national organizations now, and the international one, that defect is being somewhat remedied.

But it must be remembered that the more liberal a faith is, the harder it is to get people to join it, as Unitarian, Universalist, and Ethical Culture leaders have long since discovered. By the time a man arrives at the Humanist position, he is often so independent he thinks he needs no society or organization. There are indications, however, that the scattered and overly independent Humanists are beginning to feel the need of organization, for local chapters of the American Humanist Association are springing up in various cities of the United States and Canada.

THE FRIENDS

The Friends, or Quakers, have always sponsored many apparently conflicting ideas and attitudes. They are mystics, yet among the most active religionists. They have at times been extremely conservative, but are reckoned among the liberals in religion. They are widely known as pacifists, yet they are patriotic; and there are no more valiant fighters for freedom, and for peace which they consider essential to true freedom. They have been among the most protesting of Protestants, yet their mysticism in Quaker Meetings is nearer the Catholic type of worship than the Protestant service which features the sermon. They are among the most openminded to scientific discoveries, but they are also hospitable to the intuitions of the heart.

In the middle of the seventeenth century when the movement started, the Quakers were looked upon somewhat as the Jehovah's Witnesses are now regarded in certain quarters, and were persecuted even more, times being what they were. Their founder, George Fox, one of the world's great prophets, was six years in jail. His followers were whipped, tortured, and had their ears cut off. Between 1650 and 1689 no fewer than fifteen thousand Quakers suffered death for their faith.

They received this treatment from the authorities because they were considered dangerous revolutionaries, "the extreme left wing of the English Reformation." In both England and America, people who helped or harbored them were severely punished for collaborating in heresy and treason, for heresy is treason when church and state are united. In spite of persecution, the Quakers refused to recognize the authority either of church or of state. They would have nothing to do with church ceremonies and ritual, would not recite the creed, and even refused to attend church. They would not pay taxes used to support state-paid clergy who officiated in the "steeple-houses," the Quaker term for churches. They wore broad-brimmed hats which they refused to doff before anyone, woman, magistrate, clergyman, or king.

The reason for all this apparently rather eccentric obstinacy and recalcitrance was not that the Quakers had an anarchic opposition to any and all authority: it was simply that they recognized what they considered a higher authority, higher than either church or state. For this authority they had several names—"The Seed of the Kingdom," "The Spirit," "That of God in every man," "The Christ Within," and "The Inward Light," the last evidently from John 1:9, ". . . the true light, which lighteth every man that cometh into the world."

It is a misunderstanding of Quaker doctrine, however, to identify this inner light solely with the individual conscience, for although the conscience is obviously involved, there is much more to the process than the functioning of the moral consciousness of the individual. This is a group experience. The light comes when the Friends hold a "Quaker Meeting," sitting in silence and waiting "with one accord and in one place," like the early disciples of Christ at Pentecost. For the Friends are Pentecostalists of a sort, but not of the evangelistic Fundamentalist type. There is no glossolalia, or speaking with tongues, in a Quaker Meeting. There may be no speaking at all, just a quiet waiting period, and then an equally quiet dispersal to their homes, but with a sweet satisfaction of having been present at a deeply religious service of mystic inspiration. One Quaker scholar has called the Inward Light ". . . the Divine Presence in the midst of the worshiping group." The Presence "unites all the members into a single organic whole, the body of Christ." Not only does the worshiping individual feel himself united with an invisible Presence; he also experiences a mystical oneness with all the other worshipers.

At such exalted moments the Friends, without wine or wafer, are in communion with God and one another. They have been called ". . . neither Catholic nor Protestant, but a third form of Christianity." It may well be added that in their mysticism they are also close kin with Vedantists, Zen Buddhists, Taoists, Theosophists, and all who meditate on the Divine Love and Wisdom.

When George Fox at the tender age of twenty-three, in the year 1647, made his great personal discovery of the "Christ Within" by a mystic series of events which he called "experimental," and then began telling others about it only to find that they had had like experiences, he had no plans for establishing a religion or founding a sect, but thought only of restoring Christianity to its original form. That has been the impulse and hope of such other varied reformers as Luther, Calvin, Wesley, John Robinson, Joseph Smith, and Mary Baker Eddy. But they all, including Fox, ended up with another denomination.

The Separatists and the Seekers of seventeenth-century England became the Pilgrims and the Baptists and the

Quakers. They were all persecuted and they all grew. Individuals suffered and died, but every decade the faith waxed stronger. All three faiths crossed the Atlantic and sooner or later grew to power. Persecution died out in the freer air of the New World and the exiled and outlawed became respectable and prosperous.

The Quakers were welcomed to Rhode Island by the Baptists and soon shared in the control of that colony. They bought New Jersey in 1674 and colonized it. Seven years later William Penn was given Pennsylvania and set up such a liberal government that for seventy-five years it thrived under the rule of the Friends. In the eighteenth century they freed their slaves and thereafter worked toward the liberation of all slaves. In the next century they split over several issues, and today there are still nine kinds of Friends listed in the *Yearbook of American Churches,* but reunion is in the air. Groups formerly separated by doctrinal or sectional differences are now working together.

The Quaker Meetings have also changed. Whereas formerly there was no program and no leader but the inner light, and no one spoke save as the spirit moved him, now a chairman sometimes helps "the sense of the meeting" to emerge more rapidly. In many places there has been a more radical change to a regular Protestant-type service of worship. These congregations, called Friends Churches rather than Societies of Friends as formerly, employ professional ministers. In all Quaker groups, education and philanthropy are emphasized.

Traditionally the Friends have been objectors to war since the days of Fox, but their pacifism has been misunderstood. They refuse to fight, not only because Jesus bade men turn the other cheek and because they know that war solves no problems, but primarily because they would lose their treasured Quaker inner serenity of mind. Even in regard to war the Friends have modified their previous practice. Just as they long ago abandoned their plain gray garb and now dress like others of their station in life, and also as they have, for the most part, gradually dropped the use of "thee" for "you," so they have ceased disciplining men who enlist for military service, and now permit them freedom of choice. In World War II there were eight thousand Friends in the armed forces, besides those in non-combat and civilian service.

These various changes, however, should not be interpreted to mean that they have forsaken the leading of the Inward Light, for the "sense of the meeting" may be different in one generation from what it was the generation before. In one century conditions were not right for the abolition of slavery; in the next century, they were. John Greenleaf Whittier, John Woolman, and Lucretia Mott knew what to do in their day; and Rufus Jones knew in 1917 that it was his duty, mystic though he was, to help found and head the American Friends Service Committee. That exceptionally effective relief and reconstruction agency has served not only in war, famine, and disaster emergencies, but has organized work camps for college students and undertaken wide-range promotion of institutes to promote peace and international understanding.

In other words, the modern Quakers are most intelligently and devotedly implementing their mysticism. But they still commune in quiet meetings to renew their spiritual strength, knowing that ordered peace cannot come to the world until it dwells in the hearts of men. The 113,000 Friends in this country and the 45,000 abroad are diligently seeking for both kinds of peace.

18

THE METHODISTS

The Church of Evangelism

WHEN THE LITTLE GIRL baby had been duly christened Susannah Annesley, one of the parishioners filing out of the little English church asked just how many children, counting this one, Dr. Annesley had now. Dr. Manton, who just baptized the infant, said dryly,

"I believe it is two dozen—or a quarter of a hundred."

If the Reverend Doctor Annesley had been content with an even two dozen, there might never have been a Methodist church, for this twenty-fifth one, little Susannah, grew up to marry Samuel Wesley and bear him nineteen children, of whom the fifteenth was John and the eighteenth, Charles, the two evangelists who preached and sang into the heart of England the Methodist revival which was to sweep the world. "The mother of the Wesleys was the mother of Methodism."

Not only was Susannah Wesley one of the greatest women in religious history; she belongs among the outstanding individuals of the human race, male or female. Dr. Adam Clarke, the great Bible scholar, wrote of her:

"Such a woman, take her all in all, I have not heard of, I have not read of, nor with her equal have I been acquainted."

She had neither money nor clothes, and she knew only too well what hard work meant and scanty fare, but she was such an unusual combination of natural beauty, keen intellect, and strong moral character that she stood out in any company.

She was not only master of Greek, Latin, and French, but the pure English prose of her letters matches that of any of the great writers of her day. Girls then did not study theology, but she did avidly and with such effect that by the time she was thirteen she argued her clergyman father to a standstill and left his Church of the Dissenters to join the Church of England.

Because of her station in life and her day in history she had to do her work through her children. With foresight and patience, she trained them deliberately and even ruthlessly for their great task, especially John, of whom she wrote to his father: "I do intend to be more particularly careful of the soul of this child."

That sentence meant more than it seems to, and the Reverend Samuel Wesley caught the overtones his wife intended. Actually there came very near not being any John Wesley at all, because of a quarrel between his parents over, of all things, family prayers! But other family matters led up to the disagreement.

The Rev. Samuel Wesley had been having what his neighbors would have called a streak of bad luck; he termed it a series of "acts of God." His harvest failed; his barn fell; his cows were mutilated by enemy hands. But what troubled him most was the strange and rather expensive custom his otherwise sane wife had of presenting him too frequently with another child. When twins came, making thirteen children, it was just too much; so he wrote the Archbishop of York, telling of his afflictions, and complaining sarcastically about Susannah:

"Last night my wife brought me a few children. There are but two yet, a boy and a girl, and I think they are all at present: we have had four in two years and a day."

Samuel blamed it all on Susannah and the unfathomable acts of God, but when he got her with child again before that same year of the twins was over, she was more than ripe for rebellion.

The occasion came one evening in the Epworth parsonage when Samuel repeated the set form of prayer and came to the usual petition for the welfare of the king. She failed to respond with "Amen," as she had to the previous petitions. There was silence, prolonged and ominous. The astonished Samuel rose from his knees and demanded the reason for her silence. She said she did not consider the Hanoverian King William III was the rightful king of England.

"Sukey," said he in a temper, "if we are to have two kings, we must have two beds," and waited for her to give in. But she would not budge an inch from her decision, and he stormed away to London. Two beds it would be. Her punishment was probably not too hard to bear.

It was Samuel who finally gave in, and came back to her, his face saved by the death of King William who fell from his horse and broke his neck. He was succeeded by Queen

Anne whom the prodigal Samuel knew would be acceptable to Susannah. Indeed the baby she had been carrying was very appropriately named Anne when it arrived.

In less than a year after the birth of little Anne, another baby came, the child of the reconciliation, born June 17, 1703, and named John. Was it his father or his mother who gave him, alone of all their babies, a middle name? For he was christened John Benjamin perhaps as a sort of wishful suggestion that this child might be the last, as the Biblical Benjamin was the last of the patriarch Jacob's children.

But it didn't work; they kept coming. Charles, destined to be the great hymn-writer of Methodism, was the eighteenth; and Susannah was carrying still another, her nineteenth and last, when the famous February fire of 1709 wiped out the Epworth rectory. She managed, although too heavy to climb out the windows, to "wade through the fire, which did me no further harm than a little scorching of my hands and face."

All were apparently saved, when John was missed. His father tried to climb the stairs to the room where the five-year-old slept, but the blazing staircase fell, and Samuel struggled forth into the air to pray for the soul of his doomed son. The neighbors, however, seeing the child at the window, rescued him by forming a human pyramid. Even after, his mother referred to him as "a brand plucked from the burning," a phrase which he later adopted and used for the purpose of reminding himself that God had evidently saved him for some special high destiny.

Susannah Wesley minded most the interruption of the program she had laid out for her children, but she soon had them back in their routine in the partly restored parsonage. To be sure, she also managed all the affairs of the family, inside and outside the house, except in her husband's study. But her glory was in her own original plan of education for the souls, minds, and bodies of her children.

Methodical means "arranged in order and system," and methodical was her pedagogy. It is commonly said that the Methodists were thus nicknamed from the overly methodical habits and discipline enforced on the members of the Holy Club in Oxford some years later by John and Charles Wesley, but it was Susannah's idea which they were carrying out.

For the first three months Susannah's infants were permitted all the sleep they wanted, but at three months their daytime slumbers were limited to three hours in the morning and three in the afternoon, an allowance gradually reduced to no daylight sleep.

"When turned a year old, and some before," Mrs. Wesley later revealed her method, "they were taught to fear the rod, and to cry softly, by which means they escaped abundance of correction which they might otherwise have had; and that most odious noise of the crying of children was rarely heard in the house: but the family usually lived in as much quietness as if there had not been a child among them."

She believed that unless the will of the child was subordinated to that of the parents, their "percept and example will be ineffectual" and that therefore the child should be "governed by the reason and piety of its parents until its own have taken root and matured."

No eating between meals. No being put to bed. All marched quietly to bed at eight o'clock. If a child did wrong, but confessed, he was not punished. Girls must learn to read well before they were taught to sew. The contrary custom "is the very reason why so few women can read in a manner fit to be heard."

The big day, toward which the child looked forward as to an exciting Christmas, was the day on which he was five years old and was permitted to begin his literary education. On that day he spent six hours, from nine to twelve and from two to five, alone with his mother to learn the alphabet perfectly.

"Each of them did in that time know all its letters, great and small, except Molly and Nancy, who were a day and a half before they knew them perfectly; for which I thought them very dull."

The six hours' schooling a day was continued for five years. The day after they learned the alphabet, they started reading by spelling out the first chapter of Genesis, and all were good readers by the time they were six. She taught them languages: Hetty was fluent in Greek at the age of eight. By the time they were ten the boys were ready for "prep school" and were surprised to find themselves already as familiar with Greek and Latin as some of their teachers. The girls, when ten, helped their mother with the teaching and the housework.

Young John fitted into the system perfectly. He was quiet, studious, thoughtful. When he was but a tot and his mother offered him a pear from the rectory garden, he hesitated to take it, saying, "I will think of it." His father, who frequently upset Susannah's "methods," ridiculed her and the boy by exclaiming:

"I protest, sweetheart. I think our Jack would not attend to the most pressing necessities of nature unless he could give a reason for it."

John's superb self-control was evident as early as nine years of age, when, with four other children of the rectory, he had a siege of smallpox. Susannah wrote his father, who was, of course, in London:

"Jack has bore his disease bravely . . . like a Christian, without any complaint; though he seemed angry at the

190

smallpox when they were sore, as we guessed by his looking sourly at them, for he never said anything."

At the age of seventeen, John Wesley entered Oxford University, and remained there as student, lecturer, and fellow for fifteen years, save for two years during which he served as curate or assistant to his aging father. Charles entered Oxford six years later, and the two Wesleys, together with a dozen congenial students, formed the Holy Club, called by other students the "Bible Bigots," and later, the "Methodists," from their strict self-discipline. They studied hard, fasted Wednesdays and Fridays, walked twenty-five miles a day, prayed two hours a day, visited prisons, and denied themselves food and recreation in order to give money to the poor.

John was the most conscientious in observing the strict rules, with the natural result that his health failed, and frequent hemorrhages revealed that he had tuberculosis.

What cured him eventually was outdoor preaching, a simple and unsought remedy to which he came by a roundabout path.

His dying father Samuel left in John's care the publication of his huge masterpiece, a six-hundred-page volume on the Book of Job. It was dedicated to Queen Caroline, who interrupted her game only long enough to remark to John, who brought the presentation copy, that the book was prettily bound, and placed poor Job, unopened, on the window seat.

But on this visit to London John met James Oglethorpe, and in October, 1735, John and Charles were on board ship with the intrepid founder of the new colony of Georgia and his three hundred emigrants to America. Charles was to be Oglethorpe's secretary, while John was chaplain and parson of the expedition and the colony, as well as missionary to the Indians—quite a jump for an Oxford don.

His real and rather strange reason for going to Georgia he confided to the journal-diary he kept all his long life: "My chief motive is the hope of saving my own soul. . . ."

Why should this pious, conscientious, scholarly clergyman of the Church of England have worried about the salvation of his soul? He was supposed to have charge of the souls of others.

On the voyage, a terrible storm frightened all on board except a little company of Moravians. When the terrified John Wesley asked them why they were so tranquil, even to the singing of hymns, they told him they were not afraid to die because they knew they were saved.

When he reached Georgia, he found other Moravians, including the scholarly Spangenberg, lecturer in the great German university of Halle, who, when Wesley sought to begin academic discussions, asked that embarrassing question, "Are you sure your own soul is saved?"

During two very unhappy years in Georgia, the young preacher was a triple failure—as a parson, as a lover, and as a self-salvation-seeker. The Indians told him they didn't want to be Christians because all the Christians who had come to Georgia were liars and thieves. The English colonists told him he was too strict and High Church for the frontier. Sophy Hopkey was in love with him and he with her, but he hesitated too long, and someone else married her. John wrote his mother that he was "snatched as a brand out of fire." The phrase was significant, and perhaps the fact that he wrote it to his mother might interest a psychologist today.

What he minded most, however, was his third failure: he had not saved his own soul in Georgia, no matter how hard he had tried. He had slept on the ground instead of in his waiting bed, had gone barefoot instead of wearing his shoes, and had refused the even then lavish southern table hospitality to live on bread and water. Still his soul, he felt, was not saved. On his way back to England he wrote: "I went to America to convert the Indians, but O, who shall convert me?"

Those words seem odd indeed today when eleven and a half million Americans proudly call themselves Methodists and revere the name of John Wesley as the sainted soul who was their spiritual father!

Before he was back in England a week, whom should he meet but another of those Moravians! Peter Bohler was only twenty-five, nine years younger than John Wesley, but he seemed to have that peace of mind and soul that Wesley was now so earnestly seeking. He too was a young preacher, on his way from a German college to be a missionary in America; and stopping on the way in London to preach at Moravian meetings there.

For weeks Wesley and Bohler were almost constantly together, discussing religion, as Wesley argued for a gradual salvation by piety, Bible reading, and much prayer, while Bohler maintained and gradually proved his point from Scripture that conversion to the real Christian faith was sudden, often instantaneous, and that one knew immediately in his heart when he was saved, and was joyfully sure about it thereafter. He told Wesley to stop depending on reason and philosophy, and await the conviction and assurance of personal salvation which would surely come if he trusted in Christ.

Wesley was a great believer in finding out God's will for himself by various ways of resorting to chance, since casting lots was approved in the Bible. He would write on slips of paper several courses of action open to him, select one from his hat at random or blindly, and follow the directions it contained, as if God had spoken. Twice he lost highly desirable and willing girls that way when on the point of wedding them.

Opening his Bible at random was his favorite method, however, and in his indecision about his future and his worry about his soul, he used it often. One May morning in 1738, at five o'clock, he opened it at:

"There are given unto us exceeding great and precious promises . . ." and a little later at: "Thou are not far from the kingdom of God."

That day he walked about London in a daze, his mind still in the turmoil which was wearing him down, but that evening the great miracle happened which changed his whole life, and the religious and social history of England and America as well. Let him describe it in his own words:

"In the evening I went very unwillingly to a society in Aldersgate Street where one was reading Luther's preface to the Epistle to the Romans. About a quarter before nine, while he was describing the change which God works in the heart through faith in Christ, *I felt my heart strangely warmed.* I felt I did trust in Christ, Christ alone for my salvation; and an assurance was given me that he had taken away *my* sins, even *mine,* and saved *me* from the law of sin and death."

In the heart of London today, a little brass plate nailed to Barclay's Bank in Aldersgate Street bears this legend:

"The probable site where on May 24, 1738, John Wesley felt his heart strangely warmed. This experience of grace was the beginning of Methodism. This tablet is gratefully placed here by the Drew Theological Seminary of the Methodist Episcopal Church, Madison, New Jersey, U.S.A."

John hurried from the meeting to tell the good news to his brother Charles and found his own joy doubled, for Charles had also encountered the zealous Moravian evangelists when he had returned discouraged from Georgia, and, in the house of "a poor ignorant mechanic who knew nothing but Christ," had become converted only three days before John burst in.

Charles Wesley's Bible had confirmed the joy of his salvation by opening at a touch to a singularly prophetic verse:

"He hath put a new song in my mouth, even praise unto our God: many shall see it and fear, and shall trust in the Lord."

Already Charles had begun his "new song" by composing a new kind of hymn the day before, a hymn of wondering praise of Christ's redeeming love, and the handful of Aldersgate folk who had followed the ecstatic John to his brother's lodging knelt and sang with the happy brothers:

Where shall my wondering soul begin?
  How shall I all to heaven aspire?
A slave redeemed from death and sin,
  A brand plucked from eternal fire.
How shall I equal triumphs raise,
  Or sing my great Deliverer's praise?

The Methodist revival had begun, although none in that room knew it, and John had not yet started his real preaching. First he must needs go to the Moravian headquarters in Bohemia, whence came to England and America the missionaries who had helped him to find salvation for his troubled soul. After a summertime walk across Europe to Bohemia (now Czechoslovakia) he came to Herrnhut, "the House of the Lord," and found great peace and joy in the company of these Moravian or Bohemian Brethren, the still faithful disciples of John Huss, burned at the stake as a heretic more than three centuries before. But by September Wesley was back in England again, ready to begin his great work.

He got back to London on a Saturday night and held four public services the next day. By the next Sunday evening he had preached thirteen times, in churches, in prison, and before little evangelistic meetings like the Aldersgate one, gathered by the Moravians but consisting of people who belonged nominally to the Church of England.

This was in 1738. Wesley was thirty-five. His actions during this week marked the recurrent pattern of his life for the next fifty-two years, until he died in his eighty-eighth year. In fact, he averaged more, for he preached over forty-two thousand sermons, about sixteen a week, twice a day on weekdays and four on Sundays. And he traveled, on foot and horseback, frequently cross-country where there were no roads, over two hundred and fifty thousand miles, averaging ninety miles a week.

Very few of his sermons were heard in churches, however, for the English churches were soon closed to him and to Charles, who was also preaching. The reason given was that the Wesleys were too "enthusiastic."

That same criticism was applied to the similar and very successful preaching of another member of the Wesleys' Oxford Holy Club, the gifted George Whitefield (pronounced Whittfield), who had become converted before the Wesleys, and, immediatly after their return, had also gone to Georgia, but with altogether different results. He had preached to great crowds of delighted frontier folk who welcomed the fiery enthusiasm of his oratory.

When Whitefield got back to England, he and John Wesley "took sweet counsel together," as the latter confided to his journal, but the returning preacher, finding himself under the same ban as the Wesleys for his "enthusiasm," did something about it. He was not content to preach in crowded little back rooms to a score of people.

So George Whitefield, of whom it was said that he could be heard a mile when he preached, and two when he sang, took to the open air as he had in America. The Bristol churches refused him their pulpits, and he took the gospel of Jesus out-of-doors where it had started, emulating his Master, "who had a mountain for his pulpit and the heavens for a sounding-board."

On a midwinter Saturday afternoon, February 17, 1739, Whitefield stood on a knoll outside Bristol near Kingswood, a coal-mining district, and preached to two hundred rather surprised miners. His next audience was two thousand and soon he was preaching to twenty thousand. That wonderful voice reached them all. They listened in silence, broken only by smothered sobs as they wept for their sins. Hundreds began to rejoice in their new-found salvation. In six weeks the whole Bristol district was stirred until "men talked of nothing but religion."

Whitefield needed help. He called John Wesley to take his place in Bristol while he went on to Wales to set it aflame with the revival, then to Moorfields, a large common in London where people gathered for recreation on Sundays. He quieted and charmed the thousands, there on Sunday, by his brilliant preaching and the same evening preached to forty thousand people on Kensington Common.

It was not so easy for Wesley at Bristol. Reluctantly he entered upon "this strange way" of outdoor preaching to unwashed mobs, "having been," as he wrote, "all my life so tenacious of decency and order that I should have thought the salvation of souls almost a sin if not done in a church."

On Monday, May 2, 1739, at four in the afternoon, John Wesley preached to three thousand people his first open-air sermon on the text, "The spirit of the Lord is upon me, because he hath anointed me to preach the gospel to the poor."

That afternoon, in the electric response of his hearers, who sensed at once that here was a powerful spiritual force infinitely deeper and stronger than Whitefield's eloquent oratory, John Wesley found himself at last. His self-soul-searching was over and he no longer worried about his own salvation. Peter Bohler had once told him: "Preach faith till you have it, and then because you have it, you will preach faith."

So the meticulous priest became the fiery prophet, but he soon became also the efficient organizer. Not content like Whitefield to preach and move on, he selected from the audiences, even as he was preaching, those who seemed most sincerely moved and most capable, and quickly but carefully formed them into classes, bands, and societies. Yet he never established in England a separate Methodist church as a rival to the Anglican church which he still loved. He advised his converts to attend the sacraments of that church and always planned his meetings so as not to interfere with church service time. But when he died, he had the framework of a great people's church all worked out to minute details ready to be put into operation.

John Wesley did sponsor, especially in or near large cities, church buildings for his religious societies where he and his growing band of young preachers could preach in winter and where classes could meet and young people could sing Charles Wesley's new hymns of salvation. In fact, just ten days after his first sermon in Bristol, he laid the corner-stone for such a structure there, but another building happened to be ready first. He leased a half-ruined old foundry at Moorfields, rebuilt it, and opened meetings there with over five thousand present on November 11 that same year, 1739. Susannah Wesley moved in with John to live in one part of the rambling structure, and it became the headquarters of the growing movement. Many Methodists take the date of the opening of the Foundry Preaching House as the real beginning of the movement, but Wesley himself preferred a date a little later in the same year when "eight or ten persons came to me in London. . . . This was the rise of the United Society."

The next year he broke with the Moravians over the doctrine of "stillness," a peculiar custom they had of waiting for a blessing from the Lord, meanwhile ceasing all work, study, and even refusing to take part in church services. And the following year, 1741, he broke with Whitefield over the doctrine of "predestination."

While in America, Whitefield had been much influenced by the stern Calvinism of Jonathan Edwards, who preached that some are predestined or foreordained by God to be saved, but others to be lost. Wesley could not accept that doctrine, for he held that salvation is free to any and all who will believe. Whitefield was helped by the wealthy Countess of Huntingdon, who gave her jewels and a half-million dollars, helped build sixty-four chapels, and worked tirelessly for his cause. The Calvinistic Methodists of England today trace their origin to Whitefield, but the main wing of Methodism is Wesleyan.

Wesley and Whitefield themselves soon made up as friends, agreeing to disagree, following Wesley's life-motto, "Think and let think." And when Whitefield died, nearly thirty years later, although his body was buried beneath the pulpit of the Presbyterian Church at Newburyport, Massachusetts, his funeral sermon, at his own previous request, was preached by John Wesley in London, and repeated several times.

That motto, "Think and let think," was more than an ideal; Wesley lived up to it in unexpected ways. His theology was as different from that of the Unitarians, who did not believe in the Holy Trinity of Father, of Son and of Holy Ghost, as it was from that of the Roman Catholics, who he thought "believed more than God has revealed." Nevertheless, the facts were that both Unitarians and Catholics did lead pious lives, and, said Wesley, "I cannot argue against a matter of fact." So he recommended his Methodist followers to read biographies of pious men and saints, even if they were not Methodists. And even more unusual, in a day when all pagans and heathen were thought to be surely hell-bound, Wesley said after reading the Meditations of Marcus Aurelius that he had no doubt that Roman would be in Heaven and some nominal Christians would be shut out.

He knew the Bible well and used it much, but admitted the possibility of mistakes on the part of the gospel writers, and said plainly that many psalms and parts of many others were "highly improper for the mouths of a Christian congregation."

And although Whitefield and other Methodist preachers might occasionally resort to a sermon on hell to scare sinners into line, Wesley himself is said to have preached but one sermon on hell and forty thousand on the love of God.

In short, the essence of the Methodist religion as Wesley preached it is: "God loves us. We should love Him and each other." Here is a condensed version of Wesley's own description of the ideal Methodist:

"A Methodist is one who has the love of God shed abroad in his heart . . . who loves the Lord his God with all his heart and soul and mind and strength. He rejoices evermore, prays without ceasing, and in everything gives thanks. His heart is full of love to all mankind, and is purified from envy, malice, wrath, and every unkind affection. . . . He follows not the customs of the world; for vice does not lose its nature through its becoming fashionable. He fares not sumptuously every day. He cannot lay up treasure on the earth; nor can he adorn himself with gold or costly apparel. He cannot join in any diversion that has the least tendency to vice. . . . He does good unto all men; unto neighbors, strangers, friends, and enemies. . . . These are the marks of a true Methodist."

Besides all this, Methodist preachers had a much stricter set of rules. They were supposed to preach at least twice a day, study, read, and pray from six in the morning until noon, make pastoral calls from noon until five, and pray from five till six. The preaching came before six in the morning and after six in the evening. Wesley himself always rose at four and was preaching at five to several thousand hardy hearers who came to listen before starting their day's work.

They did things so prodigiously, these early Methodists. Charles Wesley, for instance, wrote 6,500 hymns, and his brother John somehow found time to edit them all. He tried to throw out "Jesus, Lover of my Soul" as too intimate, but the people demanded its retention, and it is still very popular today.

Wesley had to guard against too much emotionalism for the simple reason that he himself was a bundle of repressed emotions and seemed to engender emotion in others. There was uncanny power in him, and sensitive people, especially women and strong men, felt it in his presence. During his early preaching at Bristol, waves of emotion swept the crowds. As many as five hundred persons would fall in a trancelike faint at once. This catalepsy and other evidences of emotion gradually lessened, but there was always a tense rapport between him and his listeners. During one period mobs led by his opponents often attacked him bodily with curious results. Ruffians raised threatening hands to strike his head and found themselves stroking his hair lovingly instead. Sticks swung at him were strangely diverted. Wesley would fix the mob-leader with his steady gaze, whereupon the man would become his protector against the rest.

Even without Wesley this emotionalism seemed to cross the water to America when Methodism spread here. The great camp meetings in the South, so characteristic of the early missionary period, were often scenes of intense emotion, what with the loud singing, louder preaching, often by several men at once, and the cries of "Amen" which hailed every point made by the preachers. This gave rise to the popular name, "Shouting Methodists."

It was a woman who really got Methodism started in this country. To be sure, George Whitefield had paved the way, and bridged the gap between the time the chagrined Wesleys left Georgia until the time the first Wesleyan missionaries arrived.

Whitefield, in his seven visits to America, was a sort of John the Baptist for Methodism. He preached up and down the seaboard to great congregations of delighted hearers, but he was always the traveling evangelist, and left no American Methodist churches behind him.

Barbara Heck and her cousin Philip Embury, coming from Germany by way of Ireland, landed in New York in 1760. In Ireland they had heard Wesley preach and had thus become Methodists. Embury had even become a local preacher there. In New York they and a half-dozen other Methodist immigrants had slackened in their religious zeal. Five years after their arrival, Barbara came into a room and found the rest of the group playing cards. Thoroughly aroused, she swept up the cards into her apron, threw them into the fire, and told her cousin:

"Brother Embury, you must preach to us or we shall all go to hell, and God will require our blood at your hands!"

He had been thinking along that line too, but protested that he had neither church nor congregation. She said:

"Preach in your own house and to your own company first."

She herself recruited the first congregation, five persons, and he preached to them until they outgrew the little house and rented an empty room. In stamped a stout stranger, in full British uniform, announcing himself as:

"Captain Thomas Webb, of the king's service, and also a soldier of the cross and a spiritual son of John Wesley."

Webb had heard Wesley preach in Bristol, and was no mean preacher himself, so the growing New York group hired a rigging-loft on William Street, and Webb urged the Methodists in England to send preachers to gather the American harvest. Meanwhile they outgrew the rigging-loft and built a "preaching-house" on John Street, where still stands today the historic John Street Methodist Church, at Number 44.

Wesley heard the cry from America and sent Boardman and Pilmoor to Philadelphia, where Captain Webb met them and had Pilmoor preach at once on the State House steps, and then took Boardman with him to New York to preach at John Street. From then on, Methodism in this country grew rapidly, as new men came from England or were "called to preach" from among the converts here. Barbara Heck left New York and by slow stages reached Canada, where she helped establish the first Methodist church in that country, besides having started churches all along her route thither.

The itinerant Methodist preacher was in the vanguard of the westward march of Americans across the Alleghenies. He traveled over the western prairies, climbed the Rockies, and was in California in the first gold rush. He was "the man on horseback," like the great Wesley. In Washington, D.C., where three streets cross, there is a bronze statue of a rider depicting Francis Asbury, the greatest of the Methodist circuit riders, who even outrode Wesley, covering 275,000 miles.

Methodists were well known and esteemed by our presidents. John Adams heard Captain Webb preach and said he was "one of the most eloquent men I ever heard." William Henry Harrison was present at the first Methodist service held in the capital of Indiana, and held the candle for the parson.

Peter Cartwright, a huge Virginian, became a Methodist preacher at eighteen, and in twenty years had preached eight thousand sermons. While he was preaching in Nashville, in stalked General Andrew Jackson and leaned against a pillar, since all seats were filled. The nervous minister of the church nudged Cartwright and whispered that General Jackson had come in.

"Who is General Jackson?" shouted the irritated Cartwright, who knew him very well, for he had been chaplain for Jackson's army at New Orleans. "If he doesn't get his soul converted, God will damn his soul to hell as quick as he will a Guinea Negro."

And after the service Jackson said: "You are a man after my own heart. A minister of Christ ought to love everybody and fear no mortal man."

When the people of Illinois liked Cartwright so well that the Democrats named him for Congress, he found his Republican opponent in his meeting one night in a back seat. Looking pointedly at him, Cartwright preached his hardest trying to convert him, for it was well known in the neighborhood that the man was a skeptic, and no preacher had been able to get him to join a church. Finally, in his zeal, Cartwright called his opponent by name and shouted: "If you are not going to repent and go to heaven, where are you going?"

"I am going to Congress, Brother Cartwright," was the politely quiet answer from Abraham Lincoln.

Some years later President Lincoln wrote to the General Methodist Conference of 1864:

". . . It may fairly be said that the Methodist Episcopal Church, not less devoted than the best, is, by its greater numbers, the most important of all . . . sends more soldiers to the field, more nurses to the hospitals, and more prayers to heaven than any. God bless the Methodist church—bless all the churches—and blessed be God, Who, in this our great trial, giveth us the churches."

It was the Northern Methodist Episcopal Church that Lincoln was addressing, for the Methodist Episcopal Church South had been formed just twenty years before. The split had come over the issue of slavery, since southern Methodist preachers owned eleven thousand slaves, and lay-members over two hundred thousand. These two great groups reunited, however, in 1939, and, with the Methodist Protestant Church, which had split off in 1828 because its members had believed in more rights for laymen than the Episcopal system of government by bishops and preachers allowed, form today the united body known as The Methodist Church, numbering over nine million members. With the several large Negro Methodist churches—African Methodist Episcopal, African Methodist Episcopal Zion, and Colored Methodist Episcopal —numbering well over two million members, and several small denominations of white persons, such as the Wesleyan

Methodists and the Free Methodists, there are eleven and a half million Methodist members in America alone.

Several customs and practices distinguish Methodists from other Protestants. No other church has the class-meeting, which Wesley started with a group of twelve who met weekly and reported to their leader or chairman their personal problems of daily living. It was a novel sort of social confessional, somewhat anticipating modern group therapy. One had to belong to a class before he could join the church. The class-meeting has changed through the years, but is still a useful device for keeping members faithful to their vows.

No other church has changed its ministers so often. In 1804, the bishops moved a preacher, willy-nilly, to another church every two years. In 1864, the rule was, every three years; in 1888, every five years; but in 1900 the limit was removed and now the bishops reappoint the preachers from year to year as long as the man, the church, and the bishop agree that it is desirable.

Methodists differ from Baptists on such points as having bishops, going to the altar for Communion (The Lord's Supper), instead of having the deacons bring it to them, and in allowing a choice of sprinkling or immersion as the method of baptism.

In such matters as card-playing, theater-going, use of tobacco and alcohol, dancing, and amusement or recreation on Sunday, the Methodists have, historically, been stricter than the Church of England people from whom they sprang or the Episcopal Church, its American counterpart. But of late years, these debatable customs do not loom so large in Methodist sermons, and a preacher of that faith smiles when told that, after Wesley died, one of his followers, more strict than his sainted leader, destroyed a set of Shakespeare's plays, the margins completely covered with notes in Wesley's well-known handwriting.

Wesley abstained from the use of alcohol, a common practice in his day, and his followers have often been in the van of temperance and total abstinence movements, especially of late years. The Woman's Christian Temperance Union was led by Frances E. Willard, a Methodist woman; and it was largely the Methodists who, through the Anti-Saloon League, brought about the adoption of the Eighteenth Amendment to the Constitution in 1920, making Prohibition the law of the land.

Methodists of America, mindful of the fact that their church was originally a mission and built up by faithful home missionaries, give generously to their various missionary enterprises. And remembering that their faith was founded on great preaching by Wesley, Whitefield, and Asbury, they honor their ministers today, like Bishops Oxnam and McConnell, and preachers Ralph Sockman and E. Stanley Jones.

Three great things Wesley and his followers did for religion: they made it ethical, personal, and social. Their present-day leaders evidently intend to continue those three emphases.

When one reads the personal history of John Wesley, one is apt to wonder why he could not have had a happier married life. He rejected several possible life partners during his youth and young manhood. There is no doubt that he might well have married Grace Murray, who so capably helped him for years. When he did marry, rather too late, it was to a woman who was incredibly selfish, stupid, and even malicious. But his real love and devotion was reserved for his divine calling, for he was a celibate priest at heart. And as has been so truly remarked, his only child was the Methodist Church.

His long personal journal, kept in shorthand, together with his other voluminous writings, contains many remarkably fine epigrammatic sentences. The three most often quoted by his followers are:

"I have no time to be in a hurry."

"The world is my parish."

And his famous dying words: "The best of all is, God is with us."

THE EVANGELICAL UNITED BRETHREN CHURCH

Just as the Evangelical and Reformed Church was a merger of several Calvinistic Presbyterian churches of German origin and speech, the Evangelical United Brethren Church combines two German churches favoring the Arminian Methodist doctrine and polity, and belongs with the Methodists, whose beliefs need no further exposition here.

The Evangelical Church was founded in 1803 by Jacob Albright, formerly a Lutheran, then a Methodist, who preached successfully in Pennsylvania.

The Church of the United Brethren in Christ got its start from the fruitful evangelistic preaching of Philip Otterbein, a German of the Dutch Reformed Church, and his fellow-revivalist, Martin Boehm, a Mennonite. Other revivalists formed with them a fellowship of evangelists called United Brethren in Christ, elected Otterbein and Boehm bishops, and in a conference in 1817, drew up a creed and book of discipline which turned out to be pretty good Methodist doctrine and polity. After all, Wesley learned much from the Mennonites, and Methodism was spreading all through the sections of the middle states where the United Brethren were preaching and evangelizing. The Methodist flavor of the Brethren's organization was to local taste.

The merger of the Evangelicals and the Brethren took

place at Johnstown, Pa., in 1946. The resultant healthy youngster among the denominations today has 763,560 members, eight colleges, three theological seminaries, and the usual publishing houses and missionary societies. No one who studies trends would be surprised to see these evangelical Arminian brethren eventually take one more unionizing stride —into the great Methodist Church.

19

THE MORMONS OR
LATTER-DAY SAINTS

The Family Church

MISS AMERICA was a Mormon. Tall, healthy, intelligent and beautiful Colleen Hutchings, chosen at Atlantic City as Miss America of 1951, in competition with charming and talented girls from every state in the Union, was a Sunday-school teacher from Utah and very active in The Church of Jesus Christ of Latter-day Saints, as the Mormons prefer to have their church called.

To those who know Mormons, Colleen's triumph occasioned no surprise, for they have the best record of any group in the United States for health and education.

During World War II, the state of Utah, which is three-fourths Mormon in population, led all other states in the percentage of young men found fit for combat duty under Selective Service.

A healthy people has a low death rate and a high birth rate. The death rate for the United States as a whole is low compared with other countries—only ten per thousand. But the Mormon death rate is under six. The births per thousand population in the nation are twenty-four, but among the "Saints" there are thirty-eight.

As for education, several recent surveys have shown that Utah ranks first of all the states, both in the cities and in the rural areas. A Columbia University professor, after careful study, reported that as a birthplace of distinguished men of achievement, Utah surpassed the next leading state, Massachusetts, by twenty per cent, and in the number of leading men of science topped Colorado, the second-best, by thirty per cent.

Miss America of 1951 surprised the judges, reporters, and the other contestants at Atlantic City by her apparent lack of interest in what her election might mean to her personally in fame and money. She was most concerned about what her family back home in Utah, her parents and especially her six-foot brothers, would think and say about her victory. She was proud of her family and hoped they would feel that she had brought honor and credit to them.

This was a natural yet significant reaction, illustrating that Mormonism is a family-centered religion. The home is sacred. So closely integrated with his religious faith is the personal life of a Mormon that his home is literally a part of his religion.

In other words, Mormonism is not only a religion, but a unique way of life which includes every phase of community activity. In a sense, a very vital sense, a Mormon is "in church" all the time, for his Church is always in and with him, directing and governing his every decision and action.

The events that led to the founding of the American-born religion of the Latter-day Saints make a strange and interesting story. During the late 1820's, in New York State, a young man named Joseph Smith is said to have had several visions of angels between his seventeenth and twenty-first years. His angelic visitors told him that all the churches of his day were in error and that he had been chosen to re-establish God's true church on earth, based on the gospel as it would be revealed to him. Guided by the visions, young Smith declared, he discovered in a stone box or crypt on the top of a hill near Manchester, Ontario County, N. Y., a number of golden plates inscribed with strange writing. These he translated into English by using "two transparent stones" found with them, and dictated his findings to Oliver Cowdery, a former schoolteacher. The result of the translation was the *Book of Mormon*, which the Latter-day Saints believe to be the revealed Word of God.

In one vision, John the Baptist appeared to Smith and Cowdery and ordained them into the Aaronic priesthood, instructing them to baptize each other. In another divine appearance, Peter, James, and John conferred on the two men the priesthood of Melchizedek and gave them the holy apostolic keys. A year later, in 1830, Smith founded the Mormon Church in Fayette, N. Y., with as charter members six followers whom he had by that time acquired.

The Book of Mormon, which has over six hundred pages of fine print, contains what appear to be the ancient records of two great races or tribes of people, both former inhabitants of America. One race was the people of Jared, "who were scattered at the time the Lord confounded the language of the people" for building the Tower of Babel, and became the original inhabitants of this country. The other nation was "a remnant of the house of Israel," who left Palestine about 600 B. C., migrated also to North America and built up a civilization here, which largely perished by civil warfare between their two tribes, the Nephites and the Lamanites, about 421 A. D. At that time, Moroni, the last historian of the Lamanites, deposited the records in the stone box on the hillside where young Joseph Smith, under the guidance of the angelic spirit of Moroni, found them fourteen centuries later. The Prophet Joseph Smith also believed that the remnant of the second race, those Lamanites who survived the strife of the fifth century A. D., were the American Indians, and that "our Saviour made His appearance on this continent after His resurrection."

The golden plates and the sacred stones can no longer be seen. Smith said he returned them "when, according to arrangements, the messenger called for them." To authenticate this story, the Mormons name eleven other persons besides Prophet Smith who testified that they saw the plates. The Saints maintain that the Book of Mormon is as divinely inspired as the Bible, the Koran, the Vedas, or *Science and Health*. But for their best proof, they point to the wonderful civilization, unsurpassed for health, culture, and godliness, which they have built up in Utah and thereabout by strictly following the teachings of their great Prophet.

From the nucleus of six charter members of 1830, the Mormons grew so rapidly that great opposition arose from their neighbors. The very next year, they had to move from New York to Ohio, then to Missouri; from there to Nauvoo, Illinois. They kept increasing in numbers, but there was trouble inside and outside the ranks of the faithful. Disputes among them combined with persecution by hostile neighbors who resented this new, unusual religion led to the tragic death of Joseph Smith and his brother Hyrum. From Nauvoo, in midwinter, February, 1846, their new president, Brigham Young, led the long march of the covered-wagon pioneers to the valley of the Great Salt Lake in Utah. Fifty years later, the Mormon community became the State of Utah.

It might have achieved statehood sooner had it not been for the long and bitter conflict over polygamy, or "plural marriage," as the Latter-day Saints called it. Joseph Smith believed in, practiced and preached plural marriage, the duty of a man to have more than one wife at a time. That is, most Mormons believe he did. A section known as The Reorganized Church of Jesus Christ of Latter-day Saints split off from the larger group in 1852, claiming to be the true Mormon church, and that Smith never taught polygamy. In 1860, Smith's son Joseph became their president, and today they number about 129,000 as compared to over a million in the larger body.

In 1890 polygamy was prohibited by a federal law. The Mormons have strictly obeyed that law ever since, for the 12th of their Articles of Faith reads: "We believe in being subject to kings, presidents, rulers and magistrates, in obeying, honoring, and sustaining the law." The Mormon Church has been prompt to combat any attempt on the part of its members to teach or practice polygamy, and has excommunicated and prosecuted them.

The old-time Mormons defended plural marriage as having been the custom in Biblical patriarchal times. They also defended it eugenically as making it possible for a woman to marry and have children by a strong man and leading citizen, even though he might be already married, rather than have to mate with an inferior or diseased man just because he was the only available male in town. The Mormons believed that every woman had the right to have children if she wanted them and could physically do so, and that she should choose the best possible man for their father. Plural marriage made this possible. Moreover, Mormon women believe that their greatest salvation comes through marriage.

When polygamy was abolished in 1890, some plural marriages were permitted to continue, but no more such unions were allowed to be contracted after that date. It is interesting to note that when Brigham Young died in 1877, he left seventeen widows and forty-seven children. A great marble statue of him was unveiled in the National Capitol in Washington on June 1, 1950, by Mrs. Mabel Young Sanborn, his only surviving daughter, then eighty-one years old.

Toward marriage itself, Mormons have a different attitude from that of most Christians. They believe that the Christian marriage ceremony is also a bill of divorcement because the phrases "so long as ye both shall live" and "till death us do part" clearly dissolve the marriage when one party dies. So there are two forms of marriage among the Latter-day Saints, "marriage for time" for those who prefer it or who are not considered fit for "celestial marriage" for eternity, which is deemed the higher form. Such a marriage takes place within the sacred precincts of the Mormon Temple itself.

Marriage is expected of all "Saints" who are physically fit. The question of whether or not a man should marry is never debated. It is taken for granted that a Mormon will marry as soon as he has reached maturity. If he delays, he will soon feel the pressure of public and church opinion. He will find himself looked down upon as a man who has failed in his duty to the church, to the community, to his parents and grandparents, and to God, who bade men "increase and multiply."

Very few Mormon children are born out of wedlock. The census figures testify to the remarkable morality of these people. In the leading twenty-two civilized nations of the world, the average number of children born per year to unmarried mothers is seventy-four per thousand births. In the United States as a whole, it is forty; but in Utah it is only ten, the lowest of all the states. The next lowest, eleven, is in Idaho, another largely Mormon state. The low illegitimacy rate is also connected with the fact that the Mormons have a very low divorce rate, and they are trying very hard to make it even lower by continually teaching their children and young people to respect and maintain the solidarity of the family.

There is no religious group in the United States in which the home is more closely linked with the church than among the Latter-day Saints. The home is the first religious unit. Every morning in the ideal Mormon household, the entire family kneels in prayer, asking God's help in their daily work; and every night, they kneel again to thank Him. All members of the family are expected to be present at mealtime, and no food is touched until it has been blessed. Sunday morning the entire family goes to church, led by the father and mother. On Sunday afternoon, the family is together, singing songs or listening as parents read aloud from and explain the standard religious books of their church.

Regularly, sometimes as often as once a week, each Mormon family has a special "Home Evening" with a planned program of entertainment, games and fun.

A father who becomes so busy with his work or his golf that he neglects the duty of being an understanding companion to his sons, or a mother who fails to make her children's interests her own, is likely to be admonished by the church authorities, who maintain a close watch on all homes.

Every Mormon family is organized with careful division of labor and with the activities and work of each person, no matter how young or old, minutely prescribed according to the custom of the church. The head of the family is the father, whether he is the chief money-earner or not. He is patriarch, priest, judge, governor, and legislator, just as in the Bible, in Old Testament times. This is recognized as his right and duty ordained by God, and the wife and children are taught to obey the husband and father unquestioningly as part of their religion. "This patriarchal order has its divine spirit and purpose," said Joseph Smith, the founder of Mormonism, and: "It is not merely a question of who is perhaps the best qualified. Neither is it wholly a question of who is living the most worthy life. It is largely a question of law and order. . . ."

The wife's duty, privilege and joy is motherhood. Among Mormons, the glory of child-bearing womanhood is not mere Mother's Day sentimentality, but an integral part of their religion.

Mormons believe that millions of souls are waiting to be born. These souls now live as spirits with God, in the spirit world. There they try to meet the conditions and perform the duties which will qualify them to come to the earth world and get bodies of their own. They have no chance of future eternal happiness, however, until some earth woman is willing to suffer the pains of bringing them forth as human children. Thus they acquire an earthly body, forget their previous existence, and have a chance to earn eternal salvation by being brought up in a Mormon home, joining the church, and becoming a Latter-day Saint.

So, to a Mormon woman, motherhood means even more than love of husband, home and children; it means co-operating with God in his divine plan of redemption through the ages. Every child she bears helps God just that much. There is an enormous but definite number of these souls in spiritland waiting to be saved by human birth. Even God cannot save them without her assistance. So she bears all she can, and the families of the Latter-day Saints are large and the church is growing rapidly.

When these spirits are born as babes into a Mormon home, the mother welcomes the great privilege of shaping the new lives and thus, also, of influencing the community and eventually the nation. Mormons believe literally that the hand that rocks the cradle is the hand that rules the world, and that Brigham Young, their great leader, was right when he said: "A woman who would sacrifice the greatest of all earth professions, that of motherhood, which is hers by right of sex, for the silly reason of proving that she can do a man's work as well as any man, or for any other reason, is something less than a true woman, and is to be pitied as well as condemned."

If the Mormon baby, upon his arrival on earth, did not automatically forget his previous spirit existence, he would have little time to think about it. His career from cradle to grave is already pretty well planned out for him and he will be kept very busy all through his life, if he remains a good Latter-day Saint. The education and training of little "Bonnie Prince Charlie" who is already being prepared to sit some day on the throne of England is no more carefully planned and strictly supervised than that of all the thousands of little Mormon boys, his contemporaries, now being prepared to take their places as priests and missionaries, yes, and even apostles, in the Church of Jesus Christ of Latter-day Saints.

The little Mormon boy is well guided and trained not only in the home, where he is given simple but regular tasks to do almost as soon as he can walk, but he is early introduced into the nursery class in Sunday School. Soon he is promoted to kindergarten, then goes through the intermediate, junior and senior grades, and, finally, to a teacher-training class until he is himself a teacher. The Mormon Sunday schools are among the best organized in the country and have a plentiful supply of well-trained teachers, because education, both learning and teaching, is part of the religion of the "Saints." Indeed, Mormons believe that by getting knowledge, man may become like God, who was once, they think, in a condition of partial knowledge as man is today.

Besides the home and Sunday school training, the Mormon child is given highly specialized guidance by the unique institution known as the "Primary." This is weekday religious training, a sort of school, but separate from and in no way interfering with the public day school. The Primary unit, for children aged four to eleven, meets once a week after regular day school for two hours. It is not restricted to Mormons, and many non-Mormon children also attend because their parents recognize the value of the moral training, especially as a wholesome preventive of juvenile delinquency.

There are Home, Neighborhood, and Ward Primaries, depending on whether the children live in the country or town or city, but they all have the same three objects: (1) to teach religion and morality both by precept and by group activities; (2) to direct the formation of proper recreational and leisure-time habits; and (3) to train the children in health practices.

Primary children are divided into age groups with work and study adapted to their ability. For instance, the four-to-five-year-old group learns to pray, and is taught, through Bible and other stories, the virtues of reverence, gratitude, friendliness and kindness. Group Two, the six-year-olds, is taught by the study of nature and the changing seasons to appreciate the beauty of God's universe. The Zion's Boys and Girls, seven and eight years old, are given the religious training corresponding to the confirmation classes in other churches; for, by the eighth birthday, a Mormon child is expected to be ready for church membership.

But the intensive Primary training goes on for three years more. The nine-to-eleven-year-old girls are called Home Builders: Larks 9, Bluebirds 10, and Seagulls 11. Boys of corresponding age are Trail Builders: Blazers 9, Trekkers 10, and Guides 11. The Home Builders are taught four objectives or "Quests" in developing their growing personalities: Spirituality, Health, Service, and Knowledge. The Spirituality Quest develops faith in God and the church; the Health Quest requires the girl to learn how to care for her own body and keep it strong and well; the Service Quest enables her to become helpful in home, church, and town; while the Knowledge Quest gives her practical methods of learning how to observe, how to study, and how to use her hands.

The Trail Building boys, nine to eleven, have the same four objectives in self-improvement, but call them Trails rather than Quests, and seek them by somewhat more rugged methods.

At twelve, the boy goes into regular Boy Scout work, which is supported by the Mormon church. At the same age, the girl also leaves Primary, and is given careful training and direction as a Beehive Girl for three years and as a Junior Girl for two. At seventeen, she becomes a Gleaner Girl and is considered a young woman, ready to meet young men socially and enjoy the interesting life of meetings, dances, discussions, and parties so thoughtfully programmed in Mormondom for its young people from seventeen to twenty-five, a period frankly recognized as the mating age.

One thing about dances, "firesides," and other social gatherings which surprises the non-Mormon young people who may chance to attend is the close supervision of social habits. Not only is there no smoking or use of tobacco in any form, and no beer or other alcoholic drinks, but more unusual, neither tea nor coffee is served, nor even a famous drink popular everywhere else in America.

Coffee is on the list of tabooed beverages, in accordance with the dietary laws of the Latter-day Saints which are based on the *Word of Wisdom*, a revelation given by God to Joseph Smith, their great leader, on February 27, 1833. And if you smile at such strict prohibitions, your Mormon friend will smile, too, as he suggests that the observance of their health laws may have something to do with the fact that every survey shows the "Saints" to be, by far, the healthiest people in all America.

Many Protestant churches forbid dancing, but the Mormons not only permit it, they specialize in it, and always have since their pioneer forefathers made the long trek to Utah (the Ute Indian land) from Missouri and Illinois. In fact, their dancing was one reason why their orthodox neighbors in those states persecuted them. Every night on that long migration, after the wagon train had stopped and camp was made and supper eaten, they danced their weariness away before they slept. Some people think the Mormons' health record may be partly due to the tough strong stock from which they have descended.

Nowadays, the dances are practically a part of their religion; the church sponsors them and provides recreation dance halls adjacent to and often in the chapel buildings. At a jolly ward party, where the best dancer present is often the bishop himself, the latter usually takes a turn around the hall with the wife of each church member, in turn, and that member meanwhile dances with the bishop's wife. Visiting non-Mormons, locally called "gentiles," are often startled when the evening's dancing is devoutly concluded with prayer. To the Saints it seems perfectly natural, for to them, not marriage alone is sacred, but also all contacts of the sexes before marriage, especially anything having to do with the vitally im-

210

portant matter of the selection of a lifelong mate. Mormons shudder at the casual, careless, hasty and even accidental meetings, matings, and marriages among many "gentile" groups.

Every Mormon girl is most carefully prepared for marriage and so is her husband-to-be. And the strange thing about it in "gentile" eyes is the fact that the young Mormon bridegroom is almost always an elder in the Melchizedek priesthood.

At the age of twelve, when a Mormon boy leaves the Primary, he finds his prescribed program becomes increasingly heavier. He begins intensive preparation for the priesthood in addition to his regular public school studies, his Boy Scout training, and instruction in some trade by which to support his future family.

The priesthood, in its various divisions and forms, is the central and most important part of Mormonism, and the priests have greater powers given them than in other religions. Consequently, the training for the priesthood is carefully supervised and the discipline is strict.

First, the boy becomes a deacon, and serves as such during his twelfth, thirteenth, and fourteenth years. He learns primarily by doing, more than by book study, for he acts as an assistant to those in the higher grades of the priesthood—the teachers, priests, elders, and bishops.

As a deacon, he is made acquainted with the "twelve" system which runs all through the church government, based on the twelve apostles of the early Christian church. Each group of twelve deacons is a Council, and each Council has a president, assisted by a first and second counselor, these three forming the presidency of a Deacons' Council.

After three years as a deacon, the boy, if faithful and capable, is promoted to the grade of teacher and usually acts as such during his fifteenth and sixteenth years. These are the dangerous years, when juvenile delinquency crops up in American high-school youth; but the Mormon mid-teen boys have little time to get into mischief, for they are given charge of church meetings and must "see that the church meet together often, and also see that all members do their duty, . . . take the lead of meetings in the absence of the Elder or Priest, . . . and warn, expound, exhort, and teach, and invite all to come unto Christ."

These very young teachers, traveling in pairs, visit the homes of all church members once a month at least and check on the conduct and spiritual condition of old and young. They comfort and help the sick and discouraged, arrange for the needy to receive food and clothing from the bishop's storehouse, and are especially charged with quenching gossip, stopping tale-bearing and acting as peacemakers. Besides all this, these boys take care of the meeting house, run errands for their bishop, collect fast-offerings and ward funds, meet people at the door of the meeting house, usher them to seats, and distribute the sacramental bread and water.

After two years as a teacher, the boy becomes a priest, usually when seventeen, and serves as such two years before being ordained as an elder. As a priest, he may perform any of the duties of a teacher when he wishes, but he may also baptize, administer the sacrament, and ordain deacons, teachers, and other priests.

The next step upward makes the young man an elder, usually at the age of nineteen. His ordination to the rank of elder entitles him to perform the rites of confirmation of the baptized and the laying on of hands, a ceremony which is said to confer the blessing of "baptism by fire and the Holy Ghost." The elder also anoints and blesses the sick and he is on call to serve in any way which the presiding officers of the Mormon church may request. It is believed he enjoys the presence and light of the Holy Ghost within himself.

As deacon, teacher, and priest, the young man has been in the lesser or Aaronic priesthood, but when he becomes an elder, he enters the first degree of the higher or Melchizedek priesthood, which has five successive higher degrees: the seventy, high priest, patriarch, apostle, and presidency of the high priesthood. The order of the "seventy" is a selection of elders specially chosen to preach the gospel of Mormonism throughout the world under the supervision of the twelve apostles, who are the highest officials of the Latter-day Saints except the president. The "seventy" are really missionaries (over four thousand are so designated every year), who go out two by two at their own expense to make converts to their faith.

The high priests, next in rank above the seventy, are the statesmen of the church, veterans of missionary service and of rich experience in various positions. From them are chosen bishops and other officials. The patriarch comes into his office by heredity, and his work is to bless and comfort people. In one sense, he is a kind of Mormon pope, for his people believe he holds the "keys" and that what he binds or looses on earth will be bound or loosed in heaven. The higher priestly offices in the church are quite complicated in their organization.

The amazing thing to an outsider is the fact that these officials, like all the priests below them, receive no salary, and only a few of them have their expenses paid. For the Mormon priest, like the Apostle Paul, the tentmaker, earns his living at another profession, business or trade. In Salt Lake City or any Mormon town, the barber who shaves the visitor, the plumber called to mend a leaky pipe, even the lawyer or banker, is a Mormon priest of some sort, perhaps a bishop.

These men take their priesthood seriously. They believe they are God's agents, specially endowed with spiritual gifts. They assert that they receive revelations from God today just as Moses and the Biblical prophets and patriarchs did of old. They say they have the power of discernment, enabling them to detect and expose magicians, sorcerers and frauds. They claim the ability to heal the sick by the laying on of hands, anointing with oil, and praying for recovery. The Mormons usually have good physicians too, but believe that both priest and physician co-operate in helping God and nature effect the cure. They record a number of wonderful cures with no doctor present.

The *Book of Mormon* is, to some extent, the Bible of the Latter-day Saints. They use the Christian Bible too, but only "insofar as it is correctly translated," for they believe that the Prophet Joseph Smith found discrepancies in the King James version, and retranslated it. Smith's *Inspired Version* was published in a "Corrected Edition" in 1944. The *Book of Mormon* is regarded as equal with the Bible, which it supplements but does not supplant. Among the holy books of the Mormons, which they call The Standard Works of the Church, is one which was originally called *The Book of Commandments,* but now is known as *Doctrine and Covenants,* which includes the *Word of Wisdom* detailing the health rules. The fourth holy book is the popular little *Pearl of Great Price,* divided into three parts, the *Book of Moses,* the *Book of Abraham,* and the *Writings of Joseph Smith.* In the last part of the *Pearl of Great Price* is found the Mormon creed called The Articles of Faith, which differ little from the doctrines of the more orthodox or Fundamentalistic evangelistic Protestant churches, except that the Latter-day Saints do not believe either in Original Sin (the dogma that every man inherits Adam's sin) or in the Closed Canon (the doctrine that God's revelation of truth to mankind ceased when the Bible was finished). A third difference is that the Mormons believe the *Book of Mormon* to be the veritable Word of God.

Mormons consider it the duty of their church to take active care of the members not only spiritually but physically, and hold that religion is concerned with a man's body as well as his soul. They do not claim that the world owes a man a living, but think that a man ought to earn his way and that his church should see to it that he has a chance to do so. In that sense, each Mormon is his brother's keeper, and his own keeper, too.

By this mutual aid idea, the Mormons take care of their own, and it is considered shameful for a Latter-day Saint to go on government relief or accept an old age pension. To guard against "depression" and food shortages, every Mormon family is expected to keep on hand a two years' supply of staple foods.

Moreover, each Mormon ward or parish has its own storehouse of food, clothing, dishes and other essentials under the charge and responsibility of the local bishop. When need comes, the bishop takes care of the family, signing orders to release supplies. If the man of the family needs a job, the church helps him get one or tides him over until he does.

Mormons work after hours and on days off, without pay, to maintain the supplies in the warehouses by raising and canning food, making clothes, and reconditioning used shoes and clothing. What little money is needed in their church welfare program is raised by self-denial. Every good Mormon, whatever his age or occupation, fasts once a month, going without breakfast or luncheon that day, and gives to the bishop's welfare fund what the meal would have cost.

The Latter-day Saints have their own wheat mills, dairies, meat-processing plants, beet-sugar factories, lumber mills, canneries, and coal mines, all owned and operated by the church welfare organization. These industries are largely maintained by donated labor but also provide work in depression years for the otherwise jobless. In all assistance given by the church, however, care is taken to preserve the principle of the free agency of the individual.

Above all, the welfare work of the Saints gives a dramatic and practical application of their religious doctrine of the need for young and old to work. Work is considered a necessity in character-making. Idleness, laziness, and living on government doles or pensions are considered disgraceful and even sinful.

Furthermore, the Mormon who works to better himself in this world increases the glory he will have in the world to come. If he gets rich, that does not excuse him from working, not in the least; it simply increases his opportunities for working for his beloved Mormon church.

Mormon meetings are noted for their simplicity. Often they are just a sort of prayer and testimony meeting, such as is common among Baptists and Methodists at midweek evening meetings. Frequently a meeting may be little more than a speech on almost any topic, followed by a discussion in which nearly all present take part. Every Mormon child is trained in Sunday School to make two-and-a-half-minute speeches and is usually looking for a chance to speak before an audience; thus any group of Mormons never lacks for speakers, whether previously announced or not.

Even the so-called "sacramental" meetings, where the sacrament of Communion, or The Lord's Supper, is observed, partake of the same simplicity. For instance, one held recently in the North Shore ward of Chicago began with a hymn, which all present sang, sitting down. At one side, but facing the congregation, sat the two priests—selected at random by the leader of the meeting from those present—who were in charge of the sacrament. One was a business man of Chicago; the other, a sailor in uniform. The business man knelt and said a prayer asking the Lord's blessing. Then he handed to two fourteen-year old boys, young deacons, a plate of small bits of bread, which they passed among the members, each of whom took and ate a piece. Then the sailor made a short speech, and handed the boys the plates or racks holding small glasses of clear water. Each member took and drank a glass. There was no ritual. Two speakers were then introduced. One gave a moral talk on the power of a few consecrated persons, and the other spoke on public recreation as a solution of the juvenile delinquency problem. Then the congregation sang a hymn, and the meeting ended.

The Saints now number well over a million, having more than doubled in the last twenty-five years. They have eight temples: their first and great one in Salt Lake City; three others in Utah, at Logan, Manti, and St. George; one in Mesa, Arizona; one in Idaho Falls, Idaho; one in Cardston, Alberta, Canada; and one in Laie, Hawaii. Ground was broken in the fall of 1951 in Los Angeles, California, for the ninth and greatest temple of all, a multi-million dollar structure with 775-foot frontage on Santa Monica Boulevard. True to their ancient American traditions, the huge building will be of Mayan architecture, with a high tower on which there will be a statue of the Angel Moroni sounding his trumpet to remind all who behold of the revelation that came to young Joseph Smith.

20

THE CHURCH OF CHRIST, SCIENTIST

The Church a Woman Founded

IN MY COLLECTION of interesting old autograph albums there is one I particularly prize, battered and worn though it is, for among the sentimental stanzas inscribed in the tiny handwriting of the period is this one:

> May you be heaven's peculiar care,
> May you the love of thousands share,
> May all your days most happy be,
> And when far distant, think of me.
> M. B. G. 1845

Mary Baker Glover (later to be known throughout the world as Mary Baker Eddy) was a young widow of twenty-four in 1845. While it cannot be proved that she wrote these lines, it is extremely probable that she did. The little book belonged to Esther Hammond, a near neighbor, for many years, of the Bakers in New Hampshire. Like most young ladies of her day, Mary Baker Glover had her own album and wrote in several such little books in exchange, as was the custom. We know that one of her suitors, John H. Bartlett, presented her with a similar autograph album a few months later, for it is now in the historical files of the Mother Church of Christian Science in Boston, and contains many such verses by her youthful admirers.

If she did write the above verse, it was singularly prophetic for what she wished for her friend Esther came true for herself. In later years, long after Esther Hammond had gone to an early grave, Mary Baker Eddy did "the love of thousands share," yes, of hundreds of thousands of followers who deemed their beloved Leader to be indeed "Heaven's peculiar care."

The story of how Mary Morse Baker, a sickly little farm girl in an obscure village in New Hampshire, came to be the revered founder of a great American religion, with branches in nearly all countries of the world, is not only a success saga of the sort Americans delight to read, but a narrative of the triumph of a valiant human spirit over great odds after a long and heart-breaking struggle.

Arrayed against her were three formidable groups. There were, first of all, those influential people, both men and women, who maintained that woman's place was in the home and most decidedly not in the pulpit. Hadn't the Apostle Paul himself written in his First Epistle to the Corinthians:

"Let your women keep silence in the churches: for it is not permitted unto them to speak. . . . And if they will learn anything, let them ask their husbands at home: for it is a shame for women to speak in the church."

Even more outspoken in their opposition to her teaching were the orthodox religionists who called her an infidel and an atheist because her interpretation of Bible passages differed radically from theirs, and her theology spoke of God as infinite love rather than as avenging wrath.

The third and perhaps most powerful group of opponents was in the medical profession, for while the doctors did not object to this new religion saving people from sin, they did resent and fight against a faith which claimed that pain and disease were mere illusions of mortal mind, to be healed through prayer rather than by material medicine.

In spite of all this hostility, social, theological, and medical, the brave woman persisted until she had so firmly established her church that it is still thriving today, over forty years since her passing in her ninetieth year.

At the 1953 annual "June Meeting" of the Christian Scientists in Boston, seven thousand five hundred radiantly healthy delegates were present, representing three thousand churches all over the world. To them were reported case after case of recent healings, claiming complete cures through Christian Science treatment, without drugs or doctors, of such dread maladies as infantile paralysis and abdominal cancer, as well as of allegedly incurable dislocated hips and accident injuries in which the medical prognosis was death.

The listening delegates smiled and nodded in confirmation of these reports, for they too, or their friends, had been healed of various ailments and disabilities and had found peace and happiness through the principle of what they so frequently call "spiritual understanding." They maintain it is the same principle as that discovered and used by Jesus Christ in his healing ministry, rediscovered by Mary Baker Eddy, the beloved founder of their religion.

It is impossible to present an adequate appraisal of the religion of Christian Science without first relating briefly the life story of the remarkable Mrs. Eddy. Several biographies exist, but none is satisfactory. Either they are so extravagant in praise and adulation as to be incredible, or they are written by unfair critics searching out every flaw and inconsistency. Dynamic personalities are likely to be either compelling or irritating.

There is also much disagreement about the facts of her early years, probably because her public success came so late in her long life that by the time anyone thought of writing her biography, many of the really important circumstances, incidents, and impressions of her childhood and youth had been lost and forgotten, some of them even by herself, as she admitted. As has happened with all other religious leaders, devout eulogists are already spinning legends and infancy narratives bordering on the miraculous.

When the definitive biography of Mary Baker Eddy is eventually written, the author will be someone more familiar with depth psychology and the peculiarities of genius than any who have yet essayed to interpret this brilliant daughter of man.

Various records, however, and particularly her brief autobiographical sketches which she called *Retrospection and Introspection*, written when she was seventy years old, reveal enough to explain somewhat her dominant ideas and the travail of her struggling soul as she gave birth to the new religion based on her own deeply felt experiences.

A religion is born when some prophet soul, torn with long inner conflict, suddenly finds a new interpretation of life, some great unifying idea which solves that conflict for himself and for the other people of his time and place who have been similarly suffering and who, at once, flock to him as his disciples. But the prophet first must suffer his forty days or forty years in the wilderness.

It was destined to be thus with the small, fragile person christened Mary Morse Baker in 1821 in the little farm community of Bow, New Hampshire. The youngest of six children, she was sickly and subject to nervous turns from early childhood, unable to continue in school with much regularity. It is true that it was the style in the 1830's for girls and young women to be frail and weak and to faint upon the slightest provocation; but Mary Baker's frequent spells and fevers, termed "tantrums" by one unsympathetic doctor, were experiences too painful to have been deliberately pretended.

She wrote, many years later, in a short chapter entitled "Voices Not Our Own," that there were "many peculiar circumstances and events" in her childhood. She tells of one. "For some twelve months, when I was about eight years old," she wrote, "I repeatedly heard a voice, calling me distinctly by name, three times, in an ascending scale." At first, she thought it was her mother, but found it was not. The phenomenon continued, she states, "until I grew discouraged, and my mother was perplexed and anxious." When, however, the mother read to Mary the Bible story of little Samuel's similar experience, and bade her reply to the voice next time as Samuel did, "Speak, Lord: for thy servant heareth," there was no answer, but the mysterious voice ceased calling her name.

Mark Baker, her father, although he knew only part of what was going on, was naturally troubled by the odd behavior of his apparently temperamental and imaginative little daughter, and since he was, by all accounts, subject to sudden fits of anger himself, it is no wonder that the two strong wills clashed. But, in less excited moments, he accepted the family doctor's diagnosis that Mary had "too much brains for her body . . . keep her away from school all you can, and do not give her much medicine."

Mary was perfectly willing to stay out of school, for her nervous little spirit was irritated by the hubbub of the one-room country school of her girlhood; but that did not mean that she disliked books and learning. Far from it. She tells in her autobiographical notes that her very earliest recollections were of books—how her grandmother showed her and let her read "certain manuscripts containing Scriptural sonnets, besides other verses and enigmas . . . written by my great-grandmother." She recalls also that her childhood was gladdened by reading her "grandmother's treasures," old yellow newspapers and a book "printed in olden type and replete with the phraseology current in the 17th and 18th centuries." The printed word evidently had an unusual fascination for the child. Even before she was old enough to attend school, her sisters would often perch her on a table and ask her what she was going to do when she grew up, just to hear her say, "I will 'ite a book."

Her love of books began to find an outlet when her twenty-year-old brother Albert, a freshman at Dartmouth, came home for his first vacation. The nine-year-old girl embraced him in a perfect ecstasy of emotion and told him how she loved and admired him and wanted to be a scholar too, because, when she grew up, she was going to write a book.

It was an unusual school which then was started. Someone has said that the ideal university would be Mark Hopkins seated on one end of a log and a student on the other. It was something like that with Albert Baker and his sister Mary. During his vacations he taught her, and all through his four years of college she read with him his textbooks and other books he recommended. Of this early education she later wrote:

"At ten years of age I was as familiar with Lindley Murray's Grammar as with the Westminster Catechism; and the latter I had to repeat every Sunday. My favorite studies were natural philosophy, logic, and moral science. From my brother Albert I received lessons in the ancient tongues, Hebrew, Greek and Latin."

She must truly have "gained book-knowledge with far less labor than is usually requisite," as she once admitted, if she really mastered those languages and liberal arts studies along with her Dartmouth brother, for she was not quite thirteen years old when he was graduated. That would place her in the same small group of brilliant women with Susannah Wesley, the "Mother of Methodism," who, as a child, was well versed in Greek, Latin, French, and English, and at the age of thirteen defeated her clerical father in theological argument and left his church to join another.

In somewhat similar manner, little Mary Baker had violent arguments with her father and the minister when she was but a child. The strict Calvinism of the Trinitarian Congregational Church to which her parents had belonged "for a half-century" she could not accept. Her father's "relentless theology emphasized belief in a final judgment-day, in the danger of endless punishment, and in a Jehovah merciless towards unbelievers," but Mary herself, even then, was insisting that she believed in a loving God of great mercy. They disputed until the girl became really ill, and her father had to quit arguing and get the doctor for the child he thought was dying. The wise physician said it was only a fever, and prescribed a little more of mother's love and a little less of father's doctrine. Mary took refuge in prayer, already her comfort and healing. She reported the end of this episode later:

"I prayed; and a soft glow of ineffable joy came over me. The fever was gone, and I rose and dressed myself, in a normal condition of health. . . . The physician marvelled; and the 'horrible decree' of predestination—as John Calvin rightly called his own tenet—forever lost its power over me."

Mary Baker of course did not know it then, but the real and final fruit of her girlhood rebellion against the old theology was to be the future great Christian Science Church itself.

But love and marriage came first. Mary Baker's teen-age letters and poems reveal that, in quite normal fashion, her continued love of books was supplemented by a growing interest in romance and young men. Other swains were soon crowded out by "Wash" Glover, a former neighbor of the family and the building-trade partner of Mary's older brother Samuel. George Washington Glover made courting trips to the Baker home, first from Boston and then from Charleston, South Carolina, and, in December 1843, when Mary was twenty-two and a half years old, took her back with him to the South as his bride.

Mother Baker gave the bridegroom a sealed letter to be opened and read when they were halfway on their sea voyage south from Boston, a letter containing lines from the then popular poetess, Mrs. Lydia Sigourney, the sentimental "Sweet Singer of Hartford." The verses reminded Mr. Glover that "the soul of woman lives on love," and warned him:

"By all thy treasured hopes of heaven,

Deal gently with my darling child."

Mr. Glover did, but the ocean didn't. On Christmas Day, a severe storm made her "hopelessly seasick." But she made her husband kneel beside her on the cabin floor as she prayed God to save them. The wind and the sea soon subsided so suddenly that the captain called it "a miracle."

It was a brief honeymoon, however. Six months after the happy bride and groom reached Charleston, an epidemic of yellow fever took him from her, and by August Mary was back in her old New Hampshire home.

Once there again, crushed as she was by the sudden ending of her marriage, she could not long give way to grief. She had to summon all her strength for what was, in her weakness, a trying ordeal. On September 11, 1844, she gave birth to her first and only child, named George Washington Glover II for his father. She nearly died, and for some months needed as much care as the child. A neighbor woman who had just lost one of her newborn twins nursed Mary's infant; and Mark Baker himself assumed much of the care of Mary, often holding her in his arms and rocking her like a baby.

When she had slowly regained strength enough to begin taking care of her lively little son, her dear mother died. Mary wrote her brother, "Oh! George, what is left of earth to *me!*" She thought she was enduring the dark night of the soul, but her troubles and suffering were only beginning.

In less than a year, her father married a well-to-do widow, Mrs. Duncan, sister of the lieutenant governor of New York. Kind as the stepmother was, there seemed to be no room for Mary in the fine town house the prosperous Mark Baker had recently built. Mary B. Glover had no money of her own, for her husband's only tangible assets when he died were the slaves Mary had at once freed. She was too ill to do hard work. The verses and little essays she wrote for the weekly papers were good practice for her, but brought in only a pittance. She tried teaching, and started an advanced sort of kindergarten, but without success—the time for that was not ripe. Her only recourse was to go to live with her married sister Abigail Tilton.

But Abigail's four-year-old boy Albert was not too strong, and she did not wish to have the husky and noisy five-year-old George Glover in the house, too. If Mary was to live with Abigail, young George must go elsewhere. In spite of his mother's tears, prayers, and protests, the boy was sent to live with a family forty miles away.

Mrs. Glover's three years, 1850 to 1853, at her sister Abigail Tilton's home in Sanbornton Bridge (later named Tilton) were by no means tranquil. Both women were sick, Abigail with hernia, and Mary with her old trouble, "a spinal weakness which caused spasmodic seizures, followed by prostration which amounted to a complete nervous collapse." Whether the maladies of the two sisters were the cause or the effect of the arguments and dissensions would be difficult now to decide, but in such situations there is usually two-way traffic.

It was an exciting era, anyway, that middle of the nineteenth century in America. In every home there was much discussion, for interesting things were happening, and, in those days, people talked with one another more, instead of listening to other people talking on radio and television. The Fox Sisters' "rappings" in 1849 had given rise to a nation-wide discussion of spiritualism, clairvoyance, and the forms of hypnotism then called animal magnetism and mesmerism. All sorts of experiments were being conducted in large cities and small villages, attempting to discover if the Next World People were indeed signalling to the people of this world.

That Mrs. Glover practiced clairvoyance and mediumship has been both asserted and denied. If she didn't explore that field, she was among the few intelligent and clever people of the day who did not try their hand at it, but, at any rate, she later repudiated all connection with such matters.

One subject of conversation was becoming increasingly important and unavoidable, the abolition of slavery. Both Abigail and her husband, as well as Mark Baker, her father, firmly opposed abolition. Mary was just as strong for it, and the fact that she had freed the slaves left her by her husband was well known. At a reception in the Tilton home, when slavery came up for discussion, Mary kept quiet for some time, but when openly challenged, defended her minority viewpoint vigorously, ending with the dramatic statement, "Emancipation is written on the wall." The assertion shocked the gathering, especially the hostess, Abigail, who exclaimed: "Mary, do you dare say that in my house?"

With utmost dignity, in spite of the unsisterly reminder of her "poor relation" status, Mary replied, "I dare to speak what I believe in any house."

After that incident, widely discussed in the town, Mary's position in her sister's house became even more embarrassing. That she welcomed the courtship of Dr. Daniel Patterson and accepted his quick proposal of marriage because she wished to get away from the Tilton home is a possible interpretation of her act, but there were other factors in the situation. She said later, "My dominant thought in marrying again was to get back my child." And Dr. Patterson, an attractive, healthy, self-confident man, unusually well dressed for those times and parts, was a suitor not to be hastily rejected.

It is possible, however, and even probable, that another fact altogether influenced her decision more than she realized. Dr. Patterson was not only a dental doctor. He had also studied and practiced to some extent the then new and fashionable medical system known as homoeopathy. This system was based on the apparently illogical theory that the smaller the dose of medicine given the patient, the more likely it is to cure him, provided it is the drug which, in ordinary size doses, would produce the same disease in a healthy person!

It sounds sheer nonsense, but its defenders based their theory on an old Latin saying meaning "Like is likely to be cured by like." Of the same nature is the popular superstition that you can be cured by "a hair of the dog that bit you." And what are vaccination, serum, and allergy treatments but a method of insuring a patient against a disease by deliberately inoculating him with it in a mild form?

At any rate, when Dr. Patterson breezed into the Tilton home and told the beautiful but ailing young widow Glover

222

that she was altogether too delicate to be treated with heavy dosage of harsh drugs, and that he was sure she would respond to the "higher attenuations" of homoeopathic medicine, she was immediately attracted to the remedy and the charming physician. When she soon had one of her ill turns, she did respond to the new treatment, at least to some extent, and temporarily. And she married the doctor, in June 1853, although the big bridegroom had to carry her downstairs from her sickroom for the ceremony.

The marriage was a heart-breaking failure. The careless, happy-go-lucky dentist set up his practice first in one little New Hampshire hill town, then in another; and his sick wife dragged along with him, growing ever weaker and more despondent in spite of homoeopathy. She was rapidly becoming "attenuated" herself.

The long-feared Civil War came. Her husband went to Washington on a nebulous fund-raising scheme, characteristically ventured too near a line held by the Confederates, was captured and put into the dread Libby Prison. Her boy, whom her marriage had not brought back to her, except for brief visits, enlisted in the Union Army. No wonder that "the nervous seizures continued to recur with increasing violence." Her cup of sorrow was now full.

Yet she kept striving desperately, persistently, for there were moments when she thought she caught flashes of the dawnlight of healing truth beyond the dark night of the soul. Here and there she picked up illuminating bits of evidence that she might be approaching the goal she sought.

One fascinating facet of eternal truth, one clue to the secret of healing, seemed hid in this puzzling thing called homoeopathy. She was sure there was an idea there. She turned it over and over in her sharp mind, a mind now maturing through great tribulation. She would make a few homoeopathic experiments of her own, on herself and others. There were plenty of sick people around, ready to try anything.

She found one woman with dropsy, "big as a barrel in the bed." Having no medicine handy but common salt, amateur Doctor Mary attenuated it with water until there was not the slightest taste of salt in it. In all seriousness and with the proper bedside manner, she gave this "medicine" to the woman, dose after dose, and watched with amazement as the patient improved. There came a relapse, and Mary became fearful that she was giving the woman too much water. So she substituted a single unmedicated sugar pill, and the woman began gaining again. The cure was not permanent, but Mary knew she had hold of something very important. Evidently, when sick people got cured, there might be other factors at work besides medicine.

Prayer and Bible reading were helpful, she found, for

they often quieted and steadied the mind. But they didn't seem to cure sick bodies permanently. She studied all varieties of spiritualists and hypnotists, but with no abiding satisfaction. There was "something to" all such methods of groping for truth and healing, but these mediums and "doctors" were blind leaders of the blind.

There was one more doctor to try. In the autumn of 1861, Dr. Patterson had somehow secured a handbill advertising the remarkable cures without the use of medicine effected by Dr. Phineas P. Quimby of Portland, Maine. After her husband went south, Mary reread the circular carefully, noting that Quimby claimed to cure the sick by "correcting their error," and emphasized in italics that "The Truth is the cure." She felt that perhaps this man might have explored the fundamental science of healing. She told her sister Abigail she just *had* to go and see if perhaps Quimby had discovered the great truth, the scientific principle of healing.

Abigail, however, would hear nothing of Quimby "the charlatan," and instead packed her off, willy-nilly, to a respectable sanatorium, Dr. Vail's water-cure at Hill, N.H., only a few miles away. This "hydropathy," as it was called, was the "latest" fashionable cure, and featured the lavish use of water outside and in. Mary collapsed on arrival, weak and discouraged, and submitted to the treatments, although doubtful of them, repeating over and over: "I know God can and will cure me, if only I could understand His way."

Reports of Quimby's continued cures caused several to desert Dr. Vail's place; one of them was Mary, who had gradually saved small sums received from Abigail for "extras" until she had railroad fare to Portland.

It was a frail and feeble woman of forty-one who was helped up the stairs to Dr. Quimby's Portland office that October day, in 1862. His sympathy and understanding cheered her, and when he said that she "was held in bondage by the opinion of her family and physicians," and that "her animal spirit was reflecting its grief upon her body and calling it spinal disease," she listened eagerly. Then he wet his hands and massaged her head, "to generate healthy electricity," meanwhile talking soothingly and suggesting that the pain was departing and she would soon be well again. Sure enough, she felt better almost immediately under such hypnotic suggestion, and within a week, after more treatments, she says she climbed, unaided, the one hundred and eighty-two steps to the dome of Portland City Hall!

She was three weeks in Portland this first time, having treatments and daily talks with Dr. Quimby, trying to discover what there was in his therapy which cured, or at least helped, her and hundreds of others. He did not seem to know, himself, exactly. At least, he couldn't explain to her the underlying principle. It seemed to her a sort of mesmerism, but he said he had given that up. He spoke of stimulating the flow of healthy electricity by manipulating the head.

In two letter-essays in the *Portland Courier* shortly after her arrival, Mrs. Glover extolled Quimby's work which, she said, was done neither by spiritualism nor animal magnetism, but by some great principle of truth, "and just in proportion to my right perception of truth is my recovery."

Back to an amazed Sister Abigail in Sanbornton Bridge went a radiant Mary, not permanently cured but greatly impoved in health. Her husband had escaped from Libby Prison and she had happy months of reunion with him. In one of her many letters to Quimby at this time she wrote, "I am to all who once knew me a living wonder, and a living monument to your power. . . . I am quite as much of an escaped prisoner as my dear husband was."

Abigail's son Albert, now seventeen, was smoking and drinking to excess and was sent to Quimby to be cured, but with little effect, as his faith was not like his aunt's. Then Mary, always the experimenter, tried to cure the young man herself, with unexpected results. She wrote Quimby, ". . . since I have been trying to affect Albert, I am suffering from a constant desire to smoke. . . ."

Mary Patterson knew she had not yet grasped how to use the scientific principle or law of divine healing which, intuitively, she felt existed. Sometimes, it seemed to rebound on the would-be healer, as when she tried to cure Albert, and, later, when she "spit blood" while treating a tuberculosis patient. As we would say, it backfired. And there were relapses, as she knew only too well. She felt she needed more personal work and study ("pupilage" she called it) with Quimby. So, early in 1864, when Dr. Patterson went to Lynn, Mass., to set up a dental practice, she went to Portland.

From explaining Quimby's method to patients in his crowded waiting room, who didn't like the way he "mussed up" their hair, Mary soon progressed to treating them herself in their homes, spending three months with a Miss Jarvis in Warren, Maine, where she gave several lectures on Quimby's Spiritual Science. In her own busy quiet way she was preparing, intentionally or not, for her great future work.

There has been for many years a constantly recurring debate as to whether or not Mary M. Patterson, later Mrs. Eddy, appropriated P.P. Quimby's manuscripts and methods and claimed them for her own when she founded Christian Science. It is true that she owed much to Quimby, and repeatedly said so. But in her formative years, she had also been exposed frequently to Unitarianism, Universalism, Emersonian Transcendentalism, and other philosophies and religions. Her active mind had darted hither and thither for many years, like a busy bee gathering honey and pollen from all sorts of blooming flowers.

Her final religious system was her own, however, and it differed vitally from all its predecessors, as she later emphatically asserted, "by knowing the unreality of disease, sin, and death."

Quimby died in January, 1866, before he got around to formulating his theory and technique; she did give shape to and completed hers, but not immediately. She was nearer the truth before she met Quimby than he was, but she did not realize it at the time. He learned as much from her as she from him; but she put it together better, later, when she added something else, which she discovered only a few days after he died.

Quimby had been dead but two weeks when Mary Patterson had an accident on her way to a temperance meeting in Lynn. She slipped and fell on the ice "and was taken up for dead, came to consciousness . . . but to find myself the helpless cripple I was before I saw Dr. Quimby." This was her statement in a letter she wrote a fortnight later. The *Lynn Reporter*, two days after the accident, stated "Dr. Cushing found her injuries to be internal and of a severe nature, inducing spasms and internal suffering."

She had not herself called the doctor, and when she waked next day from the effects of a small dose of morphine he had given her while she was dazed by her fall, refused to take his medicine, very high attenuations of arnica. On the third day, Sunday morning, February 4, 1866, something occurred which makes that day the most important in the annals of Christian Science. It is referred to as the day of the Great Revelation, for on that day, as Mrs. Eddy wrote many years later, "I discovered the Science of divine metaphysical healing which I afterward named Christian Science."

That Sunday, as she lay on her bed helpless and suffering, she sent out of her room the sympathetic and anxious friends who had gathered there, took her Bible, opened it at random, and read in the 9th chapter of Matthew's gospel how Jesus healed a paralyzed man by telling him his sins were forgiven him and to arise and walk. Now, as she lay paralyzed in her bed, she felt as if Jesus himself were speaking to her and bidding her: "Daughter, arise and walk!"

Immediately, her pain, weakness and distress vanished. She felt suffused by love, harmony, and truth.

"It was to me a revelation of Truth, the lost chord of Truth, healing as of old. I caught this consciously from the Divine Harmony. The miracles recorded in the Bible which had before seemed to me supernatural, grew divinely natural. . . ."

Quickly, she rose from her bed, dressed, and walked into the next room where a clergyman, his wife, and other friends were astounded to see her, "almost believing they beheld an apparition." To them, it seemed as though she had risen from the dead. Twenty years later, she wrote: "It was after the death of Mr. Quimby and when I was apparently at the door of death that I made the discovery of the Principle of Divine Science. After that, it took ten years of hard work before the first edition of *Science and Health* was published in 1875."

The summer of 1866 was the summer of decision, of cutting loose from her past. Her husband left her, and there were several versions of why and how he did so. Through Abigail, he arranged to send his wife two hundred dollars a year. Abigail asked Mary to come back and live with her, and promised a cottage and an income, provided she attend Abigail's church and give up her divine healing idea. But Mary simply said, "I must do the work God has called me to." Thereafter, she had nothing to do with her family, practically cut herself off from all Quimby associates, and even changed her name back from Mrs. Patterson to Mrs. Glover.

The three years after her "Discovery" have been called "the wandering in the wilderness." In *Science and Health* she says:

"For three years after my discovery, I sought the solution of this problem of Mind-healing, searched the Scriptures and read little else, kept aloof from society, and . . . won my way to absolute conclusions through divine revelation, reason, and demonstration. The revelation of Truth in the understanding came to me gradually and apparently through divine power."

In that statement, one very important word is "demonstration," for during that important three-year period, as she moved from one boarding house or private home to another, she searched not only the Scriptures but the minds of men and women also, to discover in those minds the causes of the sickness in their bodies. She was trying to demonstrate and perfect her system of healing by removing from their minds the wrong thinking that she believed might be causing their physical ills. Nothing could block her plan now. Failures to cure did not stop her. She never doubted the scientific principle but blamed poor results on her wrong application of the principle, or the lack of cooperation by the patient.

Success in one case but spurred her on to the next. She tackled both organic diseases and functional ones. She cured a boy's bone felon, a young man's serious fever, and restored the ability to walk to a woman who had not taken a step for sixteen years. But because she used no medicines, not even in attenuated doses, did no rubbing and made no magnetic passes, the cured ones and their friends and relatives could not believe that it was Mary's system that had worked the cure. But these "demonstrations" convinced her that in spite of several failures she was on the right track.

She lived and talked and worked with the unorthodox in religion—the Quakers, Universalists, Unitarians, Spiritualists, in several towns in eastern Massachusetts: Lynn, Stoughton, Avon, Taunton, Amesbury. By 1870 she was back in Lynn again, ready to settle down and set up shop, so to speak. The wilderness wanderings were nearly over, but the hard work was not. She had learned enough now to begin to teach classes in divine healing.

So in 1870 she took the five rooms of the second floor of a Lynn house and rented a pew in the nearby Unitarian Church. A young man, Richard Kennedy, whom she had been teaching for some months, went into partnership with her and used one room for his office as practitioner; while Mrs. Glover conducted classes in mental science and worked on the manuscript she had long been carrying in her reticule, the book script which was to become *Science and Health*. What she was teaching her classes and what she had been teaching a few individuals still contained elements of Quimbyism. For instance, although apparently she herself had never used the head-stroking technique which Quimby had used on her, she had permitted her students to do so. But, in 1872, she denounced the practice as mesmeric or hypnotic, and forbade it to her students. This edict and other difficulties caused Kennedy and a few pupils to leave her. By this time, she was saying that the great principle by which mental healing worked was Deity, and that God was not Person but Principle. This idea was rather disturbing to students with an evangelical Christian background.

After Kennedy and the others left her, she gave up the rooms, and, during 1872-1875, lived quietly in boarding houses, doing a little healing and teaching of individuals, but mostly writing her book. She could now afford to spend time on it, for she had saved several thousand dollars from the fees her students had paid and from the percentage of his earnings Kennedy had faithfully handed over to her.

A new era set in when she bought the house at 8 Broad Street, Lynn, and placed over the entrance the sign "Mary B. Glover's Christian Scientists' Home." She let to various tenants all the rooms but the first floor front parlor, which she reserved for her classroom, and the one little attic room where she slept and wrote her book. No one else could enter that room until she had finished the book.

Two pupils advanced the $2200 necessary to publish the thousand copies of that famous First Edition; today, one copy of that edition would probably fetch at least one-third that sum. A number of review and gift copies were sent out, handbills were distributed, even by the author herself, but the book did not sell. The few reviewers who mentioned it at all either ridiculed it or condemned it.

The indefatigable author, nevertheless, planned to bring out a second, somewhat revised edition, and put one of her best students, named Spofford, in charge of selling it. Then, quite suddenly, she married Asa Gilbert Eddy, another good student. The quiet little ceremony was performed on New Year's Day in 1877 by the Rev. S.B. Stewart of the Unitarian Church of Lynn, where the bride had a pew. Regarding her new husband, she wrote a friend a few days later:

"Last spring, Dr. Eddy came to me a hopeless invalid. I saw him then for the first time, and but twice. When his health was so improved he next came to join my class. In four weeks after he came to study he was in practice, doing well, worked up an excellent reputation for healing and at length won my affections on the ground alone of his great goodness and strength of character."

These changes caused trouble in the little group of her followers, for Spofford had some idea of marrying her himself, but the internal strife was gradually quieted by Mrs. Eddy's firm hand.

The turn of her whole career apparently came when she began Sunday afternoon lectures in Boston, where she and her advanced ideas received a warm welcome, and people of influence and means came to her support. The Church of Christ, Scientist was incorporated in 1879 with her as president and, two years later, as pastor also. That year, 1881, when she was sixty years old, she organized the Massachusetts Metaphysical College with herself as president, and published the third and much improved edition of *Science and Health*. The next year, she moved from the little house in Lynn to a much better one on Columbus Avenue, Boston, where, in a few months, Asa Gilbert Eddy died of heart disease in spite of all the treatments he and his wife gave him.

Her husband's death greatly affected her, for he had given her the love and moral support she craved, and she retired to the home of a Christian Science friend in Northern Vermont for the summer. In the fall, after a quick emotional recovery, she was back in Boston with renewed energy and plans for expansion. These plans included the starting of regular Christian Science publications, the first of which, the *Journal*, now a monthly, began appearing in April 1883. To this, later, were added the weekly *Sentinel* and the daily newspaper, *Christian Science Monitor*, now known and respected round the world. But the immediate and notable success achieved by this dynamic woman when she descended on Boston in the fall of 1882 was the growth of her Metaphysical College. In its eight years of existence, she taught all of the classes herself, and four thousand students paid three hundred dollars each for seven lessons under her instruction. These students not only furnished ample capital for the continuation and expansion of her work, but they spread into other cities as missionaries and practicing healers, called "practitioners."

By 1888 Christian Science was firmly established. Thirty institutes and academies were training teachers and healers. Mrs. Eddy was living in a $40,000 residence on Commonwealth Avenue in the fashionable Back Bay district of Boston.

This was just the start, however, of greater growth. The sixty-seven-year-old little lady in that house was reaching out to extend the borders of her movement to the ends of the earth and digging down to establish firmly its legal, financial, and spiritual foundations. In 1895, a beautiful new church building was "demonstrated" in Boston and dedicated free of debt. She insisted this custom be followed for all churches erected in the future. There have been many, indeed, and of all types of architecture, but always dignified and impressive. Eleven years later that first "Mother Church" building was dwarfed by the vast new one erected by its side, made necessary by the steady growth of the movement. From all over the world came thirty thousand devoted "Scientists" for the dedication, marching in and out of the new building in relays, and spreading their smiling phalanxes all over Boston and vicinity as they testified how Mother Eddy had brought them health of body and great happiness of mind.

Four years later, December 4, 1910, at the close of the Sunday morning service in the great new church, when the time came for the "First Reader," Judge Clifford P. Smith, to pronounce the benediction, the people of the great congregation were surprised to hear him say:

"I shall now read part of a letter written by our revered Leader and reprinted on page 135 of *Miscellaneous Writings*:

" 'My Beloved Students—You may be looking to see me in my accustomed place with you, but this you must no longer expect. . . . I am still with you in the field of battle, taking forward marches, broader and higher views, and with the hope that you will follow. . . . You can well afford to give me up since you have in my last revised edition of *Science and Health* your teacher and guide.' "

Judge Smith paused a moment and then said:

"Although these lines were written years ago, they are true today, and will continue to be true. But it has now become my duty to announce that Mrs. Eddy passed from our sight last night at 10:45 o'clock, at her home in Chestnut Hill."

Yet her soul goes marching on, and, through her precious book, *Science and Health with Key to the Scriptures*, and

230

through her other writings, particularly the *Church Manual,* containing the "Church Tenets, Rules, and By-Laws, as prepared by Mrs. Eddy," she still controls and directs her Church and all its branches, although more than forty years have elapsed since she "passed from our sight." On the list of Church Officers of the Mother Church today, leading all the rest, is "Rev. MARY BAKER EDDY, Pastor Emeritus."

The Christian Science Church today, although claiming to be both Christian and Protestant, differs interestingly from other churches in many ways.

When you enter a Christian Science Church for the Sunday Morning service of worship, you will find the interior somewhat like that of any of the more dignified types of Protestant churches, but you will be surprised by the absence of many features common to most Christian churches.

There is no altar, for there is no Mass, and the semiannual Communion Service, celebrated in branch churches only, is entirely spiritual, with no material elements present, neither bread, wine, grape juice, nor even water.

There is no baptismal font or any baptistery, for there is no water baptism, either by immersion, pouring, or sprinkling, either for infants or for adults. Baptism, in this church, is continual spiritual purification from all material sense.

There is no pulpit, for there is no professional preacher or priest. In the early days, sermons were preached, for a while by Mrs. Eddy herself and then by clergymen who had originally been ordained in other faiths. But in 1895, when the first building of the Mother Church was dedicated, the custom was eliminated, and a unique practice substituted. Article XIV, Section 1, of the Church By-Laws reads:

"I, Mary Baker Eddy, ordain the BIBLE, and SCIENCE AND HEALTH WITH KEY TO THE SCRIPTURES, Pastor over The Mother Church—The First Church of Christ, Scientist, in Boston, Mass.—and they will continue to preach for this Church and the world."

On a raised platform at the front or chancel-end of any Christian Science Church stand two lecterns, or reading desks, in positions of equal importance, one on each side. On one rests a copy of the Bible, King James Version: on the other, a copy of *Science and Health with Key to the Scriptures,* by Mary Baker Eddy. The lectern bearing the latter book is presided over by the First Reader, and the one supporting the Bible, by the Second Reader.

The service begins with an opening hymn, followed by the reading of a scriptural selection, and by a period of silent prayer, broken by the reciting by all present of the Lord's Prayer with its spiritual interpretation as given at the end of the beautiful chapter (I) on "Prayer" in *Science and Health.* The familiar King James version of the Lord's Prayer

231

alternates, verse by verse, with Mrs. Eddy's own interpretation:

> Our Father which art in heaven,
> *Our Father-Mother God, all-harmonious,*
>
> Hallowed be Thy name.
> *Adorable One.*
>
> Thy kingdom come.
> *Thy kingdom is come; Thou art ever-present.*
>
> Thy will be done in earth, as it is in heaven.
> *Enable us to know—as in heaven, so on earth—God is*
> *omnipotent, supreme.*
>
> Give us this day our daily bread;
> *Give us grace for to-day; feed the famished affections;*
>
> And forgive us our debts, as we forgive our debtors.
> *And Love is reflected in love;*
>
> And lead us not into temptation, but deliver us from evil;
> *And God leadeth us not into temptation, but delivereth*
> *us from sin, disease, and death.*
>
> For Thine is the kingdom, and the power, and the
> glory, forever.
> *For God is infinite, all-power, all Life, Truth, Love,*
> *over all, and All.*

After another hymn, parish announcements, and a solo, the subject of the Lesson-Sermon is announced. This Lesson-Sermon takes the place of the usual regular sermon in Protestant churches. Instead of a minister preaching his interpretation of a Bible passage, however, the Second Reader, standing at the Bible lectern, reads the selected Bible verses for the day, and then the First Reader, at the other lectern, simply reads the correlative passages from *Science and Health* which have been chosen as interpreting this Bible scripture.

The collection is made after the Lesson-Sermon and is followed by a third hymn. Several of the favorites in the Christian Science hymnal were written by Mrs. Eddy. Then comes the climax of the service, the reading by the First Reader of the famous "Scientific Statement of Being" and its correlative Bible verses, I John 3:1–3. The service closes with a benediction.

The "Statement" is worth quoting here, for it is the core of Christian Science and had appeared in several versions before Mrs. Eddy hammered it into its final form:

"There is no life, truth, intelligence, nor substance in matter. All is infinite Mind and its infinite manifestation, for God is All-in-all. Spirit is immortal Truth; matter is mortal error. Spirit is the real and eternal; matter is the unreal and temporal. Spirit is God, and man is His image and likeness. Therefore man is not material; he is spiritual."

All good Christian Scientists memorize this "Statement" and get comfort in repeating and meditating on it when challenged by doubts and such illusions of mortal mind as pain and disease.

On Wednesday evenings, meetings are held which much resemble the old-time prayer and testimony meetings of evangelical churches, except that the accent is more on health than on salvation from sin.

The nearest thing to a creed are the "Tenets" which are repeated at the Communions held on the second Sundays of January and July, and are required "to be signed by those uniting with The First Church of Christ, Scientist, in Boston, Mass.," *viz.*:

"1. As adherents of Truth, we take the inspired Word of the Bible as our sufficient guide to eternal Life.

"2. We acknowledge and adore one supreme and infinite God. We acknowledge His Son, one Christ; the Holy Ghost or divine Comforter; and man in God's image and likeness.

"3. We acknowledge God's forgiveness of sin in the destruction of sin and the spiritual understanding that casts out evil as unreal. But the belief in sin is punished as long as the belief lasts.

"4. We acknowledge Jesus' atonement as the evidence of divine, efficacious Love, unfolding man's unity with God through Christ Jesus the Way-shower; and we acknowledge that man is saved through Christ, through Truth, Life, and Love as demonstrated by the Galilean Prophet in healing the sick and overcoming sin and death.

"5. We acknowledge that the crucifixion of Jesus and his resurrection served to uplift faith to understand eternal Life, even the allness of Soul, Spirit, and the nothingness of matter.

"6. And we solemnly promise to watch, and pray for that Mind to be in us which was also in Christ Jesus; to do unto others as we would have them do unto us; and to be merciful, just, and pure."

Christian Science churches keep open the year round, although those which have a second Sunday service in the afternoon or evening (always an exact repetition of the morning service) may discontinue it for the summer.

In any local church, the service on a given Sunday is the same as in all other churches, and the subject of the Lesson-Sermon is always one which was designated long ago by Mrs. Eddy itself. She selected twenty-six subjects which she believed covered the essentials of Christian Science and its application to human needs. These twenty-six subjects are repeated in the same order every six months.

For instance, on the first Sunday in January, in every Christian Science church in the world, and in many homes in towns where there is no church, the subject is always "God." If at home, good Scientists faithfully follow the service as outlined in the *Christian Science Quarterly*. On the second Sunday, a Communion Sunday, it is "Sacrament," and so on through the first half of the year with such topics as "Life," "Truth," "Love," "Spirit," "Soul," etc. Then, beginning the first Sunday in July, the same twenty-six subjects are repeated. Monotony is somewhat avoided, however, by choosing different verses of the Bible and of *Science and Health* to present different phases of the same subject, changing from "God—as Principle" to "God—as Mother," then to "God—as Father," and so on. The selection of the passages to be used, from both books, is made by a carefully chosen central committee which is strictly instructed to include nothing else in the Lesson-Sermon. Mrs. Eddy's comment is significant:

"As these discourses are made up wholly of passages from the Bible and the Christian Science text-book, they contain nothing of human opinion; they are devoid of man-made theories. . . . The gospel preached from our pulpits is not after man, neither was it taught of man, but by the revelation of Jesus Christ." From this, and similar statements, it is evident that Mrs. Eddy came to believe that her book, as the "Key to the Scriptures," is as divine a revelation as the Bible itself.

Therefore, her "Glossary" (Chapter XVII of *Science and Health*) is important inasmuch as she states that the chapter "contains the metaphysical interpretation of Bible terms, giving their spiritual sense, which is also their original meaning."

Especially interesting in the light of the many controversies over the relation of mind to matter are her definitions of both, and her distinction between mortal mind and divine Mind. Matter is "Mythology; mortality; another name for mortal mind; . . . the opposite of Truth; the opposite of Spirit; the opposite of God. . ." She defined mortal mind in part as "Nothing claiming to be something, for Mind is immortal. . . ." She maintained that, in reality, the only Mind, the only real Being, is the divine Mind, which she defines in part as "The only I, or Us; . . . the divine Principle, or God, of whom man is the full and perfect expression; Deity, which outlines but is not outlined."

The chapter after the Glossary, the last in the book, is entitled "Fruitage." It consists of one hundred pages of testimonies of those who have been healed by Christian Science. At the head of the chapter is a quotation from Jesus, "Wherefore by their fruits ye shall know them," followed by a statement that the originals of the letters thereafter quoted are in the possession of the Editor, who guarantees their authenticity.

It is a most amazing collection. The eighty-four letters include cases of cures of rheumatism, astigmatism, hernia, fibroid tumor, insanity, epilepsy, cataract, valvular heart disease, cancer, and tuberculosis, besides many minor ailments. The number of cases mentioning nerve affections, dyspepsia, stomach trouble, asthma, and other ills now classed by physicians as psychosomatic, usually due to worry and unsolved problems, would lead us to believe that Mrs. Eddy had, to a great degree, anticipated the discoveries of another woman doctor, Dr. Flanders Dunbar. Christian Scientists, however, recognize no similarity between Mrs. Eddy's methods and any kind of medical psychiatry; for the latter examines and works on the human mind, while "Christian Science is based on the understanding of the divine Mind." Besides, Christian Science is a religion and "treats all ills by prayer."

Naturally, Christian Scientists oppose compulsory vaccination for their children and compulsary medical regulations of any sort which are based on and teach the germ theory of disease. They believe the only cause of disease is mortal mind, and that the very teaching of the germ theory may create fear and bring on the disease.

As to birth control or family limitation, that is left entirely to the decisions of the married partners.

At childbirth, a regular obstetrician may be called in, and in some cases, such as bone fractures, the Christian Scientist may summon a physician or surgeon without condemnation if the injured person has not yet reached the degree of "spiritual understanding" requisite for healing it by spiritual means.

As for the "experience of death," Mrs. Eddy taught that there is no interruption of life or cessation of being or absorption into Deity, but "Mortals waken from the dream of death with bodies unseen by those who think that they bury the body." There is no prescribed ritual for a funeral. Passages from the Bible and from *Science and Health* may be read, but reading is not necessary.

Since there are no personal pastors, priests, or clergymen, Christian Scientists, in marrying, customarily follow the example of Mrs. Eddy and employ a minister of another faith. The Church Manual states: "If a Christian Scientist is to be married, the ceremony shall be performed by a clergyman who is legally authorized."

Christian Science is essentially a layman's religion. Every member is priest and preacher and healer as well. But there are special healers called "practitioners" who are trained

235

systematically for their work. They are not any different from other members of the church except that they must be approved by the Boston church, registered for public practice, and must have given evidence of success in healing. Only then are they qualified to pray for those who ask prayers. Those who ask are usually in need of healing, and the practitioners are really practiced healers. They charge for their services, but may not sue for payment, and any practioner "shall reasonably reduce his price in chronic cases of recovery, and in cases where he has not effected a cure."

The message of Christian Science is brought to the public by an efficient and able group of lecturers accredited and approved by the Mother Church of Boston. These lecturers might be called the official missionaries of the faith. Also, all Christian Science churches maintain reading rooms, where any person interested is free to browse, to obtain literature, and receive information.

The work of the Mother Church, and through it of the world-wide organization in general, is carried on by the officers, consisting of the Pastor Emeritus, a Board of five Directors, a President, a Clerk, a Treasurer, and Two Readers. The President is elected annually and usually alternates between men and women practitioners.

The branch churches are advised and supervised by the Mother Church, but have local autonomy in that they elect their own officers. But they follow the schedule of Lesson-Sermons prepared and distributed every six months by the central committee in Boston.

The real authority of the Christian Science church today lies in the Board of Directors. The directors are self-perpetuating, elect all the officers mentioned above, as well as all executives, such as the Superintendent of the Sunday School, the members of the Board of Lectureship, the Committee on Publication, and even the editors of all publications.

As for numbers, Christian Scientists obey Mother Eddy's advice, "They shall turn away from personality and numbering the people." As a result, it is impossible to get official statistics as to their membership. Over ten thousand practitioners are registered in the *Christian Science Journal*, and there are approximately three thousand authorized branch churches. In 1906, when the larger Mother Church building was dedicated, newspaper accounts estimated the total world membership to be probably a million, and Christian Scientists say it has increased rapidly since then. They consider inaccurate the figures of 268,915 members as given in the U.S. Government census of 1936, because there are more non-members studying Christian Science and attending its services than there are actual church members.

Many Christian Scientists are well-to-do, like the Parsees,

236

Quakers, and Mormons. They maintain that "there is nothing in the practice of true Christianity that requires poverty or prohibits wealth," and that "prosperity and sufficiency of supply are the natural outcome of the spiritual understanding which enables one to overcome lack, limitation, and other material beliefs." Such material beliefs "deny the goodness of God and the abundance which belongs to man as His expression." They point proudly to the example of their Pastor Emeritus who suffered poverty for years but, finally, by God's help and her spiritual understanding, overcame limitations to such an extent that she left an estate of over two million dollars. The general idea among her followers seems to be that poverty is a sort of disease, but God is rich and can help one cure it.

Mrs. Eddy established the business, administrative, and financial base of her Church so carefully that it is now a wealthy institution with an increasing income, derived from the enormous sales of her books and the gifts of grateful members. The only required contribution is the annual "per capita tax of not less than a dollar." Usually, of course, it is much more. Some members give one-tenth of their income. It has sometimes been gently suggested that, since a Christian Scientist has no doctor's bill to pay, that amount could well be added to what one would normally give to the church.

When all is said and done, the fact remains that, by common consent, Christian Scientists are acknowledged by even their most outspoken critics to be happy, sweet-tempered, considerate and tolerant of others' opinions though firm in their own, cooperative in community affairs, socially conscious, and excellent citizens. They maintain that their religion makes them that way, and they give credit and great praise to Mary Baker Eddy and the little book which, after great tribulation and much earnest thought, she did manage to "ite," as she prophesied when but a tiny girl.

Appendix 1

OTHER CHURCHES AND
RELIGIOUS GROUPS

THERE ARE A number of religious organizations having some affinity with the churches and denominations already discussed which nevertheless do not quite belong in the same category with those faiths. They have individual characteristics of interest to the student of religion, however, and so deserve at least brief mention. Other groups not included even here are, in a sense, of equal importance, but in the interests of brevity must be omitted. Even the valuable *Ency-*

clopedia of Religion and Ethics, with its thirteen volumes, each three times the wordage of this manual, omits reference to some religions. The ones included in this appendix might each be given a separate chapter because of the interesting material available.

JEHOVAH'S WITNESSES

These most interesting and devoted people were successively called Russellites (after their founder, Pastor Charles Taze Russell), International Bible Students, and Millennial Dawnists, before they were named Jehovah's Witnesses, in 1931. Their present president, Nathan Homer Knorr, who followed Russell's successor, Judge Rutherford, at the latter's death in 1942, says that "Jehovah's witnesses of modern times have not arbitrarily assumed this God-given name, but the facts concerning their activity prove it applicable to them, that they are living up to it." By "God-given," he refers to Isaiah 43:10, 12 in the American Standard Revised Version:

"Ye are my witnesses, saith Jehovah, and my servant whom I have chosen; that ye may know and believe me, and understand that I am he: before me there was no God formed, neither shall there be after me. . . . I have declared, and I have saved, and I have showed; and there was no strange god among you: therefore ye are my witnesses, saith Jehovah, and I am God."

It is an important passage, for the Jehovah's Witnesses refer to it as their scriptural justification for denying the Christian doctrine of the Holy Trinity. They assert that not only is that doctrine not taught in the New Testament, but it is specifically prohibited in this Old Testament passage. For them, consequently, Jesus is not God or the second Person of the Trinity, but a sort of agent, sent to set up Jehovah's kingdom, to maintain that God's name is Jehovah, and redeem mankind. And the Holy Ghost is not considered to be the third Person of the Trinity, but simply the unseen "power of Jehovah" on earth.

After Armageddon, which is coming soon (millions now living will never die), they believe that Christ will lead the hosts of heaven, the holy angels, the army of righteousness, and defeat the army of Satan, while the righteous watch the great battle.

They have no churches and no professional ministers and claim not to be a religion, but they have a smoothly functioning organization of regional, zone, and company "servants," and every Witness is regarded as a sort of missionary minister, and, therefore, exempt from military draft. Witnesses give allegiance only to Jehovah, and so have run into trouble by refusing to vote, do jury duty, or salute the flag. The Supreme Court of the United States has vindicated them in the flag-saluting dispute. In many states and countries they have suffered much persecution, including stoning, whipping, and the burning of their homes; but they rejoice in this, expecting it, and knowing that the word "martyr" is Greek for Witness.

Their publications have wide circulation, largely through the mail and the hands of street-corner and house-to-house "publishers," and, in one year recently, twelve million magazines, eighteen million tracts, and twenty million books and booklets were distributed. They have their own version of the New Testament, published in 1950, which they prefer to call the "New World Translation of the Christian Greek Scriptures." In 1953 they published the first volume of their Old Testament, the "New World Translation of the Hebrew Scriptures," in a first edition of a half-million copies. Apart from a few semantic peculiarities like translating the Greek word *stauros,* as "stake" instead of "cross," and the often-startling use of the colloquial and the vernacular, the anonymous translators have certainly rendered the best manuscript texts, both Greek and Hebrew, with scholarly ability and acumen.

A convention of the Witnesses at the New York Yankee Stadium in 1953 for a week had a daily attendance surpassing crowd records for baseball. Four thousand six hundred and forty converts were immersed within five hours in a swimming pool in one great mass-baptizing. All meetings were so well conducted that the police called the visitors the most polite and best-behaved gathering they had ever seen, and New Yorkers in general got the impression that while the Witnesses had some unusual ideas about religion, they certainly were sincere and pleasant people, and excelled some other faiths in such matters as sales organization and public-relations technique. No official statistics of membership are issued, but there are probably at least a half million Witnesses in the world, of whom a little over half are in the United States. The nearest to an official statement of membership was an announcement in the *Watchtower* of April 1, 1953, reporting "a new peak reached in 1952 of 456,265 ministerial publishers in the field!"

ADVENTISTS AND NEO-FUNDAMENTALISTS

There has always been an apocalyptic, millennial strain in the Christian religion, recurring in times of war and other crises, whenever a prophet or group of religious leaders interprets literally the promise of Jesus Christ to return to earth and the many other Biblical references to the end of the world and the coming Kingdom of God.

The Jehovah's Witnesses are "Second Coming" people, but they are not exactly in the true orthodox line of Adventists,

239

Pentecostalists, and Neo-Fundamentalists, for unlike these the Witnesses do not accept Jesus Christ as God and Savior.

The Adventists (with a capital A) had their origin in America when a New York upstate farmer, William Miller, using only his Bible and concordance, set the date for Christ's return between March 21, 1843, and March 21, 1844, basing his prediction on his interpretation of the prophecies of Daniel. In spite of the passing of that year and the subsequent return of many Millerites to their former churches, enough remained to form a millennial movement in Albany in 1845. This movement has spread and divided over various doctrines until there are now six Adventist bodies, of which the largest is the Seventh Day Adventists, numbering a quarter million members,

They take their name from their observance of the seventh day, Saturday, as the Sabbath, and are very conservative in doctrine and strict practice. They forbid their members to dance, play cards, attend theaters, or use tobacco or alcohol. They practice adult immersion baptism, give one-tenth or more of their income to their church, and are strong for religious freedom and the total separation of church and state.

Besides the Adventists, there belong in this group of very orthodox denominations usually holding millennial views a number of churches also emphasizing Pentecostalism. That is, they lay great stress on trying to reproduce today the phenomena described in the Book of Acts as occurring on the Day of Pentecost in the early church: the "speaking with tongues," the descending of the Holy Spirit, the wholesale baptisms, the healings and prophesyings. Speaking with tongues is rapid, ecstatic speech, usually unintelligible even to the speaker, but sometimes explained by one who has another Pentecostal gift, that of interpretation. Evidence of the descent of the Holy Spirit is seen by Pentecostalists in the bodily rhythmic or spasmodic movements common at country revivals and camp-meetings. Healing, another evidence of the presence of the Holy Spirit, is by prayer, massage, and rubbing with oil. Prophesying is preaching, but preaching is not prophesying unless it be very fervent and full of familiar Bible quotations accompanied by many gestures.

The Neo-Fundamentalists hold to all the orthodox literalist views of the well-known Fundamentalists of the 1920's, but require the belief in and practice of the *charismata* or Pentecostal gifts as well. Along with this emphasis, great stress is laid on personal holiness, usually interpreted as refraining from all worldly pleasures, and spending all one's spare time in prayer, Bible-reading, and church-going.

Over and under all other doctrines in these churches, however, like a rolling cloud above or subterranean rumblings, is the Adventist belief in the imminent Second Coming of

Christ on the clouds of heaven. It is stressed in every sermon and the favorite Bible passages are the Apocalypses in Daniel, Ezekiel and Isaiah, the Book of Revelation, and the "Little Apocalypse" of Jesus' words in St. Mark 13 and the parallel passages in Matthew and Luke.

Converts by the thousand are joining these various Adventist-type religions, not only because of the atom- and H-bomb threat, but also because the ministers and lay-people of these Neo-Fundamentalistic faiths put vastly more of their time, energy, money, and devotion into their religion than do the preachers and members of the old-line denominations.

Organized since the beginning of the twentieth century and achieving their greatest growth in the last decade, the size and strength of the Neo-Fundamentalist churches is not realized by the general public.

The 1953 *Yearbook of American Churches* gives the following statistics: (1) the Churches of God have 305,043 members and 530,511 in their Sunday Schools; (2) the Assemblies of God have 370,118 members; (3) the Church of God in Christ, 328,304; (4) the Pentecostal Assemblies, 300,070; (5) the Churches of Christ have 1,500,000; last year, the membership was 1,000,000; (6) the Church of the Nazarene, a merger, in 1908, of three Holiness groups, opposes the Pentecostal practice of speaking with tongues, but is otherwise orthodox and has been termed "the right wing of the holiness movement." It has 243,152 members and 503,415 in Sunday Schools.

With the many smaller Adventist, Pentecostal, and Holiness denominations added, there are already nearly four million members in this rapidly growing type of religion. In many American towns, it is the only kind of religion functioning at present.

THE NEW THOUGHT MOVEMENT

The public generally is not aware of the strength of the religious movement loosely known as New Thought. This is explained partly by the fact that a great many members of well-known Christian denominations are also members of New Thought groups, finding there, they often say, the inspiration and optimistic atmosphere they sometimes miss in their "regular" churches. Many a Baptist or Methodist pastor calling on invalids and shut-ins finds on a table near the bedside a well-thumbed copy of *Unity* or *Science of Mind* or a book by Emmet Fox, for the many New Thought organizations and Unity centers put the postman on the pastoral staff long ago and have built up a large mail-order following.

New Thought groups, although emphasizing the same general teachings, have many different names, and that is another reason why their numbers are underestimated. On the

241

program of the Thirty-eighth Annual Congress of the International New Thought Alliance, held in July 1953 at the Hotel Astor, New York City, there were representatives not only from New Thought and Unity Temples and Churches, as one would expect, but also more from Centers and Schools of Metaphysics, Truth, Understanding, Divine Science, and Religious Science.

On the West Coast, Drs. Robert H. Bitzer, Frederick Bailes, and Ernest Holmes have impressive churches and schools; and in New York City, Drs. Raymond C. Baker, Paul M. Brunet, and Ervin Seale, three young preachers with large followings, are also among the leaders in the progressive wing of the New Thought movement.

New Thought contains several strains of thought, not all new, for they come from varied sources. The great American native prophet, not yet accurately appraised, Phineas P. Quimby (1802-1866), was one source, and has been called "The Father of New Thought." His early disciples, such as Rev. Warren F. Evans and the Dressers, Julius, Mrs. Julius, and Horace, differed from Mrs. Eddy's Christian Science by not denying the reality of matter, considering it the expression of mind. Modern New Thought leaders have gone still farther from Christian Science by leaning more toward the psychological and psychosomatic than to the theological emphasis in religion.

New Thought differs also from orthodox Christianity in general by avoiding the dualistic idea of man *vs.* God, and by excluding such doctrines as total depravity, original sin, vicarious atonement, or any mediation between man and God by priest, minister, saints, the Virgin Mary, or even Jesus Christ. If they deny the sole divinity of Christ, they affirm the divinity of all men. They have derived much of their teaching from the Unitarians, Channing and Emerson. And since Emerson himself taught as much Hinduism as Christianity after Henry Thoreau had told him about Eastern mysticism, there is likely to be some esoteric Brahmanism in certain New Thought schools.

Among the pioneers, and those who shaped and influenced New Thought are Emile Coué, Julia Seton, Elizabeth Towne, Mary E. T. Chapin, Ernest Holmes, W. John Murray, Judge T. Troward, Ella Wheeler Wilcox, Orison Swett Marden, Villa Faulkner Page, Ralph Waldo Trine, Emmet Fox, Harry Gaze, and Harold Sherman.

Unity School of Christianity, one of the largest organizations in the New Thought movement, with a 1300-acre garden-city headquarters just outside Kansas City, was founded by Charles and Myrtle Fillmore, and by them named Unity in 1891. It differs somewhat from the I.N.T.A. units, from which it seceded in 1922, by laying more stress on the healing of mind, body, and even of poverty. It affirms, with Christian Science, that God is Principle rather than Person; it teaches reincarnation; it has telephone and mail prayer-service, handling as many as a half-million requests a year; and it emphasizes Bible study, but interprets it symbolically.

New Thought people do not know their own strength; but Dr. Barker estimates their adherents as five million, with an actual active membership of two hundred thousand.

SPIRITUALISTS

From the animistic beginnings of religion and in every culture since there have always been Spiritualists or Spiritists, however much frowned upon by priests of other faiths. The scriptures of Jews and Christians and all other Bibles contain reports of spiritistic phenomena. But as an American religion, now organized in several assemblies and conferences with about 175,000 members and at least a million fringe adherents, it started in 1848, when the Fox sisters of Hydesville, N. Y., heard strange knocks in their cottage, now a national shrine.

Today, séances are held by circles with a medium to contact the spirits, but Spiritualism functions as a religion, with churches, ministers, worship-meetings, hymn-books, and rituals for baptisms and funerals. In side-street chapels in many cities, message-bearing pastors hold nightly meetings and often render helpful service as advisers. Periodically, psychic investigators examine mediums to detect fraud, which sometimes exists but may be unconscious. Psychologists are at last paying more attention to psychic phenomena as probably originating in the little known areas of the human psyche called the subconscious or unconscious; but scientists have yet to explain certain occurrences and evidence satisfactorily to Spiritualists.

Since it advertises in Spiritualist papers and was formerly the United Spiritual Science Church, there might be included here the rapidly growing Christ Unity Science Church, listed in the *Yearbook of American Churches* as having 682,172 members in 1952 and 1,112,123 in 1953. It flourishes in the Southwest, emphasizes "Christian ontology (metaphysics) and divine healing," and has 4,181 churches and a Sunday School enrollment of 471,154.

THEOSOPHISTS AND RELATED GROUPS

Of the three methods of apprehending truth—reason, revelation and intuition—Theosophists depend primarily upon the last. For this reason they are classed as mystics, but they combine with intuition a great deal of philosophical speculation and reasoning. Later Theosophists are also inclined to regard the writings of earlier ones as in the nature of revealed truth.

Literally, theosophy is a Greek word meaning knowledge of things divine, and, as generally used, implies secret wisdom or vital information obtained only by student initiates after a lengthy process of indoctrination.

Ancient in origin, Theosophy stems not only from the Neoplatonists like Plotinus (who held that the physical universe, nature, and man were all emanations from God, to whom man might be reunited by ecstatic trance), but derives also from the still older Hindu and Buddhistic search for the divine knowledge which they called *Brahma-vidya*, the exact Sanskrit equivalent of Theosophy.

Early mystics like the Chinese Taoists, the Christian Gnostics, and the Jewish Cabalists were often theosophical; so was the Renaissance genius Paracelsus and, a century later, the German cobbler mystic Jakob Boehme, who got much from Paracelsus and gave much to George Fox and the early English Quakers.

Theosophists today generally teach the universal brotherhood of all mankind, seek to spread the knowledge of comparative religion, study the laws of nature, and affirm that man's powers, though latent, are almost limitless. Man may progress through the seven Theosophic levels from the merely physical to the perfect Universal Self, but in the process must transmigrate through a number of existences.

Madame Helena P. Blavatsky founded the Theosophical Society of America in New York City in 1875, and, in 1877, published *Isis Unveiled,* in which she revealed her remarkable, original theories regarding the evolution of man and his religions. Two years later, she went to Madras, India, and established her Society there. When she died, in 1891, she had one hundred thousand followers. Her disciples, now divided into two international societies, still commemorate the day of her death, May 8, as "White Lotus Day."

There are three divisions of American Rosicrucians, all teaching mainly theosophical doctrines. The Societas Rosicruciana has an office in New York City, the Fraternitas Rosae Crucis has one in Quakertown, Pa., and the Ancient Mystical Order Rosae Crucis (AMORC) one in San Jose, Cal.

Rosicrucians belong to secret fraternities and have mystic symbols, like the pyramid, the swastika, and the rosy cross. The last is sometimes represented by a cross within a circle, but the AMORC has a red rose on a golden cross. The name Rosicrucian has been traced to the symbol, but it has also been derived from the name of a German scholar and noble, Christian Rosenkreuz, said to have founded the brotherhood in 1420, after long travel and study in Damascus, Egypt, and

Spain. It is asserted that the early Rosicrucians were alchemists, hypnotists, almoners, and healers of the sick.

Brothers of this order are found today in all parts of the British Commonwealth as well as in America; and some of them are still interested in such unconventional means for the relief and cure of disease as hypnotism, vegetable drugs, and colored lights. They teach a sort of pantheism, believing that the Creator is still in every tree, plant, and rock, for the whole universe is instinct with life, according to the supreme design of the Master Mind.

Bahaism, like Theosophy, has its roots in Gnosticism and Neoplatonism, especially in the Persian and Zoroastrian strains of those types of east Mediterranean mysticism. It also has elements of Sufism, the Moslem mysticism of contemplation which developed in Persia in the 11th century. But its immediate origin was in Babism, a nineteenth-century mysticism, both Persian and Moslem, when Mirza Ali Mohammed took the title of Bab ed-Din (Gate of Faith), and announced himself the successor of Moses, Christ, and Mohammed. His teaching of a combination of Judaism, Christianity, Islam, and Parseeism, plus Gnostic elements, aroused opposition, and he was imprisoned and finally shot, in 1850. Babism went underground, but reappeared, in 1868, as Bahaism with Baha Ullah as the Bab's successor and the next prophet. After years in prison, where he wrote several books, he died in 1892 and was succeeded by his son, Sir Abdul Baha Bahai, who, before his death in 1921, appointed his grandson Shogi Effendi as the next Guardian of the Bahai Cause.

It was under the latter's able leadership that the Bahai Assemblies in America were organized into a National Spiritual Assembly and a large and beautiful Bahai Temple built at Wilmette, Ill., near Chicago. This Temple of Peace is a nonagon in shape, with nine great pillars of white quartz to symbolize the nine living religions of the world. Like Theosophy, Bahai emphasizes the teaching of Comparative Religion. It also proclaims that the foundation of all religions is one, and teaches world peace, universal education, and the equality of the sexes. It advocates an international auxiliary language.

There are said to be 700,000 Bahais in Persia, but there are only about five thousand in the United States. A recent interesting development is the creation by the New History Society of New York, a Bahai group, of an international Caravan of East and West, a youth correspondence peace society with 1,300 chapters in thirty-seven countries and a membership of one hundred thousand.

Emanuel Swedenborg (1688-1772) was one of the most amazingly versatile geniuses who ever lived, a veritable Swedish Leonardo da Vinci. For the first half of his long life, he was a scholar, inventor, engineer, and an advanced scientist in the fields of physics, anatomy, physiology, economics, astronomy, paleontology, geology, and metallurgy. He anticipated several recent developments and predicted others. Kant and Laplace have been credited with being the first to adduce the nebular hypothesis theory to account for the formation of the sun and planets, but Swedenborg had published that theory in one of his books in 1734, twenty years before Kant and sixty before Laplace.

In 1747, he suddenly resigned his government position as Assessor of the Royal College of Mines which he had held for thirty years and devoted himself to theological and spiritual matters, declaring that heaven had been opened to him. First, he had been instructed in dreams, then had seen visions and heard voices. In his full illumination or theophany, after visiting heaven and hell and talking with angels and spirits, the Lord gave him full instructions as to the symbolic meaning and interpretation of the Scriptures.

Swedenborg had no idea of establishing a religion or sect, and felt that any member of any church could remain in his faith and still belong to the New Church which God had revealed. But the system which he set forth in his book, *Divine Love and Wisdom*, was, as the very title reveals, distinctly theosophic. His other books, such as the *Arcana Caelestia* and the *Apocalypse Revealed*, disclose the inner, secret, esoteric, and symbolic meaning of the Bible from Genesis to Revelation. The origins and causes, as well as the final destiny of all things, natural and spiritual, are in the Divine Mind. God is the Divine Man, manifesting himself in Christ's glorified humanity. All things (in true theosophic fashion) are emanations from God. From God comes the sacred sphere which is the spiritual sun and from the spiritual sun comes the physical sun. Swedenborg carried this concept of the "correspondences" between the spiritual and the natural throughout his whole system. In the Swedish prophet's doctrines of discrete degrees and continuous degrees on separate planes of existence, we recognize the type of theosophic thinking characteristic of Gnosticism and Neoplatonism.

Robert Hindmarsh organized in London, in 1783, the first Swedenborgian society and called it the New Church; the first in America was formed in Baltimore in 1792, and a General Convention was held in 1817. There are now sixty-nine Churches of the New Jerusalem, as the Swedenborgian groups are generally called in America, with a membership of nearly seven thousand, and foreign missions in fourteen countries. The somewhat abstruse teachings of Swedenborg have been simplified in America in five brief doctrines: "1. That there is one God, in whom there is a Divine Trinity; and that He is the Lord Jesus Christ; 2. that a saving faith is to believe in Him; 3. that evils are to be shunned, because they are of and from the devil; 4. that good actions are to be done because they are of and from God; 5. that these are to be done by a man as from himself; but that it ought to be believed that they are done from the Lord with him and by him."

Swedenborg's influence, however, has not been limited to the church which was established after his death. Men of science still explore his voluminous writings, and men of many faiths find inspiration there.

The Vedanta Society in America is based on a Hindu philosophy which, in some aspects, is theosophic. Of the six philosophical systems of the Brahman, three are connected with the development of theosophical doctrine; the Sankhya, the Yoga, and the Vedanta; of these the Vedanta is the most widespread. The word means the "end or final aim of the Veda," the great sacred literature of the Hindus. The great commentator on Vedantist philosophy was Sankara, who lived about A. D. 800. Most educated Hindus in India today are Vedantists, and the great majority of them accept Sankara's interpretations. The central teaching of Vedanta is that each man's *atman* or soul is identical with the Brahman, the All-Soul—it is not a part of the Brahman, nor an emanation from the Brahman, but is Brahman. Any apparent experience or appearance seeming to indicate the contrary is an illusion, a dream-image.

There are many modifications of this doctrine, especially those resulting from contact with the western world. Swami Vivekananda brought one variety to America, in 1893, and expounded it at the World Columbian Exposition, where it was received with such enthusiasm that the Vedanta Society of America was founded. Today it has twelve hundred members in eleven local societies, holding meetings and otherwise explaining their doctrines. Their teachings are an attempt to harmonize science, philosophy and religion in an East-West synthesis. The result is a pleasing blend of Unitarianism and Ethical Culture with restful mystic and quietistic Oriental overtones. The Vedanta societies are influential in cultural and intellectual circles, far beyond what their small numbers would indicate.

SALVATION ARMY and VOLUNTEERS OF AMERICA

In 1865, a Methodist minister, William Booth, began preaching in the London East End slums, but soon decided that his street-corner preaching was the wrong technique with which to reach the ill-fed, ill-clothed and ill-housed people. He changed his methods and was soon nicknamed by the regular clergy, "the Soap, Soup, and Salvation Preacher." He had found that washing and feeding people first had much to do with their willingness to listen to his message of salvation. He discovered, too, that the usual leisurely methods of parsons were too slow to cope with the continual emergencies arising in this type of work, so, with himself as General Booth, he set up a military religious organization, with converts as recruits, then cadets, and later as officers.

The idea was a great success. It spread throughout the British Isles, then to America in 1880, where it now numbers over two hundred thirty thousand members. It has five million in all, in ninety-seven countries. The theology taught and preached is evangelically orthodox, emphasizing salvation as God's cure for man's sin, man's never-failing hope in Christ, and the need of sanctification as well as salvation. The Army still feeds hungry people, serving millions of meals annually. It helps the sick, the homeless, the unemployed, criminals, children, old people, and unmarried mothers. Hospitals, service centers, homes, nurseries, clinics, and summer camps give practical, needed, Christian help. In wartime its prompt and fearless service is especially notable.

The Volunteers of America, founded by Ballington (son of William) and Maude Booth in New York in 1896, is democratically managed and retains only a semi-military form of organization, but does work somewhat similar to that of the older Army. It has 183 churches, 448 service units, and twenty-five thousand members.

Appendix 2

STATISTICS OF RELIGIOUS BODIES

No ONE KNOWS how many denominations and religious bodies there are in the United States, or how many churches, temples, and synagogs, or how many members there are of religious organizations of all kinds. There has been no religious census by the federal government since 1936, and it is doubtful if there will soon be another, for that one was unsatisfactory and incomplete due largely to the refusal of 40,000 churches to cooperate. Many ministers considered the census a violation of the constitutional separation of church and state.

There is always, too, the problem of definition. What is a denomination or religious body? What is a church? And what, indeed, is a church member? Is any statistical comparison of the numerical strength of two denominations based on "membership" fair when one denomination includes as members all baptized infants and children and the other counts only adults? Again, some churches reckon as members only those who have really professed belief in the tenets of that church and have publicly "joined" it; whereas other churches include as members persons who are only "adherents" or "attendants" or "supporters" or "members of the parish" whose only appearance in the church will be at their own funeral.

As for the individual churches, how many years may a church remain on the "inactive" list and still be counted as a church in the annual reports of its denomination? Then, too, the size of the churches varies. The Church of the Nazarene denomination with its 3,710 churches would naturally be thought much larger than the Polish National Catholics with only 156, but the Poles average 1,704 members per church and the Nazarenes only 66, giving the latter a total membership of 243,152, fewer by far than the 265,879 of the Poles. There are some even greater contrasts: the Independent Baptists average only 17 members per church and the Cumberland Methodists, 15; whereas the Roman Catholics have 1,924, the Armenian Orthodox 2,280, and the Greek Orthodox 3,125 members. The over-all average, nationally, is 323, if one takes the figures of the 1953 *Yearbook of American Churches*, but only 250 according to the 1953 *World Almanac*.

In the absence of official federal government figures, one must rely on these two sources, both of which are, of course, forced to use estimates in many instances, especially when the church officials are negligent in sending information. The *World Almanac*, edited by Mr. Harry Hansen, bases its figures on replies to its own questionnaires and makes some use of the *Yearbook of American Churches*, edited by Dr. Benson Y. Landis, Associate Executive Director of the Central Department of Research and Survey of the National Council of the Churches of Christ in the United States of America. The Yearbook is based on information accumulated in Dr. Landis' office, such as directories, statistical and historical data, and the official reports of the statisticians of the various denominations and religious bodies.

The 1952 *World Almanac* listed, as of October, 1951, 265 religious bodies in continental United States with an estimated 265,583 churches and a total membership of 89,391,076, including 28,634,878 Roman Catholics and 54,482,603 Protestants. But the 1953 issue of the Almanac listed for 1952 only "about 230 religious bodies," 325,856 churches and 81,355,494 members, with 29,407,520 Roman Catholics and only 48,853,367 Protestants. These figures represented in one year a loss of 35 denominations, a gain of 60,273 churches, a loss of 8,035,582 members, a gain of 772,642 Roman Catholics, and a loss of 5,629,236 Protestants.

The 1954 Almanac, however, reports a total membership of 90,860,779, a gain in one year of 9,525,285. Obviously, the figures must be wrong somewhere. The churches did not lose eight million members one year and gain nine and a half million the next year.

Contrast those figures with the Yearbook statistics. The 1952 Yearbook gave these 1951 reports: 252 bodies (244 reporting), 284,592 churches, 88,673,005 total membership, including 29,241,580 Roman Catholics and 52,162,432 Protestants. The 1953 Yearbook listed the 1952 figures as follows: 261 bodies (251 reporting), 285,277 churches, 92,277,129 total membership, including 30,253,427 Roman Catholics and 54,229,963 Protestants, a gain in all directions.

Part of the discrepancy between the two sets of statistics may be due to the fact that the Almanac is published the first of the year and the Yearbook, not until August. Again, the church officials may respond more willingly to a religious than to a secular inquiry. But even the National Council of Churches, through Dr. Landis, has difficulty in eliciting up-to-date information, as is seen by the fact that in the latest Yearbook record, for 1952, twenty-one small denominations are listed as having made no report since 1940.

The Almanac gives the 1950 membership of Jewish Congregations as 5,000,000, the 1951 membership as 4,500,000, and the 1952 membership as 1,485,000. The Yearbook is still repeating the round number of five million.

There is need for both these books of religious statistics to reconsider the question of what is to be considered a denomination. Instead of 230 or 261 sects, denominations, or religious bodies in the United States, there are probably at least a thousand, if the same criterion is used for the neo-Fundamentalist and Pentecostal groups as is taken for the better-known and older denominations. If the Primitive Friends with only nine people in its total membership, the Independent Baptists with fifty, and the Cumberland Methodists with sixty, are reckoned as three separate denominations, then the same criterion should be applied to the various new Churches of God, now considered in both Almanac and Yearbook as but one denomination, although that group contains "at least two hundred independent religious bodies," according to the 1951 edition of Mead's *Handbook of Denominations*, and those independent bodies average 1525 in membership.

Neither the National Council's Yearbook nor the World Almanac recognizes the many New Thought, Unity, Divine Science, and Religious Science churches, centers, and temples as religious bodies, although these new sects are certainly as religious as the Buddhists, Spiritualists, Unitarians,

Universalists, and the Vedanta and Ethical Culture Societies and have as many followers.

It should be carefully noted by all who depend for their information upon either of the two books mentioned that neither editor has the staff or financial resources necessary to make the extensive field investigations requisite to check the figures submitted to them by the representatives of the various religious organizations. Denominational statisticians, themselves, must depend largely upon the figures sent them by local pastors or church clerks. Recently, however, the growing practice in several denominations of apportioning to each local church a quota contribution toward national denominational expenses based on the claimed local membership has been very effective in promoting accurate annual reports. Hitherto there has been very little dishonesty, but considerable carelessness.

INDEX

absolutism, 180-1
abstinence, 107
Adler, Felix, 177-8
Adventists, 239-41
Africa, 11, 83
Akhenaten, 13
Alexander the Great, 38, 53
Allah, 12, 13, 14, 15, 23, ch. 8
Allat, 12, 82
American Ethical Union, 178-82
American Humanist Ass'n 181-84
Analects, The, 58
Ancient Chronicle of the Mud Sea, The 46
Andover Creed, 173, 176
angels, 37, 39, 203, 238, 246
Anglican Church, ch. 14, 196
Angra Mainyu, 39
animism, 9-11, 13, ch. 7, 80
Antiochus Epiphanes, 25-7, 34
Apostolic Succession, 112-4, 148
Aquinas, St. Thomas 30, 97
Arabia, 12, 23, 82
Aryans, 17, 42
ascetiscism, 17, 23, 49
Ash Wednesday, 105
Assemblies of God, 240
Assumption of Mary, 100
Atenism, 13
Atheism, 15, 19, 216
Athens, 12, 41
Augustine, St. 30, 90
Baal, 12
Babylon-ia, 38, 41
Bahaism, 244-6
baptism, 10, 15, 91, 111, 124, 144, 160, 164-7, 200 211, 231, 239-40
Baptists, 92, ch. 16
Beecher, Henry Ward, 160
Bhakti, 18, 23
Bible-s, 28-9, 32, 36, 42, 65, 67, 80-2, 144, 152, 165, 192, 196, 204, 212-3, 231, 239, 243, 246

birth control, 235
bishops, 86-7, 112-3, 136, 200, 212
Blavatsky, Helena P., 243-4
Book of Mormon, 204, 212-3
bo-tree, 45, 50
Bradford, William, ch. 15
Brahm-a 18, 23, 243
Brahman, 16, 49, 242, 247
Brewster, William, ch. 15
Browne, Robert, 152-3
Buddha, The ch. 4, 19, 65, 77
Buddhism, ch. 4, 20, 24, 64
Bunyan, John, 165, 170-2
Burma, 53, 211, 213
Cabalists, 244
Cabrini, St. Francesca, 93-5
Calvin-ism, John, 131-43, 165, 173-6, 196-204, 219-20
Campellites, 172
caste, 16, 17, 23
catechism, 107, 128, 140, 220
celibacy, 52, 128
Channing, W. E., ch. 17, 242
China, 53, 82, 95, ch. 5-6
Christ, 14-6, 85, 232-3
Christian-ity, 13, 14, 24, 27-8, 34, 36-43, 80, ch. 9
Christian denomination, 162
Christian Science, ch. 20
Christmas, 34, 90, 161
Christ Unity Science, 243-4
Chuang-Tse, 68-70
Churches of Christ, 241
Churches of God, 241
Church of Christ, Scientist, ch., 20
Church of God in Christ, 241
Church of the Nazarene, 241
circumcision, 28
The City of God, 90
Communion, 105, 125, 126-7, 133, 142, 214, 230
Communism, 63, 71, 72, 117
confession, 15, 103-4, 111, 126, 146
confirmation, 107, 128, 211

252

253